LATE ROMANTICISM AND THE END OF POLITICS

In the late Romantic age, demands for political change converged with thinking about the end of the world. This book examines writings by Lord Byron, Mary Shelley, and their circle that imagined the end, from poems by Byron that pictured fallen empires, sinking islands, and dying stars to the making and unmaking of populations in *Frankenstein* and *The Last Man*. These works intersected with and enclosed reflections upon brewing political changes. By imagining political dynasties, slavery, parliament, and English law reaching an end, writers challenged liberal visions of the political future that viewed the basis of governance as permanently settled. The prospect of volcanic eruptions and biblical deluges, meanwhile, pointed toward new political worlds, forged in the ruins of this one. These visions of coming to an end acquire added resonance in our own time, as political and planetary end-times converge once again.

JOHN OWEN HAVARD is Associate Professor of English at Binghamton University. He is the author of *Disaffected Parties: Political Estrangement and the Making of English Literature, 1760–1830* (2019). His articles and essays on the Byron circle, party politics, political emotion, and the future of democracy have appeared in *ELH, Nineteenth-Century Literature, The Byron Journal, The New Rambler,* and *Public Books*.

This series aims to foster the best new work in one of the most challenging fields within English literary studies. From the early 1780s to the early 1830s, a formidable array of talented men and women took to literary composition, not just in poetry, which some of them famously transformed, but in many modes of writing. The expansion of publishing created new opportunities for writers, and the political stakes of what they wrote were raised again by what Wordsworth called those 'great national events' that were 'almost daily taking place': the French Revolution, the Napoleonic and American wars, urbanization, industrialization, religious revival, an expanded empire abroad, and the reform movement at home. This was an enormous ambition, even when it pretended otherwise. The relations between science, philosophy, religion, and literature were reworked in texts such as *Frankenstein* and *Biographia Literaria*; gender relations in *A Vindication of the Rights of Woman* and *Don Juan*; journalism by Cobbett and Hazlitt; and poetic form, content, and style by the Lake School and the Cockney School. Outside Shakespeare studies, probably no body of writing has produced such a wealth of commentary or done so much to shape the responses of modern criticism. This indeed is the period that saw the emergence of those notions of literature and of literary history, especially national literary history, on which modern scholarship in English has been founded.

The categories produced by Romanticism have also been challenged by recent historicist arguments. The task of the series is to engage both with a challenging corpus of Romantic writings and with the changing field of criticism they have helped to shape. As with other literary series published by Cambridge University Press, this one will represent the work of both younger and more established scholars on either side of the Atlantic and elsewhere.

See the end of the book for a complete list of published titles.

LATE ROMANTICISM AND THE END OF POLITICS

Byron, Mary Shelley, and the Last Men

JOHN OWEN HAVARD

Binghamton University

CAMBRIDGE
UNIVERSITY PRESS

CAMBRIDGE
UNIVERSITY PRESS

Shaftesbury Road, Cambridge CB2 8EA, United Kingdom

One Liberty Plaza, 20th Floor, New York, NY 10006, USA

477 Williamstown Road, Port Melbourne, VIC 3207, Australia

314–321, 3rd Floor, Plot 3, Splendor Forum, Jasola District Centre,
New Delhi – 110025, India

103 Penang Road, #05–06/07, Visioncrest Commercial, Singapore 238467

Cambridge University Press is part of Cambridge University Press & Assessment,
a department of the University of Cambridge.

We share the University's mission to contribute to society through the pursuit of
education, learning and research at the highest international levels of excellence.

www.cambridge.org
Information on this title: www.cambridge.org/9781009289207

DOI: 10.1017/9781009289160

First published 2023

A catalogue record for this publication is available from the British Library.

ISBN 978-1-009-28920-7 Hardback

Contents

Figures

Acknowledgments

How nice – and how strange! – to recall the circumstances that produced this book.

First, the women. Penny Fielding offered a warm welcome in Edinburgh and enquired brightly about "Darkness." Claire Connolly kept us up late talking about funerals. Emily Rohrbach, the Romanticist's Romanticist, offered steely support and friendship from a distance. Jessie Reeder has been my lifeline to the Victorian age. Stephanie DeGooyer is my corrective lens. Sandra Macpherson is still the best. Abi Ward and Kathleen Fearn brought precision and keen intelligence to the final manuscript. Liz Armstrong and the mammals of the Laguna de San Ignacio gave me a blissful week not thinking about this book as I reached the last stages. My mum put me up when I was getting started. One day, we will all go to the pub.

Jim Chandler and I first talked about this project five summers (and five long winters) ago. It is an honor to be joining this series and to be part of the scholarly world it has made possible. I think of Lauren Berlant when I read Byron's remarks on "our earthquakes – our politics." Reconnecting with Jerry McGann in Berkeley has been an unexpected delight: We are not worthy! Peter Mileur has been a huge support, as have Joe Keith and the rest of my treasured department. From Chicago to California to Binghamton and back to Cambridge (although, unlike Byron, they wisely never let me in). Time flies.

I thank Emily Paterson-Morgan, Tricia Matthew, Jonathan Kramnick, Tobias Menely, Jason Moore, and Di Gildea for opportunities to engage the questions I take up here. I owe Mark Canuel and Jon Mee belated thanks for last time.

The discussion of Swift in Chapter 1 incorporates material from my "Swift's Political Climates," forthcoming in *The Eighteenth Century: Theory and Interpretation*. The first section of Chapter 5 draws on my "What Freedom? *Frankenstein*, Anti-Occidentalism, and English Liberty,"

Nineteenth-Century Literature 74.3 (2019): 305–31. Several paragraphs in Chapter 3 are from my "'Blustering, Bungling, Trimming': Byron, Hobhouse, and the Politics of *Don Juan* Canto I," *The Byron Journal* 49.1 (2021): 29–41.

I thank the anonymous reviewers of this book for reports that were models of encouragement, support, and care. At Cambridge University Press, Bethany Thomas has been a pleasure to work with, as has George Laver.

My friends mean the world to me. I hope they know who they are. I give special thanks to Brad Anderson, Ben Bateman, and Ben Steverman for love and encouragement on both sides of the Atlantic. Chuck and Alyse spread the love from Texas. Hugh and Selga – and the tinkers – remain my anchors.

Last and not least, I thank my man, Nathan Vernon. I was lucky to spend the strange times in which I wrote much of this book with him – and Blemie, now in that place where "in the long evenings" there are "a million fireplaces with logs forever burning." I take some solace in this and other losses imagining some other world where "one curls oneself up and blinks into the flames and nods and dreams, remembering the old brave days on earth."

Abbreviations

BLJ	*Byron's Letters and Journals*, ed. Leslie Marchand, 12 vols. (London: J. Murray, 1973–82).
CPW	*Complete Poetical Works*, ed. Jerome J. McGann, 7 vols. (Oxford: Oxford University Press, 1980–93).
Hansard	Hansard, UK Parliament Online.
JMS	*The Journals of Mary Shelley, 1814–1844*, eds. Paula R. Feldman and Diana Scott-Kilvert, 2 vols. (Oxford: Oxford University Press, 1987).
LM	Mary Shelley, *The Last Man*, ed. Anne McWhir (Peterborough: Broadview, 1996).
LMS	*The Letters of Mary Wollstonecraft Shelley*, 3 vols. (Baltimore: Johns Hopkins University Press, 1980).
ODNB	Oxford Dictionary of National Biography Online.

Where Will It End?

Henry Brougham had little time for "thoughtless optimists" when it came to politics. Writing for the *Edinburgh Review* in 1818, he praised a recent book that advocated for emigration to the United States. Brougham was awed by Morris Birkbeck's account of the scale and dynamism of the new nation. "A broad, deep, and rapid stream of population is running constantly towards the western parts of the Continent," he wrote, casting emigration as a force of nature. He observed, dubiously, that "vast states" were forming "towards the Pacific Ocean, the growth of which as much exceeds in rapidity what we have been wont to admire on the shores of the Atlantic." All this left at an "immeasurable distance" the "scarcely perceptible progress of our European societies." It was little wonder that England had been left behind. Ravaged by poverty and austerity, Birkbeck's book had suggested, the beleaguered nation was headed for political disaster. An English farmer (like the land-bound *villeins* "of old time") had "no voice in the appointment of the legislature unless he happens to possess a freehold of forty shillings a year." With "no elective franchise," he could "scarcely be said to have a political existence" and had no concern with "public affairs." It was thus "quite reasonable and just to secure a timely retreat from the approaching crisis – either of anarchy or despotism." America's population was exploding, while England faced decline and even catastrophe. But where, Brougham asked, was "this prodigious increase of numbers, this vast extension of dominion, to end?"[1]

Anticipating Alexis de Tocqueville a decade later, Brougham claimed that politics was less of a distraction in America. Men had "abundant occupation of their own, without thinking of the State." But the success of the United States could also be attributed to something else: its "total want" of a familiar breed of politician. "The race of mere statesmen," Brougham wrote, "so well known among us in the Old world, is wholly unknown in the New." There was no shortage of political feeling; the Americans were ("no doubt") "decided partisans, and warm political combatants; but what project or chance can counterbalance, in their eyes, the benefits conferred by the Union, of cultivating their soil, and pursuing their traffic freely and gainfully, in their capacity of private individuals?" The "cautious and economical character" of the federal government seemed "admirably adapted to secure its hold over the affections of a rational and a frugal people." Indeed, "until the whole frame of society alters," Brougham ventured, "even a great increase of political characters will not enable those persons successfully to appeal to the bulk of the community, with the prospect of splitting the Union." A "preacher of insurrection" might "safely be left with such personages as the American farmers."[2]

We have become more familiar, in the years since Brougham wrote, with the prospect that established political unions will come to an end. In our own moment, long-standing decline and growing inequality have been met, on both sides of the Atlantic, by "preacher[s] of insurrection" and explosions of fervent feeling. We have become more familiar, too, with the prospect – if not the impending or already unfolding reality – that the world as we know it will come to an end. The fantasies about Western supremacy and perpetual growth that shaped previous centuries now confront acute challenges. This book took shape in the shadows cast by these developments. But its emphasis falls not only on decline and prospective disaster but on how closing horizons and ending lines provide opportunities to reexamine the targets of governance and the objectives of political activity: what we might call the ends of politics. In *The Last Man* (1826), Mary Shelley imagined a pandemic that destroys the human race, in what can be considered the first end-of-the-world novel. But in contrast with other fictional apocalypses, the dissolution of mankind begins, in *The Last Man*, with the peaceful unwinding of political institutions. In a version of the dynamic described in Brougham's review, the dwindling of the population restores England, in turn, to a kind of quasi-rural existence, as vocal male politicians suddenly vanish and new communities take shape in the rubble.[3]

This book examines writings by Lord Byron, Mary Shelley, and their circle that confronted the prospect of the world ending, from poems by Byron that pictured fallen empires, sinking islands, evacuated planets, and dying stars, to the making and unmaking of populations in *Frankenstein* and *The Last Man*. Those writings, this study shows, intersected with and enclosed reflections upon political change. While overshadowed by the past – not least in the guise of a reconstituted Tory elite – the late Romantic age saw long-standing tensions come together with new prospects for political mobilization and legislative change. This book focuses on the period bracketed by Britain's 1815 victory at Waterloo and the passage of the 1832 Reform Act. From reform of parliament and the abolition of slavery to the ascent of liberal ideals and free trade, politics in the early nineteenth century underwent considerable and dramatic changes. My interest, however, is less in tying literary texts to historical specifics than in exploring literature's engagement with the multiple temporalities and vectors of change that "politics" enfolded.[4] In early nineteenth-century England, a newly democratic *ethos* (and liberal *telos*) promised an end to politics as usual. These political changes – which entailed, among other things, profound challenges to the standing of elite political men – amounted to endings, whether welcome or otherwise, that were also fresh beginnings. They converged, in the writings I examine here, with visions of the world coming to an end.

The "end of the world" can mean the failure of institutions and collapse of society, the end of the human species, the ruin and demise of Planet Earth, and the biblical Apocalypse that ends historical time. These formulations are distinct but overlapping. They coincide (and clash) in complex ways. The collapse of political and social institutions, for example, may have a negligible impact on nonhuman animals and natural environments; indeed, fewer people and less human activity may have beneficial consequences for planetary life writ large. Approached from the perspective of ecocriticism, environmentalism, or "the Anthropocene," we have only one world: Planet Earth.[5] But more than one world may be at issue in talk of the "end of the world." The demise of this planet, in some versions of evangelical Christianity, hastens the onset of the world to come. Rather than fixing this planet, meanwhile, some techno-utopian fantasists have focused on the prospect of escaping to Mars or the moon, turning their back on the problems of this world in the pursuit of another. Apocalyptic rhetoric has become especially widespread in discussions of contemporary politics. "The only thing that is the end of the world," Barack Obama stated in the final weeks of 2016, "is the end of the world."[6] What we call the "end of the world," Obama's comments remind us, almost invariably falls short of irrecoverable collapse, let alone the Apocalypse of biblical eschatology (the "End of the World" that structured Christian thought in the premodern West).[7] Yet catastrophe and world-ending continue to infuse our perception of present-day reality and to inflect our understanding of prospective futures. That may result, as Obama seems to imply, in overblown analogies and an inflated sense of doom. Recent developments have accentuated a belief that established institutions and existing forms of political agency are exhausted. The already shaky claim that mankind had reached the end of history has now been further discredited. But the claim that the end of the world is nigh might be said to have taken its place. Where before, the only way was up, or straight ahead, into a fantasized state of irreversible stasis – with the supposed global triumph of liberal democracy – now, the only way ahead can seem to be a series of slow or steep declines, accelerating and converging catastrophes.

Claims that the world is doomed may be no less dubious – at least in political terms – than claims that we have reached history's end.[8] In teasing apart these converging rhetorics, separating out these visions of the end of the world, we not only maintain a sense of proportion. Crisis may also provide practical opportunities and imaginative vehicles for change, prompting reevaluation, and opening pathways for other possible futures. Those futures can, of course, amount to more of the same – or worse. As Naomi Klein has stringently argued, crisis affords special opportunity to vested interests, who exploit disorienting "shock" to entrench inequitable systems.[9] No sane person wants to see catastrophe. Yet as Klein has also shown, crisis may afford the opportunity to revisit our political priorities. Disasters, whether natural or man-made, may reaffirm the need for local organizing and international solidarity, creating new political, social, and economic orders while further discrediting neoliberal capitalism and related hegemonies.[10] The global response to Covid presents a recent example of the elusive potential nested within unexpected disruption. Although plenty of people were still forced to go into work, the onset of the pandemic also saw relentless activity and global interchange give way to somnolent streets and empty skies. Indeed, the early phases of lockdown witnessed tableaus eerily reminiscent of Shelley's *Last Man*, as iconic sites from the Vatican to Wall Street fell silent and animals took over abandoned streets, reclaiming a world evacuated of mankind.[11] Literature, this book argues, creates disaster-free spaces of rethinking, in which the world can be confronted and imagined anew, whether by way of the impasses created by sudden ruptures and looming absences or through more subtle changes and adjustments: tremors of anticipated transformation, fleeting disruptions to the status quo, flickering glimpses of an alternative world.[12] *The Last Man* plays out at length one version of what might happen when the world as we know it ceases to be. Both in elaborate and more understated ways, all the writings discussed in this book contemplate what might result from dislodging or uprooting things as they are. That begins with the political systems organized around individual men.

"This is not the apocalypse," President Obama told White House staff members the day after the 2016 presidential election.[13] But despite hopeful assertions to the contrary, a sense of dread, decline, and doom remained pervasive for the remainder of that decade (and, it seems safe to say, beyond). Recent events, from the vote for Brexit to the election of Trump, had shown that political upsets and the abrupt collapse of certainties – amidst a gathering whirlwind of global upheaval, technological change, and dis- and misinformation – could feel very much like the end of the world. In *The Origins of Totalitarianism*, Hannah Arendt showed how the cascade of events might coincide with torrents of false information to wash away any sense of fixity and truth, unleashing violence and terror.[14] In our own time, the chaotic state of politics has (so to speak) drowned out and sucked the oxygen of attention away from environmental catastrophe. Partisan and ideological division obscure collective predicaments, distracting from the need for large-scale action in the face of environmental peril. Political failure can redouble feelings of impotence, giving rise to depression and helplessness rivaling that of once-hopeful radicals after the failure of the French Revolution. But as this book sets out to show, there are many ends of the world – each demanding that we reimagine the ends of politics. Literature, at the same time, imagines its own worlds. Beyond their ultimate political implications, the endings and fresh openings explored here give rise to meditations on mankind and its limits, including the reorientation of perspectives beyond our species and this world altogether – to alternative sources of meaning or the broken solace that comes from staring into the void. The writings of Byron, Mary Shelley, and their circle will not offer solutions to what ails us. But they serve as a prelude to more recent efforts to think and feel our way through a newly hopeless-seeming human condition. They also make valuable contributions to that undertaking in their own right, as fusions of political thought and literary poetics able to administer, as Keats wrote of the scenes sealed on the Grecian urn, to those "in midst of other woes."[15]

Shelley's "Tale" and the Spirit of the Age

In February 1825, Mary Shelley approached a sitting member of parliament with a modest proposal. "I have often wished to be present at a debate in the House of Commons," Shelley wrote to MP John Cam Hobhouse. Expressing particular interest in a recent debate between Brougham and George Canning over a petition supporting Catholic rights, she stated that the "animated discussions now going on" and "the splendid eloquence displayed" were "beyond words objects of attraction." Shelley emphasized

her capacities as an attentive listener of animated men in the 1831 introduction to *Frankenstein*. ("Many and long were the conversations between
Lord Byron and [Percy] Shelley," she recalled of her time at Lake Geneva,
"to which I was a devout but nearly silent listener.")[16] But Shelley's letter to
Hobhouse, while ostensibly demure, was also quietly assertive. Attendance
at parliament would be invaluable, she wrote, for the "Tale" at which she
was then at work. Her letter concluded by conveying her desire to attend
the "strangers gallery" where visitors were permitted to observe parliamentary debates: "I hear that there is a place, over the roof of St. Stephens where
you senators permit us to hear, not seen." She concluded by apologizing in
advance for seeming too forward in her request to visit the hallowed
chamber of English politics and to view its lofty "senators."[17]

  The Spirit of the Age appeared the same year. William Hazlitt's group
portrait of the late Romantic period featured extended depictions of
Cobbett, Godwin, and Wordsworth – to name just the prominent
Williams. As that subset of eminent men makes clear, Hazlitt included
figures from the world of letters and from the world of politics. Alongside
Sir Walter Scott and other literary lions, Hazlitt profiled political figures
ranging from Godwin and Cobbett to the aging radical Horne Tooke and
the conservative cleric Thomas Malthus. *The Spirit of the Age* also included
shorter sketches of Canning, Brougham, the radical stalwart Sir Francis
Burdett, and the evangelical abolitionist William Wilberforce. The opening pages of *The Spirit of the Age* referenced Hobhouse as a vigorous
exemplar of popular "hustings" politics. The book began with a portrait
of Jeremy Bentham, presented as a political thinker who cast his eyes on
wide horizons and distant nations. The portrait of "Lord Byron" had
a special status in the collection, which appeared the year after the poet's
death in Greece.

  In 1826, the year after the appearance of Hazlitt's book, Shelley published her novel heralding the end of the world. *The Last Man*, set in late
twenty-first-century England, witnesses the human species succumb to
a mysterious wave of global illness. But the opening volume of Shelley's
novel had, as I have noted, a prominent political dimension. Anticipated in
her desire to visit the House of Commons – this was the "Tale" at which
she was at work when she wrote to Hobhouse – the book depicts factions of
"royalists," "aristocrats," and "democrats" contending to lead England
after the abolition of the monarchy, which the book optimistically dates
to 2073. The futuristic world of *The Last Man* alluded, in both direct and
veiled ways, to contemporary political debate, from brewing arguments for
parliamentary reform and expanded suffrage to the more radical visions of

change associated with the French Revolution and independence movements taking shape across Europe and the Americas. Aside from its engagement with Godwinian radicalism and Benthamite reform – and its glimpses at the kind of male-dominated worlds familiar to Shelley and her mother, Mary Wollstonecraft – the novel includes characters based directly on Percy Shelley and Byron. *The Last Man* scrambled and recombined these various elements of the late Romantic age, which Shelley exported to a distant future and presented against the backdrop of dramatic changes to mankind's standing in the world, amounting to the end of "man" as such.

In the second half of this book, I offer a reading of Shelley's novel that takes seriously its attention to politics. Two features of that argument may be outlined here. In the first instance, *The Last Man* focuses on the last *men*. The opening volume is overshadowed by the Byronic politician Lord Raymond and former heir to the throne Adrian, an effete idealist who shares features with Percy Shelley. An unduly narrow approach to the novel has led critics to brush past these early scenes. But read in more expansive terms, they draw our attention to a second feature of the book: the complex political resonances that accompany its picture of a world without mankind. *The Last Man* invites readings that attend to universals and current preoccupations, with recent interpretations emphasizing viral illness, interspecies community, refugee crisis, natural disaster, and apocalypse. To be sure, the ultimate horizons of Shelley's novel strayed far beyond politics. But in leaping to totalizing frames, universalizing questions, and current concerns, critics have obscured the political dimensions of *The Last Man*. Even the novel's account of a prepolitical, natural state and its visions of an evacuated planet, I propose, have complex political implications.

No less than *The Spirit of the Age* the previous year, *The Last Man* drew together the competing impulses, time frames, and agendas – as well as some of the specific personalities – that were reshaping politics in early nineteenth-century England. Like *The Spirit of the Age*, the novel engaged Godwin's political utopianism, Cobbett's populist rancor, Wordsworth's rustic idealism, and Bentham's visions of the "New World." Yet the novel's overarching narrative and the wider theme announced by its title also leave us with a puzzle. Why did Shelley make the fulfillment of certain radical ambitions (and debates about the viability of political institutions, even after their reform) the starting point for a novel concerned with the demise of mankind? Why portray recent changes to the ends of politics in proximity to mankind's final days on Earth? *The Last Man* joined with other works by Mary Shelley and Byron, this study argues, in imagining the spirit of the age as the sense of an ending. These writings and the wider print-political and cultural-affective spheres in which they took shape countenanced various prospects for the end of the world, from the dissolution of institutions and collapse of society to the demise and extinction of the human species to the exhaustion (or conflagration) of the planet. These reflections on world ending were intertwined, this book proposes, with thinking about the future of politics at the outset of the nineteenth-century "Age of Reform."[18] As the first half of this book emphasizes, that began with the nuts and bolts of politics: parties, institutions, and legislation, practical reforms, radical aspirations, and conservative reaction. Rather than pointing only to catastrophe, encounters with ends and endings could be generative, pointing to the waning importance of political lineages rooted in the past (waning importance that, as we know from our own experience, does not preclude stubborn persistence) or challenging efforts to sweep resistance and unrest into a buried past. Endings offered a means, in particular, to reflect upon the gains and losses associated with the transition into a new era of liberal governance. These reflections on coming to an end acquire renewed importance during our own time, as visions of political and planetary end-times converge once again.

Byron's Lastness and the End of the Race

Although this book is not, for the most part, concerned with the Americas, the early United States offers some instructive ways of thinking about political modernity. In local histories starting in the 1820s, Jean O'Brien has detailed, "New Englanders scripted themselves as modern people looking to the future, creating order out of chaos and forging modern societies and cultures that broke from the past." The Indigenous peoples of those lands had no continuing place in those stories, which "implicitly argued that Indians and Indian ways could not be acknowledged as legitimate, ongoing, and part of the landscape of the future." "Firsting" and "Lasting" became critical tools in what O'Brien, adapting Bruno Latour, frames as a battle over who and what gets to be "modern." James Fenimore Cooper's *Last of the Mohicans* (1826) exemplified a wider tendency to dwell upon the supposed "Last of X" as a means to consign Indians to a premodern or uncivilized past (and to erase or elide the challenges their continued presence posed to this newly evacuated modernity).[19] In his final published poem, *The Island* (1823), Byron imagined an encounter with native peoples that evaded these tendencies, I argue in this book's final chapter, by imagining a world in which England

and *its* institutions no longer existed. In *Frankenstein*, I argue in the same chapter, Shelley had her characters retreat to the North Pole as a site beyond Europe and its ruinous political legacies. But both authors were going against the grain. In the coming century, a growing emphasis on forward movement made little room for alternative trajectories – an emphasis that became especially acute in America and related imperial contexts. Apparent across a "broad canvas of cultural expression in the nineteenth century" and exemplified by sentimentalized appeals to dying races, "lastness" produced progress narratives and racialized conceptions of historical time that helped shape a future closed off from the past.[20]

The late Romantic age in England saw varied and clashing visions of the future. In the late eighteenth and early nineteenth centuries, a concern with progress was shared by philosophers, historiographers, and the newly emergent mass public.[21] The conjectural history of the Scottish Enlightenment had advanced a stadial theory for human advancement. But the upheaval of the global age of revolutions radically reconfigured – and even exploded – existing progress narratives.[22] With the French Revolution, Reinhart Koselleck writes, "the previous world of social and political experience, still bound up in the sequence of generations, was blown apart."[23] During the late Romantic age in England, overlapping groups of activists, artists, philosophers, and visionaries remained invested in ideas of human progress. Those investments – whether inflected by philosophical thinking and conjectural history or driven by radical hopes and popular mobilization – were bound up with the practical belief that politics could continue moving forward: what we would today recognize, broadly speaking, as the tenets of progressive politics. Although indebted to the spirit of change inaugurated by the French Revolution (including self-described "Jacobins" and such groups as the London Corresponding Society), the early nineteenth-century emphasis on forward political movement had multiple axes, from the "march of intellect" to evangelical abolitionism to Bentham's elaboration of Godwinian ideals into practical agendas for reform. Demands for parliamentary reform had deep histories and complexly overlaid networks while antislavery organizing and demands for abolition were driven by an expansive transatlantic coalition, including the writings of Black Atlantic authors. Politics in this moment was driven, that is to say, not only by stadial theories or the world-historical force imputed to events in France but by diverse actors and heterogeneous networks engaging multiple time frames and vectors of change.

Reformist views were not universally held, of course, even among those on the "Whig" end of the political spectrum. Many resisted the disintegration of old structures and the ushering in, whether gradual or instantaneous, of a transformed political future. There were also those who fell into none of these camps. The figures on whom I focus in this book tarried around visions of the last men in and beyond politics. But that did not mean they were wholly resistant to change. These backward-looking reflections, neither fully reactionary nor entirely hostile to progress, were infused with an indeterminate political promise. That was the case, this book argues, for reflections by and upon one man in particular. The death of Lord Byron in 1824 echoed like a thunderclap through the age memorialized by Hazlitt the following year. Byron's exile from England and eventual death in Greece were widely discussed and mourned. Contemporary representations established Byron's reputation down to this day, from rakish dandy and early celebrity to globe-trotting dilet-tante and freedom fighter.[24] His death saw personal outpourings of grief and the renewal of scandal. The later years of Byron's life and responses to his death also brought his importance as a political figure into renewed focus. He became a symbol of doomed revolutionary hopes. But what Byron's lifelong commitment to "opposition" would have looked like, had he lived, also became an intriguing question. Looking to events during his lifetime and developments since his death, writers developed speculative accounts of Byron living into subsequent decades. Those accounts – which included fictionalized treatments of the poet's future life – imagined Byron returning to England to revive his political ambi-tions or voyaging elsewhere in the globe and portrayed him, variously, as a radical reformer and populist figurehead or as an aristocratic relic and political dinosaur (who had turned out, despite his Whig credentials, a "Tory at last," as he had jibed of Robert Southey). Byron, for his own part, remained haunted by his retreat from Whig politics. But he did not remain wedded to any static political role. The public efforts to imagine his political future echoed the private writings and personal reflections in which Byron asked what he might have accomplished politically by returning to England rather than seeking out revolutionary movements and other horizons overseas.

As Byron anticipated in his 1816 poem "Prometheus," he became "a symbol and a sign" of resistance. But his writings also capture a more elusive and ambiguous sense of faded possibility and renewed potential. Both tendencies can be discerned in one of his final poems. Written in January 1824, the poem known as "On This Day I Complete My Thirty-Sixth Year" has been overshadowed by the fact that Byron died a few months later. In his 1830 edition of Byron's writings, Thomas Moore presented these lines as a living, breathing relic:

> Taking into consideration every thing connected with these verses, – the last tender aspirations of a loving spirit which they breathe, the self-devotion to a noble cause which they so nobly express, and that consciousness of a near grave glimmering sadly through the whole, – there is perhaps no production within the range of mere human composition, round which the circumstances and feelings under which it was written cast so touching an interest.[25]

But the clashing registers of the poem – in which Byron writes both of fading leaves and molten passion – exceed the terms of Moore's effusive retrospective reading, which surrounds the poem with a halo of political hope and devotion. Byron can equally be seen approaching what turned out to be his final birthday in a spirit of self-erasure, giving the poem's de facto lastness less settled significance. Revolutionary hope gives way here to stepping aside and letting go.

Byron had traveled to Greece at the behest of his various political circles including the London Greek Committee, Italian resistance forces, and the leaders of the struggle in Greece, to whose "Cause" he made ever-increasing commitments. The poem on his final birthday stages a turn from love to valor. But the relinquishing of love also occasions its paradoxical reassertion. In the poem's early stanzas, stalled movement couples with renewed "fire," reworking, at a geological level, one of Byron's repeated images: the scorpion stung by its own tail. A "lone . . . Volcanic Isle," his overflowing passion finds no outlet, consuming him. But that self-immolation couples with a stony heart: "unmoved" and no longer moving, untouched by and unable to touch others, Byron is an island or world unto himself, chained like Prometheus to his own self-regenerating pain. Political struggle is placed front and center in the second half of the poem, which describes revolutionary awakening as already in motion. Byron's seeming turn to military valor in the poem's closing stanzas was, in turn, made immortal by events. By dying three months later, he suffused this allusion to death with ironic vitality, making the "Soldier's Grave" of the poem's final stanza ring not with loss but with valedictory potential. Yet the contingency of events risks obscuring the multiple levels of resonance here, including those that point away from death's straightforward rehabilitation as revolutionary spirit. In continuity with the earlier lines of the poem, the speaker may instead remain in a contradictory state of impassivity and self-enclosed potential, such that the world moves on without him.

Whether or not Byron foresaw his own death in this particular poem, he routinely imagined his life enveloped by death. Andrew Bennett has pointed to the "strange rehearsal" for his passing undertaken throughout his lifetime, which included lying in empty graves and treating his exile as a kind posthumous existence.[26] Three years earlier, on his thirty-third birthday, Byron had written his own epitaph, which imagined him (following "lethargy" and a "lingering disease") being "interred in the Eternity / of the Past."[27] Reading "On This Day I Complete My Thirty-Sixth Year" with a view to Byron's wider investments in lastness shifts its political resonances. The poem's concluding stanzas introduce the revolutionary context that allows him to revive his "spirit." But the parenthetical reference to Greece immediately corrects and clarifies the opening injunction: Greece *is* "awake." Byron indulges in Macbeth-like grappling with conscience. But this gives way, in the end, to a "Rest" whose precondition was the future Greek nation already in formation. Byron's implied role was simple: to get out of the way. In this close-to-final poem, Byron imagined his own passing. But the poem that became Byron's parting statement on his identity as a lone political man also imagines him "look[ing] round" at a scene evacuated of his presence, taking his earned repose. His disappearance echoes within a changed reality, a different world. The poem's admirers have placed the emphasis on last confession and undying passion, while its critics have flatly dismissed its mawkish self-pity and "tawdry, worn-out rhetoric."[28] But "On This Day I Complete My Thirty-Sixth Year" also stages a deliberate and poignant vanishing act: overtaken by and subsumed within a larger cause, Byron lets his active presence give way to uncanny echoes of his already-anticipated absence.

In approaching writings by and about Byron, this study attends both to the imprint and to the erasure of actual and imagined political agency. Rather than choosing between presence and absence, demonstrated agency or unactualized potential, I keep both possibilities in view when sounding out the complex political valences of Byron's life, works, and reputation. Byron often presented himself as a relic and a remnant – an archaic, belated presence. Accounts of his death honored and amplified these tendencies. But they also risked obscuring the strange potential that inhered in these backward-facing appeals. "The best of Prophets of the future," Byron wrote in 1821, "is the past." As with the tortured journal entry in which he made that assertion, Byron's writings developed a unique poetics of lastness that wove past together with present, absence with presence, lost potential with its prospective reactivation in other futures.[29] Mary Shelley developed her own related poetics. In her fiction, dynamics recalling those coiled into Byron's poems and compressed into his journal entries echoed out across longer time frames and through more elaborate geographies. For all their differences, generic and otherwise, their respective writings were, to some extent, inextricable, materially entangled by their circumstances of composition. In much the same way that the Byron–Shelley circle borrowed themes from each other – from the Prometheus myth to lost Miltonic Edens to visions of the end of the world – they also developed a related set of aesthetic concerns. These crossings find one point of convergence, this book argues, in Byron's reflections on lastness, lost pasts, and ending worlds.

Romantic studies has long been preoccupied both with the draw of moldering pasts and with the promise of budding futures. Ruins, relics, Gothic histories, and undead spirits have been seen to infuse Romantic texts with dark undercurrents that challenge enlightenment, modernity, and reason. The mirrors cast by futurity onto the present, critics have similarly shown, break open familiar temporalities and redirect the world onto unknown courses.[30] But aspirations for the future were bound up – then, as now – with attachments to the past. Ending lines and closing horizons frequently entered into reckonings with the coming state of early nineteenth-century England and the wider world. Those meditations, this book argues, had purposes beyond merely lamenting or celebrating a lost past (and embracing or fearing an uncertain future). They revealed writers and publics at once excited and unsettled by the loss of former certainties. Those visions of coming to an end intersected, in turn, with newly emergent ways of thinking about man's place in the universe, including dramatically revised timescales for the age of the planet (and thus of the human species). Those revelations, tied to proto-Darwinian discoveries and geological exploration, meant that prospective absences and mourned losses echoed within and across massively expanded voids of space and time. Rather than indulging simplistic fantasies of declining species, dying lights, and empty planets, however, the writers I examine here embroidered these visions of world ending with poignant reflections on loss and change, making lastness, I set out to demonstrate, the site of revived possibility.

Lastness, for Jacques Khalip, offers a means of encountering – without "fear, foreshadowing, or catastrophe" – a kind of impossible stasis and emptiness: "the unthinkable but unavoidable limit of our lives and worlds." But that which we *call* "last," Khalip reminds us, need be nothing of the sort. The last may also be that which endures, the second-to-last, "all the more auratic and fetishized as the condition of repeatedly *not* being over ... the perpetuation of the valediction."[31] Khalip attends not to the ways that lastness can be ethically – let alone politically – useful but to the ontological and epistemological questions raised by that (non)threshold. The practices of unwinding and letting go – whose political resonances I stress here – extend in his account to the dissolution of philosophical categories, including those that structure the subject and the world in the first place. Jonathan Sachs takes up the related but distinct question of decline, attending to the timelines that asymptotically approach inconceivable loss and large-scale collapse and offering a nuanced account of how narratives of declension help, paradoxically, to give affirmative shape to the future. Rather than serving as the simple inverse of progress, decline helped late eighteenth- and early nineteenth-century writers and thinkers to imagine an unknowable world. Romantic ruins, approached in this light, "join time past and time present and thus serve both as a discursive counterweight to and a sentimental icon of decline."[32]

Attending to interweaving pasts and futures and the poetics of lastness, this book joins with these studies in paying special attention to Romantic literature as a privileged site at which colliding time frames and converging losses take shape. Poetry became especially crucial to engagements with a newly empty-seeming world. The lastness that extends, for Khalip, beyond humanity as such finds uncanny echoes in empty landscapes, lightless voids, and gaping skies. Sachs situates these barren scenes in relation to the geological discovery of "deep time." In the context of commercial acceleration, the unearthing of massively expanded chronologies and endless pasts thus helped give rise, Sachs maintains, to a compensatory – and hortatory – emphasis on "*slow* time," whose influence can be discerned in Wordsworth's rocks, Coleridge's icicles, and Keats's urn. The emphasis on *ending* presented writers, I propose, with complex spaces of reflection that fall somewhere between absolute lastness and projected lines forward, in which the impending loss of one world coincided with its provisional rehabilitation in an unknown futurity. Looking backward offered a prospective challenge to visions of the future that imagined politics as freshly renovated, the basis of governance as permanently settled. But nothing was guaranteed: the endings that challenged closed views of the future also carried an ominous sense of lastness that challenged the premise of futurity as such. To adopt a poetic image from various writings considered here, we might compare this paradoxical situation to a statue falling in a desert, with both somebody and nobody around to hear it.

For Shelley's father William Godwin, sepulchers, monuments, and other relics promised to revive associations with the past. Literature had a special role in this argument, which framed reading and writing as a means, quite literally, of keeping the deceased alive. Godwin argued against remaining cut off from ancestors and their inheritances, contending that the "desire to start afresh" coupled with the "fact of ending too soon" kept the world "from moving forward."[33] Byron advanced his own darkly contrarian view, resisting monolithic ideas of progress but cultivating uncertainty as to whether the world left behind by a ruinous past would be able to carry forward its desirable legacies. Shelley made this dynamic of failed transmission damningly specific, imagining a future inhabited by an ever-dwindling number of people. In *The Last Man*, remnants of the past echo in a world progressively emptied out of anybody able to hear them. But the unwinding of society and dwindling of the population at least sharpen the ambiguous resonance of those losses. Whether or not *The Last Man* imagines a future in which any readers remain to make sense of its prophetic vision is uncertain. However, the answer is more clear for Shelley's writings themselves. *The Last Man* imagines a world, in some sense, outside time. But we find a concrete analogue for the novel's bearing on Shelley's political present in Byron's writings, which had their own life after death, a counterintuitive dynamic wherein loss and lastness activate real potential in the here and now. The end of the line becomes the site of restless energies, unfinished business.

In political terms, Byron had an idiosyncratic stance, looking back to the fading importance of aristocratic political elites and the former generations of "Old Whigs," including Edmund Burke and Richard Brinsley Sheridan. He teased Hobhouse, his friend from the Whig Club at Cambridge University, for having lent himself to "Hunt and Cobbett – and the bones of Tom Paine."[34] But Byron's attachments to older types of political men (and his aversion to political modernization) were not, I propose, merely reflexive or uncritical. Byron had an acute understanding of changing political roles in England, this book will argue, and his embrace of the past, while self-consciously retrograde and increasingly elegiac, channeled hopes for a different future. Those political ambitions were bound up with reflections upon dying races and ending lines that cut against and complicated existing progress narratives. In his final years, one account claimed, Byron continued to identify with a "tribe of Mohawks" from his earlier life, "not knowing that this tribe was extinct."[35] That claim sought to disparage Byron's investments in the past. But at a time when Whigs confronted an emboldened Tory elite and prospective replacement by a new breed of liberal politician, those reflections brought alternative trajectories into view, neither looking backward to a settled past nor forward to a predictable future. In *The Last Man*, Shelley made that potential explicit, having the hopes of Lord Raymond – an explicitly Byronic figure, modeled on the poet – reverberate against a backdrop of political ending and the dawning of a permanently changed world, in which the place of both individual men and "man" as such was no longer assured.

Political Biography and the Byron Circle

While neither, strictly speaking, a work of political history nor a literary biography, this book seeks to test existing accounts of Byron's politics – and to contest some of their conclusions about the directions and intensities of his political commitments. Paying close attention to Byron's political interlocutors and expanding the geographical terrain of his political thought from England and Europe to the Americas and the South Seas, I revise accounts of his belated "Whig" politics and the scope and intensity of his revolutionary ideals. Chapters 2 and 3 pay fine-grained attention to organized partisanship and political debate while also attending in detail to printed works and literary texts. As such, these chapters examine the changing field of political positions at a time when parties were in flux and new orientations were taking hold (including with respect to the British Empire). The purpose of these discussions is not to offer a new account of Byron's politics per se. Rather, I use "Byron's politics" to open up a fuller account of the period, from the changing contours of political leadership to the wider cultural-affective field. This book accordingly brings detailed attention to politics together with attention to the literary milieus, print spheres, and the wider cultural arenas in which both politics and literature took shape. Attending to actualized and potential political positions, I draw upon fictional and imaginative works, interpersonal dynamics, and intertextual transmission. In doing so, I seek to advance an expanded approach to political biography.

Samuel Johnson may serve as an example of a literary author with a more familiar kind of "political biography."[36] An essayist, lexicographer, man of letters, and cranky *bon vivant*, Johnson voiced staunch Tory views and wrote proministerial pamphlets on topics of heated debate in the years leading up to the American Revolution. In a previous study, I used Johnson's Toryism to stake a claim about what it means to study the "politics" of a literary author (as distinct from – but inevitably entangled with – the political significance attached to their writings). "Certain facts remain beyond dispute," I wrote, "based on the available record of his statements and actions – which are all we have to go on in assessing the politics of Johnson or anyone else."[37] Colin Jager has taken issue with this claim. "To be sure," he writes, "statements and actions are a crucial part of politics. But 'all we have to go on'? Well, no. Among the many things ignored here are the words on the page themselves, and therefore the manifold ways that those words can be taken up, mis-understood, interpreted, reinterpreted – in short, the entire world of *reading*."[38] Unless I misunderstand Jager here, he appears to suggest that any reader's reading of an author's words should be included within an account of that author's politics – even and perhaps especially when those words are interpreted anew or "mis-understood." That approach does not seem likely to generate an intelligible account of an author's politics, let alone a meaningful one. I stand by my assertion about the "record" of an author's "statements and actions" being "all we have to go on" in giving an account of their politics. (What else would we go on?) But two points are worth emphasizing. First, accepting my claim does not preclude an author's writings being interpreted in ways that go against – and that even point to complications or contradictions within – their demonstrated political views.[39] Second, the record of actions on which we base an account of an author's politics can and should include what we know about their reading. For her part, Shelley discerned political resonances within Byron's works that she elaborated upon in private written reflections and published works. Those intuitions and reflections, I will propose, have an important bearing on her engagement with political activity and debate. But they do not somehow belong, as Jager would have it, in an account of Byron's politics. They are all Shelley's own.

When it comes to an assessment of his politics, Byron, like most people, presents a mixed record. He had well-documented entanglements with various causes and movements, justifying his revolutionary reputation. But his writings also include many statements attacking the "rabble" and bloodthirsty Jacobins. Byron's politics are further complicated by the fact that his dazzling life and early death gave rise to much speculation about what, in a different turn of events, he would have done (or had, in fact, been planning to do). When they come from his immediate circle, those speculations help to clarify what options were available to him. That Byron could seemingly have become a successful Whig MP, leader of a popular movement, or even head of an overseas republic helps to establish where he deliberately turned away from such opportunities. In limning the contours of Byron's actual, potential, or imagined political biography, these speculations also point to the role that "Byron" played in a wider cultural-political field. Both kinds of speculation are important to this book.

Where a traditional political biography would seek to separate Byron the
man out from the wider field of representations – while recognizing the
role that available guises of political agency played as enabling conditions
for his politics – this book ultimately has more interest in approaching
Byron and "Byron" as entangled and to some degree inseparable. Another
way to say this is that I am as concerned with imagined Byronic political
trajectories as with Byron's actual politics. Beyond questions about docu-
mented political orientation and involvement, this book adopts an
approach to political biography that looks beyond ideas and actions
narrowly defined and proposes an approach to political formation that
includes literary production and creative expression and that draws, in
turn, upon a range of material, from posthumous depictions to intertextual
echoes. *Pace* Jager, I do not want to suggest that an author's politics can be
whatever we might want to imagine them to be. But while seeking to
maintain clarity around that question, I also seek to push it to its limits,
asking whether we might find traces of an author's politics in absence and
erasure, fleeting imaginings and vanished imprints, what is not there as
much as what is.[40]

The benefits of this expanded approach become apparent with Mary
Shelley. By a narrower set of criteria, Shelley did not have a political
biography. But approached in the expanded terms of this study, she
emerges as one of the most sophisticated political thinkers of the age –
and as one of its most nuanced observers of politics. Teasing out Shelley's
unique perspective and authorial stance requires some careful work, however. In her compelling study of Mary Shelley, Godwin, and
Wollstonecraft, Julie A. Carlson has emphasized the inseparability of
their lives and writing. Expanding upon precursors including William
St. Clair's collective intellectual and political biography, Carlson returns
to view psychic ties and affective bonds, collectively held ideas and borrowed tropes – a kind of shared viscera that binds the lives and works of
England's "first family." Shelley's writings were not only inseparable from
the ideas and influence of her parents. Those works and to some degree
Shelley *herself* as a thinking, writing, feeling individual were inextricable,
Carlson demonstrates, from her familial milieu and its concerns with the
publicity of private sentiments, for example, or the forces shaping personal
identity and habits of thinking. This book takes inspiration from Carlson's
powerful study and its account of authorship as transpersonal and transfer-
ential, bridging persons and books, affects and ideas. At the same time,
I place the emphasis on Shelley's estrangement, including her cultivated
distance from the men around her.[41] These features of her identity

converge in her reflections upon lastness. Byron's bombastic presence and haunting death inform the depiction of Lord Raymond in *The Last Man*. Following Barbara Johnson, Shelley's depictions of fictional men in her writings may even be considered part of her *own* political biography.[42] At the same time, Shelley's writings betray self-consciousness about her relative invisibility, as marked in her silent listening at Lake Geneva and promises to be a demure observer of parliament. But in these quiet and self-effacing gestures, I propose, she paradoxically asserted her unique perspective on politics.

The journal entry in which Shelley imagined herself as "the last man" has been read in narrowly gendered terms, locating her as the barren end point of a fertile line of literary creation.[43] But in *Frankenstein* and *The Last Man*, this book argues, Shelley made her experiences of loss and isolation into the crucible for powerful imaginative reflections on the ends of politics and the future of mankind. In parallel with its focus on Byron, this book argues for an approach to so-called second-generation Romanticism reconstellated around Shelley's perspective. That includes her obliquely critical perspective on a political world organized by and around men. This study takes cues from Shelley in looking at that world askance, leveraging a focus on men into alternative, critical perspectives. In shifting Shelley's homonymic elision of maleness with the entirety of the human race into a slant rhyme, my attention to the last *men* seeks to anatomize the political and literary culture that affirmed the dominance of men over women. Men still dominate the pages that follow. But as Shelley showed in *Frankenstein*, such a focus can sheathe a damning critique of masculine hubris and failure. While devoting attention to Byron and other male figures – alongside the sidelined literary and political contributions of Shelley – this book also recognizes that this was a period in which one of the most influential reformers and most important novelists of the age was invisible to some of her contemporaries (Hobhouse described Maria Edgeworth as the "smallest and most insignificant person I ever saw – very plain," adding that "she said nothing that I heard" upon meeting her at a party).[44] The author of *Emma* elicited the approval of Walter Scott. But the full talents of Jane Austen, Shelley's rival as the author of the period's most enduringly important works, were discernible only to her immediate circles, her sister, or nobody at all.

While attending to individual literary works in their own right, this study equally adopts a horizontal approach, thinking less in terms of genealogical and diachronic models of influence than in terms of lateral and multidirectional movements within the same period and between literary writings, political activity, and the wider cultural-affective field. Shelley once again demonstrates the merits of an approach attentive to these interrelationships. Although her contributions remain to some degree under erasure, written in the invisible ink of silent observation, reading, and editing, we may begin to return her perspective to view by way of the emphasis on influence, intertextuality, allusion, and collaborative aesthetics that has maintained a steady drumbeat through the last half-century of Romantic criticism.[45] Even Shelley's transcriptions of works by members of her circle – beginning with *Childe Harold's Pilgrimage* – may be considered transformative, imaginative acts.[46] This book may thus be considered, among other things, an intertextual study of Byron and Shelley that takes reading and allusion to be as central to political thought as they are to creative process. To return Shelley's political thought to view, this book contends, we must work through her complex ties to the lives, ideas, and sentiments of others, in particular her attachment to the poetry and person of Byron – and its enfolding into her own aesthetics.

Late Romanticism and the End of an Era

The late Romantic age saw core features of the political past swept away. The early nineteenth century witnessed brewing unrest in England, as increasingly bleak realities on the ground belied the revolutionary promise of previous decades. This was "a period in which a largely patriotic wartime populace changed to a reform-seeking, internationally aware public."[47] As Byron ascended to poetic fame, idealistic hopes gave way to the stark realities of the Napoleonic wars and subsequent suffering and repression at home and abroad. Far from the French Revolution having ended history, the past seemed to have returned with full force.[48] Yet this was also a period of dynamism and change.[49] Historians have debated whether the passage of the 1832 Reform Act marked a dramatic break with an *ancien régime* or a quietistic effort to preserve much of the status quo. But we do not need to accept that everything was transformed – nor affirm that nothing much changed – to recognize that the years leading up to and directly following Reform witnessed a multifaceted sense of nationwide housecleaning and ground clearing.[50] A print from 1832 entitled "The Managers Last Kick, or, the Destruction of the Boroughmongers" (Figure 1) cast the passage of Reform in just those terms. The Reform Act brought long-awaited changes to the practice of elections, expanding the franchise to men who met income and property thresholds, and set the country on course for political modernization. Reform's success witnessed

Figure 1 Charles Jameson Grant, "The Managers Last Kick, or, the Destruction of the Boroughmongers" (1832). BM 567777001. © The Trustees of the British Museum.

a Whig elite still dominated by aristocratic patronage networks operate in tandem with the new generation headed by Sir John Russell and nationwide reform agitation to vanquish opposition from the Duke of Wellington and the right wing of the Tory party. In the print, King William rides to victory on a white horse (identified as "Good Old Grey," after the Whig leader) while Russell taunts his rivals, trumpeting the "Purge" of around one hundred MPs from the rolls. Wellington and his fellow Tories, meanwhile, sit stewing on their benches in parliament (presented as the "Bedlam" insane asylum) while the "rotten boroughs" eliminated by the Reform Act tumble into a version of John Bunyan's "Slough of Despond." But disenfranchised boroughs and discarded remnants of the Tory elite are not alone in falling into the abyss. The tangled mass of bodies also includes disappointed radicals and reformers including Henry Hunt and his Irish contemporary Daniel O'Connell. The image thus heralds not only the arrival of Reform but the passing away of radical hopes, swallowed up by the ground beneath as a renovated future took hold.

Earlier that year, Hunt addressed the House of Commons. As if in fulfillment of Shelley's prophecies in *The Last Man* – where an aggressive populist eventually takes power – Hunt had been elected two years earlier as MP for Preston, defeating future prime minister Edward Stanley.[51] Hunt continued to press for recognition of the "working classes." The Reform Act, passed in 1832, after innumerable setbacks and false starts, ultimately had narrower concerns. But Hunt had another cause in mind when he rose to speak: a further inquiry into the 1819 "Peterloo" massacre. "Twelve years had elapsed since these atrocities were committed," Hunt informed the chamber, "and in twelve years events had occurred, which, though they did not prevent him from still demanding justice, had completely eradicated the desire for revenge." This claim was less than entirely convincing. Hunt's Wordsworthian repetitions notwithstanding ("twelve years had elapsed . . . and in twelve years"), his outrage had not lessened. In response, another MP claimed the proposed inquiry had "no other tendency than to rip up old grievances, and to revive animosities, which he had trusted would ere now be put to sleep by the soothing hand of time." Hunt's demands were, as Wordsworth wrote of poetry, emotion recollected in tranquility. During a long, rambling speech, he veered between paranoid accusations about the government's incitement of the violence at Manchester and self-righteous appeals to the injustice of his own imprisonment. But vengeance was subsumed within vindication. "Revenge on the authors and abettors of the outrages of that day," Hunt bluntly stated, "he had already had enough." The Manchester meeting had been a proreform rally. Hunt had now lived to see a bill brought to parliament "which, though it might not give to the people the relief which he wished them to obtain, still admitted that all the allegations which he had at that time made were correct, namely, that the House of Commons did not represent the people, but only a corrupt portion of placeholders and boroughmongers."[52]

More importantly, all his enemies were dead. "Who was the Prime Minister of that day?" Hunt asked, referring to Lord Liverpool. "Where was he?" Dead. George Canning? Dead. While imprisoned, Hunt had received the not-unwelcome news that Castlereagh had committed suicide. At an early demonstration of the railway, William Huskisson was killed by a train. Hunt proceeded with still more daring allusions to the recent monarch ("King George the 4th – he who had thanked the Magistrates with such breathless haste – where now was he?") The former regent, much derided by Byron, had passed with little fanfare in 1830. While the House of Commons had "refused to do justice between the people and their oppressors on this melancholy occasion," Hunt concluded, "the hand of Providence had already inflicted justice, where justice was due," and he had "already witnessed enough of the discomfiture of his adversaries to sate even the keenest appetite of revenge." With an eye still on the "yeomanry" who attacked the crowd, he "yet trusted to live to see the day" in which those who had "instigate[d] the people to acts of violence" and "throw[n] discredit upon Reform" would face their reckoning. But he had received vindication, at the level of political debate. Hunt had lived to see "the Members of that Government, which had gone to war with France to stifle the call for Reform, compelled to sit night after night in weak and ineffectual struggles against the progress of a measure which in itself was nothing but the commencement of Reform." Hunt concluded that he "might even now say, 'the Lord's will be done: I have lived long enough, for I have lived to see the borough mongers brought upon their knees before the people whom they have so long insulted.'"[53] Hunt not only channeled radical disappointment at Reform's concessions to moderates; he also sought to preserve a "Romantic" excess of feeling – the kind of recalcitrant affect discernible, I argue in Chapter 3, in the wake of the following year's Slavery Abolition Act.

The Reform Act was experienced as a dramatic rupture with the past. As the legislation was gathering steam, Hobhouse visited his brother in the country, where the local MP was "one of those old courtiers who inquires only what the King wishes." There were, Hobhouse heard, "still many" such men. But in London, he added, "the race is nearly extinct."[54] Yet the political elite was not so much dissolved and destroyed as renovated and reconfigured. As the "Destruction of the Boroughmongers" print (Figure 1) suggested, Reform eradicated swathes of corruption. But what the print imagined as the "Last Kick" of entrenched political interests also risked becoming the last gasp of the radical movement. Hunt's speech pointed to the complex resonances of this outcome. "In vain had that arrogant and insolent party sent Reformer after Reformer to prison," he railed of the Tory elite, "in vain had they gagged the Press by acts as alien to the practice as they were novel to the theory of the British Constitution – in vain had they passed Bills to prevent public meetings, and to put down the right of petitioning; for, in spite of the menaces of the law, and the terrors of the dungeon, the cause of Reform had proved *a giant too powerful* for them to cope with."[55]

Hunt may well have been picturing another daunting creation: that of Victor Frankenstein. He would not have been alone in connecting Shelley's 1818 novel with recent political innovations. Hunt had, in fact, recently been referenced in a print that made just that connection. The previous year, "Political Frankensteins. Alarmed at the progress of a Giant of their own Creation" (Figure 2) depicts Daniel O'Connell as a bulked-up but seemingly good-natured "Giant," several feet taller than the men seeking to restrain him.[56] Those men include Edward Stanley, whom Hunt had defeated at election in 1830. "This is even worse than being Hunted out of Preston!" Stanley exclaims, alluding to that defeat, as the radical Irish organizer and activist breaks through their efforts to restrain him with legislation, waving calls for "Repeal of the Union" and "Agitation

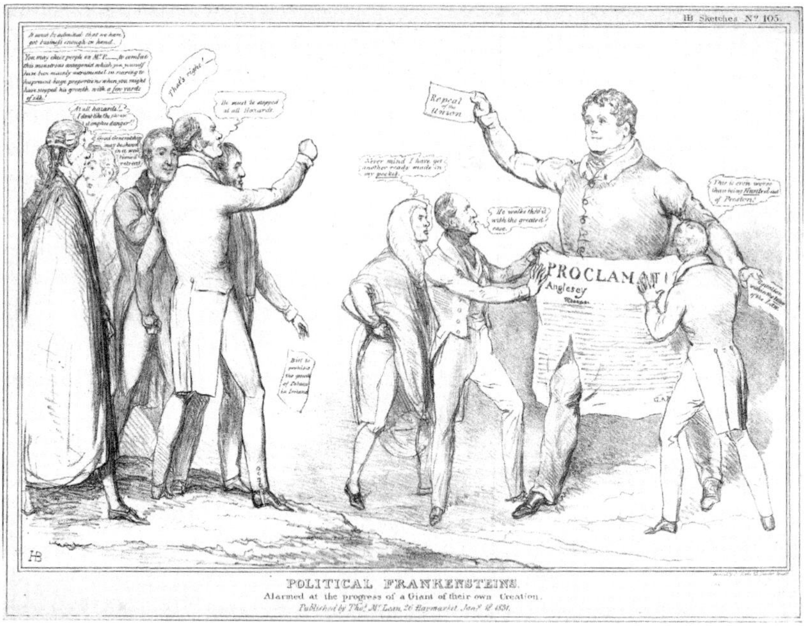

Figure 2 "Political Frankensteins. Alarmed at the progress of a Giant of their own Creation" (1831). BM 765726001. © The Trustees of the British Museum.

within the <u>letter</u> of the Law." The passage in 1829 of legislation that allowed O'Connell, a Catholic with a huge popular following, to take his seat in parliament had fractured the Tory party, helping to pave the way for the Reform Act. But while setting in motion further reformist measures and socioeconomic changes over the coming decade, the short-term implications were more sharply curtailed. The not-yet-fully enfranchised demos confronted a new world far from hospitable to their interests, as did not-yet -fully emancipated enslaved persons overseas. For his part, Hunt "trusted to live still longer, and if he did live a few years more," he told parliament, "he should live to see justice inflicted on all who committed and abetted the massacre at Manchester." But these spirited calls for the undying pursuit of "justice" aside, the coming era saw a new breed of quiescent politicians preside over newly regulated populations, at home and abroad.

Liberalism would go on to adopt multiple guises, from those stressed in Michel Foucault's still-invaluable account of institutional apparatuses, instrumental rationalities, and population management to master narratives about the "end of history."[57] The ideals of classical liberalism came into sharper focus with eradicated corruption and an expanded franchise, in tandem with the growth of industrial capitalism and free trade. The Whigs endured into the early decades of the Victorian age. Lord Melbourne, the young Queen Victoria's first prime minister, coexisted with the new generation heralded by Russell but had strong ties to the old Whig houses (not least through his mother, a scandalmongering society lady and confidante of Byron). As the nineteenth century went on, however, a renovated political elite took hold. The liberal politician's dispassionate reason would be cast as the antidote to a rowdy mob, leading more respectable members of the emergent mass public to become a core constituency of the Liberal party. Reformers had imagined the uprooting of an entire political system, for which aristocratic Whig lineages became totemic symbols. But with the transition into the mid-Victorian age, those resonant absences were soon filled in, as new edifices of control and management took hold at home and abroad.

These changes in the political elite coupled with a new understanding of literature. As Elaine Hadley and Amanda Anderson have demonstrated, mid-Victorian liberalism witnessed newly quiescent, modest, and humbled ways of imagining both the political domain and the sphere of letters.[58] The early nineteenth century saw the consolidation of new ideas of the literary realm, variously defined by nonpartisanship, a (paradoxical) remove from commercial imperatives, the feminization of affect, and the masculinization of literary authority. These decades also saw a move beyond the interchange between literature and politics that was a hallmark of the preceding period. As I argued in my previous book, *Disaffected Parties*, resituating the Romantic age in the long eighteenth century highlights the agitated, disaffected energies that continued to shape literary authorship, even as the literary domain became increasingly defined against – and insulated from – the world of politics. Attending more closely to the transition between late Romanticism and the Victorian age deepens our appreciation of the relationship between Romantic writing and the pre- and post-Reform mood of acquiescence, equipoise, and lastness.

Walter Scott died in 1832, having devoted his final years to publishing *Tales of a Grandfather*. Jeremy Bentham, who died the same year, donated his body to the newly formed University College. Hazlitt had long been on the ropes and died at the outset of the decade. The three men made very different ghosts. Scott's spectral presence in the literary field gave way to the robust fictional marketplace his works had helped to consolidate.[59] The uncanny presence of Bentham's waxen corpse, meanwhile, offered a ghoulish gloss on Hazlitt's assertion that he "legislated for future times." Mary Shelley was aghast when she saw Hazlitt shortly before his death, recalling responses to the hollowed-eyed Romantic visionaries and failed creators that haunt her novels. In his 1825 collection, Hazlitt had presented a vivid tableau of reformers, visionaries, poets, and politicians variously animated by the "Spirit of the Age." But those energies had given way to what Hobhouse (echoing Byron) termed "the *cant* of the age."[60] The moment a "writer of talent" got into good company, Hobhouse wrote in 1830, "he [*sic*] was told that he must adopt unfashionable opinions." Thomas Babington Macaulay (who gave what Hobhouse derisively termed "essays" in the House of Commons) points to the consolidation of new orthodoxies. In tandem with the Anglocentric Victorian worldview of his *History of England* (1848), Macaulay exported a narrow version of Benthamite legal theory to India, where he helped advance new forms of political repression and cultural imperialism.[61] Following life as a dandy and author of "silver-fork" fiction, Edward Bulwer-Lytton turned to imperialist fantasies and racialized utopias, becoming the bestselling novelist in the post-Reform decades, his fiction rivaling Dickens's in popularity for the remainder of the century. Shelley wrote to Scott in 1829 seeking assistance with her historical novel *The Fortunes of Perkin Warbeck*, before deepening her concerns with domestic virtue in her final novels.

By 1832, John Keats and Percy Shelley had been dead for a decade. Wordsworth and Coleridge hobbled on, reduced versions of their former selves. In 1830, Arthur Henry Hallam, a member, with Alfred Tennyson, of the "Apostles" at Cambridge University, published a promising book of poems; Tennyson published his own *Poems Chiefly Lyrical* the same year. But poetry had begun to undergo a wider sea change. Albums and anthologies flooded the poetry marketplace, fueling uncertainty about literature's role.[62] That changing literary-cultural field made room, fleetingly, for new flavors of Byronism. Female poets now reignited the poet's spirit under their own lights. "L.E.L." burnished her reputation through acts of poetic "self-fashioning," Susan Wolfson enthuses, which embraced "Byronism" as "living and then dying portraiture."[63] The hero of *Childe Harold's Pilgrimage* continued to animate the souls of female readers and poets (and even some men). But these were, Wolfson contends, reflections on poems and images, self-conscious engagements with Byron as "author" and emphatically not, in any sense, brushes with the man himself.

Byron now belonged to a different age and a closed past. Despite acquiring further layers of notoriety in the years after his death, he had become, in Wolfson's wonderful phrase, a "generic drug."[64] Floridly imagined as a dandy and figure of scandal, Byron served as proxy for an era that was decisively over, entombed in his former reputation, soldered to an epoch that was consigned to a vanished past.[65] Whatever we conclude about Byron's spirituality, the grandiose monument to the poet overseen by Hobhouse spoke volumes about the priorities of a new age.[66] The same went, in another register, for Moore's mammoth biography and collected works. For all their animation of fresh controversy about his marriage, Moore's labors were to sit on a changing kind of bookshelf alongside Leigh Hunt's disillusioned account of the poet and John Wilson Croker's freshly repackaged *Life of Johnson*. Byron's ex-wife became a prominent antislavery campaigner, attending the 1840 World Anti-Slavery Convention and corresponding with Harriet Beecher Stowe (whose *Lady Byron Vindicated* inserted further nails in the coffin with respect to Byron's personal reputation). These revivals of earlier disputes notwithstanding, the poet began to be passed down, in the ever-dwindling units of anecdote, anthologized extract, portrait, imitative poem, and epigram. Byron's tortured journal entry about the "best of prophets of the future" being "the past" was repackaged as a digestible, conservative-friendly sentiment, cited by US senators and at least one Republican President.[67]

Watching Percy Shelley's skull burn and crack in his funeral pyre, Byron had hardened his poetic purpose. In his 1832 speech to parliament, Hunt made his own Hamlet-like gesture, holding up, for dramatic effect, a piece of skull belonging to one of the Peterloo victims. But these remnants notwithstanding, Byron and the spirit of his age had begun to pass into the ether. Even for those still with a foot in popular radicalism, the political skies had settled into a new palette. The radical excitement of the 1790s, the eminence of the Whigs, and even the Tory party were not long for the world – even if refashioned Whig politicians and new brands of Tory*ism* would have formidable afterlives. The moralistic tendency that some observers discerned in Chartism (no drinking!) carried across to the ortho-doxies of political Liberalism.[68] The New Poor Law and Robert Peel's Metropolitan Police heralded new guises of social control and moral discipline. Hunt may have called for an inquiry into Peterloo, in an effort, over a decade later, to keep past struggles alive. But an event earlier the same summer as the violence in Manchester stamped that year with importance for an altogether different reason. May 24, 1819, saw the birth of Alexandrina Victoria, future queen of England and figurehead of a globe-spanning empire, the first woman of a changed world.

The Victorian age witnessed imperialism and free trade extend and further deepen British control across the globe. Hobhouse inherited a baronetcy and went on to ascend the colonial administration, navigating conflict in Afghanistan as secretary at war and overseeing India as president of the Board of Control. Governance had begun to take on a new stripe, in tandem with ascendant liberal ideals, economic shifts, and biopolitical norms. Politics, in short, had new ends. Robert Peel, presiding over the transition from Toryism into Conservatism, effected a radical break with the past when he opposed the Corn Laws in the name of free trade. These developments coincided, among other shifts, with increased fossil-fuel consumption. In the "Managers Last Kick" print, Peel appears among the tangled mass of figures falling into the "Slough of Despond" at the bottom of the image (close to Hunt, who has fallen into a bottle of the "blacking" ink he marketed in an effort to revive his career). The image of these political relics falling into a black pit had its own dark irony. In fact, the opening outward of the Earth's core, through the industrial-level extraction of coal, would help to redraw Britain's electoral map and transform politics over the coming two centuries (changes only now coming to an end with Labour's waning hold over the former mining heartlands of northern England and south Wales). In his 1871 novel *The Coming Race*, Bulwer-Lytton's American narrator travels down a coal mine, where he discovers an alien species living at the planet's core. Their perfected society portends a wiping clean of the Earth's surface and the vanquishing of political conflict.[69] The conspicuous black core of the "Managers Last Kick" points, instead, to the various, clashing forces that would roil politics in the decades to come.[70] John Bull stands on a shelf of rock, cheering at the renovated political elite. But the ground beneath his feet gives way to a pool of darkness, hinting at the buried energies that would transform both politics and the face of the Earth in the years to come.

The End of History and the End of the World

In a now notorious 1989 essay, Francis Fukuyama proposed that the end of the Cold War had witnessed the "end of history as such": "the end point of mankind's ideological evolution and the universalization of Western liberal democracy as the final form of human government."[71] "We who live in stable, long-standing liberal democracies face an unusual situation," Fukuyama elaborated in the book-length version of his argument:

> we have trouble imagining a world that is better than our own, or a future that is not essentially democratic and capitalist. Within that framework, of course, many things could be improved: we could house the homeless, guarantee opportunity for minorities and women, improve competitiveness, and create new jobs. We can also imagine future worlds that are significantly worse than what we know now, in which national, racial, or religious intolerance makes a comeback, or in which we are overwhelmed by war or environmental collapse. But we cannot picture to ourselves a world that is *essentially* different from the present one, and at the same time better. Other, less reflective ages also thought of themselves as the best, but we arrive at this conclusion exhausted, as it were, from the pursuit of alternatives we felt *had* to be better than liberal democracy.[72]

Fukuyama makes clear that his claim about the triumph of Western liberal democracy does not mean that the world might not become "significantly worse." It is perhaps just as well. Recent challenges to the political status quo, including the turn against globalization and the resurgence of illiberal populisms, have presented substantive empirical challenges to claims for liberalism's triumph.[73] At the same time, we have been reminded that some cannot imagine a better future than liberalism.[74] Climate change may have effected a more permanent disruption to the premises of Fukuyama's argument, extending beyond his prescient fears of "environmental collapse." Far from history having ended, we now confront uncertainty about what kind of future mankind has and questions about how our political institutions can evolve (or whether they will endure) to meet coming challenges. The "end of the world" has become our new "end of history." But reflecting on the world ending might equally help to dislodge monolithic arguments about the future in favor of multifaceted reflections on the changing ends of politics. Rather than debating whether liberalism has triumphed or giving way to similarly reductive claims that "man" faces certain doom, the exigencies of the current moment force us to countenance a range of possibilities for what remains of the future.

Fukuyama developed the arguments of his essay in a 1992 book entitled *The End of History and The Last Man*, where he expounded at greater length on the naivety of socialism. "In our grandparents' time," Fukuyama wrote, "many reasonable people could foresee a radiant socialist future in which private property and capitalism had been abolished, and *in which politics itself was somehow overcome*."[75] Rather than a constitutional break or dramatic rupture, political institutions and procedures give way, in this scenario, to a larger set of collective processes (along with, we can assume, "radiant" visions of shared plentitude and mutual contentment). These changes in the organization of society, eliminating the need for private ownership, come together with the similarly expansive, if more elusive, transformation to which Fukuyama alludes when he speaks of a future in which "politics itself was somehow overcome." That phrasing sets up the blissfully naive idea of ("somehow") overcoming politics as the fantastical and ludicrous counterpart to his own more hard-headed and chastened claim about liberalism heralding the end of history, exemplified in the melancholic fact of there never being a perfected "Last Man" (a further addition to the original essay, borrowed from Nietzsche, which provides the book with its locus for ambivalent reflections about the futility of world-altering ambitions).

Yet for all his deepened criticisms of utopian naivety, Fukuyama leaves his own argument open to critique on exactly the same grounds. His appeal to a posthistorical moment in which the "final form of human government" has been decided *itself* amounts to the assertion that politics has, effectively, ended. Assuming that we identify the political with anything other than – and in addition to – fairly frequent multiparty elections, ballot boxes, and full enfranchisement under the rule of law, then Fukuyama also describes a society in which politics has been, as he writes of socialism, "somehow overcome." As with a static socialist utopia, his argument imagines a world in which politics has been absorbed into a larger set of procedural norms and economic practices. This is the mindset to which Emmett Rensin alludes in a pungent 2017 jeremiad against neoliberal technocratic elites. It was "all going so well just a moment ago," Rensin writes, followed by a free-indirect paraphrase of Fukuyama's argument, which slyly adjusts its tense to the perfected past: "History *was* over." In the wake of Trump, Brexit, and other shocks, however, the charts of the expert elites "lie abandoned by the roadside."[76]

Politics appears here as a broken-down vehicle, a junked-out car. At first, Rensin characterizes liberal governance, grounded in free trade, stable laws, and limited regulation, as a streamlined system and well-oiled machine. But he sets up these metaphors only to discredit and recontextualize them: "Liberalism is not working. Something deep within the mechanism has cracked. All our wonk managers, our expert stewards of the world, have lost their way. They wander desert highways in a daze, wondering why the brakes locked up, why the steering wheel came off, how the engine caught on fire." Describing flailing political elites as drivers of a broken-down car billowing smoke at the roadside, Rensin's metaphor also encloses a further, more literal layer of reference, collapsing liberal governance back into an image of a stalling, petroleum-fueled global economy. Both technocratic leadership and a carbon-based economy have, simultaneously, the argument implies, reached the end of the road. Yet in contrast with the fictional dystopias that stage irreversible collapse as sweeping tableaus of rusted cars and trash-can fires amidst a howling void, these desert scenes also offer a qualified opportunity. This breakdown may still give way to a reimagined future, even as wandering "desert highways in a daze" might also suggest increasingly unbearable temperatures. In any case, overturning simplistic narratives about achieved final states in favor of the *end* of the end of history, the moment after postpolitical politics, the brink of ruin but not yet a state of disaster, leaves us in open territory, under wide horizons.

In expanding our appreciation for the range of political positions that Byron, Shelley, and their wider circles made imaginable, we develop new lines of approach to their concerns with coming to the end. The various images and themes that accompany the reflections on ending in works by these authors – stolen fires and dying stars, serenely closing horizons and unspoiled idylls – not only intersected with and informed their thinking about politics. Their emphasis on endings also became a means, I argue, to register uncertainty (if not flat-out unease) concerning the onset of economic and political liberalism. This book's newly integrated account of politics and the Byron circle yields fresh interpretations of works including Shelley's novels and the cluster of late writings in which Byron reflected upon eschatological, apocalyptic, and otherwise cataclysmic themes. Drawing these interrelated writings together with a cross-section of contemporary political activity and debate, I return to view an underexplored nexus of late Romantic literary activity and political thought: a unique moment of convergence that brought both the inherited political past and the future of liberal governance under the spotlight. Beyond politics, these writings also help to disclose further, subterranean shifts, at both national and planetary scales, including the onset of a carbon-fueled economy.

Byron and his contemporaries did not experience impending ecological catastrophe. But they did confront an analogous predicament to that posed by the "Anthropocene." Without knowingly experiencing climate change, they lived through the advent of industrial modernity and voiced fears and more muted premonitions that technological change and capitalist expansion were unalterably deforming the planet. In the process, they imagined "the world" coming to an end. That prospect was informed by growing realizations about the extinction of species and geological speculations that the world had already "ended" several times before. Byron and his circle elaborated millenarian, apocalyptic, and proto science-fictional scenarios, including fantasies of escaping this planet altogether. Their writings featured myriad reflections upon the prospect of a world without, before, or capable of proceeding without, mankind. To this extent, they may be said to inhabit an "Anthropocenean moment" cognate with our own, in which we confront the prospect of a world without mankind (and, at the same time, our prospective incapacity to reverse or ultimately prevent that outcome).[77] While that "moment" has found paradigmatic expression in our own time, the experience of living on in the face of irreparable damage, continuing impotence, and even future "extinction" also inflects the various writings examined by this book. At the same time as they open up ways of thinking anew about the changing ends of politics, then, these works also reveal the generative – or at least reparative – possibilities that may follow from coming to the end.

Chapter Summaries

The first three chapters focus closely on politics, paying detailed attention to political activity and debate (including developments on the ground) while introducing the biographical, literary-historical, and conceptual frameworks that inform the book as a whole. Chapter 1, "The End of Politics and the End of the World," backs away from the specifics of the late Romantic age to examine the convergence between world-ending rhetoric and political change across a wider canvas. Approaching the "end of politics" as related to but distinct from both the "end of the world" and the "end of history," I examine the disrupted political worlds and partially realized utopias in works by Jonathan Swift and William Morris before turning to the convergence of endings unique to the late

Romantic age. In addition to the dramatic breaks and historical rupture associated with the French Revolution (and more subtle visions of disruption and uprooting like those found in Morris and Swift), late Romantic authors embraced entirely new ways of imagining freshly opening "worlds." Even Byron's poem "Darkness," I propose, uses the death of the sun to fleetingly imagine the futures that might take shape at the moment when politics ends. Chapter 2, "The Last Whigs," turns to the bustling terrain of political activity with a focus on the changing roles available to political men. Examining published and unpublished writings by Hobhouse and Byron, I explore the vanishing space available to the Whigs as the traditional party of opposition as "the people" gained ground as a political force – and the space that would come to be occupied, later in the nineteenth century, by the "liberal" politician. The chapter concludes with Byron's meditations upon images of eminent Whig politicians and orators from the recent past and a reading of his *Monody on the Death of the Right Honourable R. B. Sheridan*. Chapter 3, "Byron, Brougham, and the End of Slavery," examines poetic and political disruptions to the wider affective public sphere during debates over the abolition of slavery – and asks how they intersect with the recalcitrant feeling attributed to formerly enslaved people between the late Romantic period and the onset of the Victorian age. The early drafts of Byron's sprawling satirical masterwork *Don Juan* included a sketch of Brougham, whom the poet mocked for his zealous, often-erratic commitments. In contemporary depictions, including antislavery caricatures, those energies aligned Brougham with Black resistance, helping to keep the last enslaved people in view as a new world order began to take hold.

The remaining two chapters bring these frameworks for approaching politics and futurity together with detailed attention to longer literary works. Chapter 4 offers an extended reading of Shelley's *The Last Man*. In the first half of the chapter, I ask how political men modeled after Byron channeled poignant failures and elusive hopes in the context of post-reform futures. Where George Eliot's *Felix Holt* emphasizes the unsuitability of a Byronic politician's elite bearing and crass populism to post-1832 politics in England – betraying both Eliot's Victorian prejudices against Byron's poetry and her liberal worldview – Shelley made a subtly different case when she imported Byron to an imaginary twenty-first-century future. Lord Raymond becomes an early locus for loss in *The Last Man*, anticipating the eventual demise of mankind. But this Byronic figure also channels fading prospects for unity that become intertwined with this proleptic sense of absence, shaping a complex orientation toward the political future.

The second half of the chapter – focused on the marginal figure of Lionel Verney and his sister Perdita – asks what conclusions we can draw about the politics of Shelley's novel as a whole. *The Last Man*, I propose, implies qualified support for the dissolution of monarchy while adopting a quietist perspective on popular, reformist demands. At the same time, the novel presents a multilayered return to the natural state imagined to precede politics, scrambling stadial narratives and promising to dislodge and even uproot politics as usual.

Works by Byron and Shelley traced movements beyond Europe and the Americas, extending to the escape from this planet. Chapter 5 expands the book's geographical reach beyond England to examine writings by Byron and Shelley within a global frame, including the ways that they imagine the earth as emptied-out and subject to ruin, deluge, and destruction. "New Worlds: *Frankenstein*, *The Island*, and the Ends of the Earth" asks how the doomed voyages and evacuated landscapes in Shelley's first novel and Byron's final long poem reflect back upon the condition of England. In *Frankenstein*, Shelley presented a grim picture of the destruction wrought by European institutions, whose influence can be discerned from South America to the North Pole. *The Island*, by contrast, offers a more fruitful vision of renewal and possible escape. Brougham may have been premature when he imagined new American states bordering the Pacific. But in extending his imagination to the South Seas and an unspoiled Tahitian paradise, Byron offered glimpses of the future world that might come from leaving England and its institutions behind. The Coda turns to *Don Juan*, examining the unique spin that Byron's poetic masterpiece placed on lastness and (not) coming to an end. With their emphasis on ending lines, sinking islands, and foreign shores, Byron's final writings imagine a world in which existing institutions, nations, and peoples no longer exist. In the process, they bring new ends for literature into view.

CHAPTER I

The End of Politics and the End of the World

A Leaf from the Future History of England, on the Subject of Reform in Parliament (1831) presented a prophecy of collapse with origins in the political present. "In the year of 1831," the author stated, "now above a century ago, began that English Revolution, so fatal a disaster to that country, so useful a warning to others." A "long period of peace and security" had made the people "almost insensible to blessings, which, by constant use, had grown as familiar to them as light and air": "They were tranquil at home, they were respected abroad. Their constitution, above all, had long been to foreign nations the object of admiring envy." But while "unshaken by hostile violence," England's constitution was "not proof against domestic faction": "it was safe from murder, but it fell by suicide." The anonymous pamphlet went on to describe a speculative future, in which heated public feeling converged with incendiary populism to issue in sweeping transformation. The author took contemporary events as the point of departure. On March 1, 1831, MPs led by Sir John Russell debated a Reform Bill that would redraw England's electoral map along more equitable lines and expand the franchise to most male ratepayers. *A Leaf from the Future History of England* referenced these contemporary debates. But from a perspective located 100 years into the imagined future, these moderate reforms marked only the start – and what would come to be seen as the beginning of the end.[1]

Five years later, the pamphlet explained, the franchise was universal and electoral freedoms expanded. But the arrival of democracy coupled with a descent into tyranny. The new British National Convention gave way to an English Emperor, who presided over a reign of terror. The state introduced its own take on the guillotine, murdering rebels and political enemies. William Cobbett, the demagogic radical, was put into power – only to swiftly face execution as another faction took over. The country, meanwhile, fell into ruin. *A Leaf from the Future History of England* conceded some flaws with the existing political system, acknowledging that Manchester was not represented in parliament during the first three decades of the nineteenth century. But 100 years later, that once-burgeoning industrial city was a mere "village," the surrounding country barren. In 1831, Russell and the Whigs, helped along by agitation in the country at large, were pushing demands for parliamentary reform to the center of the political agenda. Even Tories opposed to reform acknow-ledged the need for some changes. But viewed from a vantage point located 100 years hence, the imperfect political situation of the early 1830s was made to appear in a radically different light. "How often, in the days of anarchy and bloodshed that ensued," the pamphlet lamented, "did the English people look back, even to these defects, with deep and bitter regret; how often did they wish that, by the same or ten times greater imperfec-tions, they could regain some portion of the peace and prosperity which they formerly enjoyed, – some few of the blessings which they rashly flung away!"[2]

A Leaf from the Future History of England provides a vivid illustration of how ending politics as usual might lead to the end of the world. The 1832 Reform Act fell short of transforming the social order. But *A Leaf from the Future History of England,* written the previous year from the right wing of the Tory party, cast *any* reform as prospective disaster. Bringing the current workings of politics to an end here initiates the beginning of the end of human society: a bleak, dystopian future that includes the tyrannical, quasi-totalitarian rule that suspends or erases the possibility for politics. The ravaged landscapes here, moreover, recall other ruinous visions of the end of the world. More recent fictional dystopias that engage with crum-bling societies and failing institutions (including so-called Cli-Fi or cli-mate-change fiction) present political collapse as inextricable from environmental catastrophe, with one creating, or giving way to, the other. But while the end of politics can be catastrophic, it may also appear, especially in theoretical, imaginative, and speculative works, as a necessary reform or reset, which places society on a better footing. At its most expansive, the dissolution of the old order may usher in a transformed world no longer hampered by established structures of governance, nor in any need of politics as such. That may entail returns to the "state of nature" imagined to precede human society, the onset of a perfected postpolitical society, or other kinds of ecological and societal reworking. The prospect of politics ending need not be fully realized or articulated, moreover, to suggest a reoriented world. Even momentary suspensions of existing polit-ical certainties may – like a calendar left on the wrong day, or the stuck hand on a clock – suggest prospects for renewal or transformation, as when a Mormon law clerk in Tony Kushner's *Angels in America* accidentally goes to court on a Sunday[3] or the grumpy protagonist of *Groundhog Day* confronts the same twenty-four-hour period over and over.[4] These freshly opening prospects and momentarily glimpsed alternatives need not be the antitheses of a pervasive emphasis on endings, but their corollaries. That is to say, visions of closing horizons and newly opening ones may coincide.

This chapter examines some of the ways that writers have imagined worlds no longer organized by existing political structures in tandem with visions of the world coming to an end. Before turning to the Romantic age, I explore two literary works from the adjoining periods: Jonathan Swift's *Gulliver's Travels* (1726) and William Morris's *News from Nowhere* (1890). From the early eighteenth and late nineteenth centuries respectively, these fictionalized journeys to other worlds supplement and reorient the emphasis on apotheosis and rebirth in the wake of the French Revolution. Rather than singular ruptures and radical breaks, they offer more equivocal and suggestive visions of disruption and uprooting along-side clean breaks and starting over. Swift's writings imagine worlds subject to pluralized apocalypses with few guarantees around what is to follow. Morris, by contrast, brings an at-once abrupt and seamless transition into an imagined future together with the radical reconfiguration of human society. From here, the chapter returns to the Romantic period, beginning with the so-called first generation who experienced revolution firsthand. The authors addressed by this book did not draw, or did not only draw, upon revolutionary utopianism and appeals to perfected consensus, as had been more typical for the previous generation.[5] Rather, they invoked a variety of timescales and vectors of change to create richly polyvalent visions of political endings and fresh beginnings. Drawn together with new ways of imagining "the world" in time and space, their reflections echoed across expansive geopolitical vistas and through an unimaginably vast future. In conclusion, I turn to Byron's "Darkness" to ask how even a poem about the death of the sun uses the demise of the planet to imagine the resetting of the world after politics ends.

Clean Slates: Disruption and Uprooting in *Gulliver's Travels* and *News from Nowhere*

In *Gulliver's Travels* and *News from Nowhere*, Swift and Morris create literary spaces in which politics and its ends come in for dramatic reevalu-ation. While indebted to the utopian tradition, both works keep actual political institutions in the near distance, hovering in a kind of suspended animation, as they imagine new worlds and clean slates. These authors imagine dramatic ruptures. But they also look beyond narrow and monolithic understandings of revolution, at one extreme, and the simple overcoming of political contention, at the other. Instead, they attend to disruptions, at various scales, which reorient political systems and to the uprooting, whether sudden or gradual, of existing institutions. At a remove from the dichotomies of the early Romantic age, these works call attention to the moment immediately prior to rupture or revolution, in which change is in the air and collapse seems imminent. (Morris's novel begins with a rowdy debate between a group of socialists, several with "Anarchist opinions."[6]) They focus, in turn, upon the multiple temporalities entailed by dramatic political change, or its failure, from Morris's timeless-feeling spaces of empty daydreaming to the doom-laden Swiftian mindset that further hastens on the world to come (even if that world consists of nothing at all). In the process, they show, paradoxically, how rupture need not be total and all-consuming. Even the end of the world might provide an occasion to pursue new ends.

Jonathan Swift experienced a life of political disruption. Arriving in London from Ireland, he witnessed the birth of modern political culture. Swift became an influential pamphleteer during the "First Age of Parties," confronting dramatic changes of political control and heated constitutional debates (including over imperial policy). Following the death of Queen Anne, Swift returned to Ireland – an exit from the metropolitan centre of power that he portrayed as involuntary exile to a blighted landscape. That experience gave rise to his most celebrated satires: *Gulliver's Travels* and *A Modest Proposal*. Swift formulated a master narrative about the debased political system that had taken hold over his lifetime. Accounts of the "Glorious Revolution" as consensual and nonviolent have given way to a recognition that the events of 1688 to 1689 were and remained highly contested – with added implications for imperial policy.[7] The modernizing ("Whig") innovations associated with the 1688 Revolution had, in Swift's view, led to political disaster, imposing the foreign Hanoverian monarchy on England and paving the way for the political corruption exemplified by Robert Walpole. Swift was similarly scathing about modern imperialism and global commerce. Aside from generic critiques of corruption and luxury, Swift pointed to a nefarious trade system that had led to the despoiling of the Irish "nation." The ravaging effects of colonial policy and exploitative global trade sharpened the satirical teeth of his *Modest Proposal*, which proposed cannibalism as an ironic solution to Irish overpopulation. These contexts were similarly relevant, in more oblique ways, to *Gulliver's Travels*.

Swift is also known for satirical critique of another order. His vicious condemnation of modern politics – and growing attention to its implications for the Anglo-Irish economy – became inseparable from his expressed hatred of the world as such. *A Modest Proposal* and *Gulliver's Travels* made partisan points, attacking specific systems and policies. But Swift's famously unstable satire also converged, in these late writings, with a caustic, all-consuming misanthropy, such that the reader cannot quite be sure whether to take his dark proposals seriously. In both his published writings and private correspondence, Swift's critiques of contemporary politics and governance were thus inseparable from his jaundiced perspective on his surroundings, the Irish people, and the human species *tout court*. Indeed, as much as he sought to challenge and even tear down specific existing political systems, Swift also countenanced and even welcomed the prospect of mankind's extinction. "Drown the world!" he wrote to Alexander Pope on November 26, 1725, "I am not content with despising it."[8]

In the final voyage of *Gulliver's Travels*, published the following year, Gulliver confronts the projected extermination of the Yahoos: a bestial, pest-like species that doubles for mankind. These calls for drowning, forced extinction, and (in *A Modest Proposal*) mass cannibalism witness Swift at his most extreme. They coincide with and take shape through condemnation of his surroundings. Yet in a further twist, Swift's criticisms of the Irish landscape and Irish people – the Yahoos have red hair and a Gaelic-sounding name – were inseparable from his critique of English colonial policy. Swift also used "Yahoos" as a term for the blinkered followers of English politics, the statesmen, authors, calculating projectors, and (worst of all) *lawyers* he deemed responsible for the ruinous state of his surroundings. A similar equivocation factored into his perception of politics more widely, which he subjected both to generic complaints (grumbling about the state of "politicks") and more specific and pointed criticism. The critiques that Swift lodged, like sticks of dynamite, into the edifices of the modern world promised various kinds of disruption and destruction. But his equivocation between specific and generic, Ireland and England, the world around him and the world as such, created qualified room for other possibilities.

Gulliver's Travels presents its hero with constant disruptions, thrusting him into a series of outlandish political worlds. That whiplash was true, in some respects, to the experience of contemporary politics, where the growing sense that new hegemonies were settling into place coupled with the prospect of sudden changes and renewed upheaval. The continued contestation of 1688 aside, those changes did not yet take the guise of revolution, at least as that concept has come to be understood since the late eighteenth century. Fellow Scriblerus Club member John Arbuthnot wrote to a disenchanted Swift the year after his return to Ireland:

> I should have the same concern for things as yow, were I not convinc'd that a comet will make much more strange revolutions upon the face of our Globe, than all the petty changes that can be occasioned by Gover[nment]s and Ministrys, and yow will allow it to be a matter of importance to think of Methods to save ones self & family in such a terrible shock when this whole earth will turn upon new poles & revolve in a new orbite.[9]

Arbuthnot contrasted these "strange revolutions upon the face of our Globe" with more frequent changes of government and ministers. But revolution, here, did not yet mean an all-consuming, time-altering event. The word "revolution," Hannah Arendt notes, had its origin in thinking about the literal revolving of planets and could equally mean a return (as with the "Revolution" that restored Charles II to the throne in 1660).[10] Swift had a tendency to view the world in absolute terms, a tendency he coupled with a growing sense of decline, political and otherwise. But in his writings and those of his circle, visions of demise and doom also come together with the prospect that dramatic changes might yet shake up the status quo, a prospect even discernible in his rhetorically inflated call for a biblical deluge. The "strange revolutions" anticipated by Arbuthnot promise to reorient and even supplant existing political systems, even as they offer little reassurance about what that change might portend.

In the third voyage of *Gulliver's Travels*, a comet gives rise to reflection upon the end of the world. Gulliver finds himself transported to "an Island in the Air, inhabited by Men, who were able (as it should seem) to raise, or sink, or put it into a progressive Motion, as they pleased." Laputa's inhabitants can hover above the clouds, avoiding the weather even as they create the climate below for the neglected land of Balnibarbi. The Laputans are also strangely distracted. The "Minds of these People are so taken up with intense Speculations," Gulliver notes, "that they neither can speak, or attend to the Discourses of others, without being rouzed by some external Taction upon the Organs of Speech and Hearing." The satire in the third voyage of *Gulliver's Travels* has multiple targets, from the Royal Society and Hanoverian monarchy to speculative projecting and scientific endeavor writ large. Laputa clearly represents features of colonial policy, recalling the brutal subjection of Ireland to the prerogative of English rulers. The floating island can block the sun from the land below, deepening the toll taken by Laputa's governance from afar (on top of its promotion of wasteful, ruinous projects). But Swift supplies an added layer to this critique of insularity and neglect. The Laputans are not only scientific cranks and impractical kooks, but political junkies. Aside from their "great Faith in judicial Astrology," Gulliver tells us, he "chiefly admired" (while finding "altogether unaccountable") the "strong Disposition [he] observed in them towards News and Politicks." That obsession becomes entangled with their fears about a planetary crisis, having to do with unexplained events in the sky. The people of Laputa, Gulliver writes, "are under continual Disquietudes," concerning their fears of comets and the death of the sun. As a result, they never enjoy "a Minute's Peace of Mind."[11]

The Laputans' obsession with potentially catastrophic change to the face of the planet makes them ignore the consequences of governing systems in their own present.[12] The mistreated land and neglected people of Balnibarbi pointedly echo Swift's wider critique of English rule. As Carole Fabricant notes, the Whigs and their financial quixotism were seen to be "systematically converting the British soil into a wasteland." The more immediate locus for this critique was Ireland, where colonial neglect coupled with the dumping of unwanted goods and legacies of colonial oppression.[13] Read with a view to its lofty speculations about changes to the face of the globe and these more down-to-earth contexts, the third part of *Gulliver's Travels* – originally intended as the final voyage – acquires double-pronged significance. That begins with the Laputans' fretting about the death of the sun. Swift opens out this doom-infused, science-fictional scenario into a damning vision of a political world characterized by absolutist rulers, insulated politicians, destructive innovations, and disposable populations. Fears about the end of the world here converge with and ultimately enable a totalizing vision of oppressive political systems. But Swift thereby reminds us, as he does throughout *Gulliver's Travels*, that the survival of any political system remains highly contingent, even if what comes next remains uncertain. The state of politics, like the state of Ireland, may appear desperate. But whatever else it represents, the end of the world at least represents the end of *that*.

In the published book, Gulliver's final voyage takes him to the land of the Yahoos and the Houyhnhnms, their hyperrational horse masters. The final part of the book as written, the episode of the floating island concluded the *Travels* with closed-off yet highly contingent political worlds and their destructive influence upon the global environment. By contrast, the final voyage as published subsumes these critiques of particularized political and economic systems beneath condemnation of the human species (even as the Stoic horse-people maintain their own ascetic society, which pointedly excludes trade with "modern colonies"). *Gulliver's Travels* thereby looks ahead to anthropocentric approaches to the climate crisis. The "Anthropocene" not only names a new stratigraphic age. Under that banner, mankind's role in creating a new epoch in planetary history has also been cast as a radical conceptual and philosophical break. Appeals to the "Anthropocene" have thus frequently acquired a moralizing and quasi-religious cast (human beings are flawed, sinful, fallen creatures who know not what we do) amounting, in some cases, to a so-called *mis*anthropocene, in which concern for the fate of the planet gives way to self-lacerating laments about our terrible species (we deserve everything we get, even as those harms are unevenly distributed across current and future generations, such that "we" are not by any means all in the same boat). These appeals to the awfulness of mankind and the deserved doom of our species are eminently Swiftian.

They are also eminently political. In his account of the "Capitalocene," Jason Moore has puckishly challenged the very terminology that organizes current debate. Replacing the Anthropocene with his own Swiftian port-manteau, Moore points to a *longue-durée* history of extraction and coercion dating back to the onset of global capitalism.[14] Swift's emphasis on man-kind's ruinous influence on the planet – from the expansion of global trade to our hypocritical failure to confront the wasteful products of our own excesses – resonates, in turn, with attempts to grapple with the toll of those developments, which were set into motion or considerably ramped up during his lifetime. Arguing that "the Anthropocene may stand for all the climate problems we face today collectively," Dipesh Chakrabarty enumer-ates a Swiftian catalogue: "global figures for population, real GDPs, foreign direct investment, damming of rivers, water use, fertilizer consumption, urban population, paper consumption, transport motor vehicles, tele-phones, international tourism, and McDonald's restaurants (yes!)"[15] Chakrabarty has his eye on a later period, around 1945 to 2015, "'The Great Acceleration' in human history." But we may tie these developments both to familiar episodes of industrial advancement and a deeper history of colonial expansion and resource expropriation. The foundations for the exponential increases of the postwar period were laid in preceding centur-ies. Swift's was thus an anticapitalist perspective on ecological devastation *avant la lettre*.[16]

Gulliver's experiences jolt him out of established ways of thinking, as he confronts political systems that resemble, in distorted and distended fashion, his own. *Gulliver's Travels* similarly dislodges the reader from the political present, not least with the increasingly utopian and fantastical nature of the book, from the floating island to the anticommerce horses. Swift turned a withering eye on the politics of his lifetime even as he imagined the world being wiped clean of its present corruption. He rooted himself ever-more fixedly in his Irish surroundings even as he used Ireland to ground his most shocking proposals. His reflections ultimately became inseparable from his misanthropic critiques of the world and mankind more widely, such that the ultimate solution could look only like a world washed clean of man, his politics, and his despoiling influence on the planet. But in making apocalypses multiple, he helped to bring the ends pursued by politics (and the paths not taken) into focus, pointing to other possible worlds than this one.[17]

News from Nowhere presents a more recuperative picture. This futuristic "Romance" quietly reveals how the ills of the modern world might be overcome. At the same time, Morris points to dramatic change beneath the surface of the placid world he imagines, change whose revolutionary currents may yet roil the world of his imagined reader. Morris made use of the utopian tradition that also lies behind *Gulliver's Travels*, but with some important differences. Gulliver's sequential voyages progressively alienate him from his home country and leave him without a safe place to land. The "strange revolutions" portended by politically disruptive comets might, Arbuthnot noted, force the world to "revolve in a new orbite." But as the book goes on, we are left with a vision of the world redeemable only by biblical deluge or mass extinction. By contrast, Morris imagines a sudden, painless transition into a new and improved England. *News from Nowhere* begins with protagonist William Guest returning from a rowdy meeting of the Socialist League on a crowded underground train, "the means of traveling which civilization has forced upon us like a habit."[18] The next morning, he awakes on a sunny day over a century into the future. The "Nowhere" in which Guest finds himself represents a wholly new world, almost unrecognizable except for the Thames and freshly overgrown forests. Factories have closed down, ugly urban housing has been replaced. He finds himself rowed at a leisurely pace in a sailboat rather than wrangling with cab drivers or underground stations and encounters neat gardens and tree-lined pathways where once there had been grimy, crowded streets. But nested within this easeful transition are tremors of more dramatic upheaval.

The transformed environment of *News from Nowhere* finds a violent counterpart in Richard Jeffries's novel *After London; Or, Wild England*

(1885).[19] Where Guest awakes peacefully into a changed world, Jeffries's book begins in the wake of an unspecified catastrophe. Evacuated of people, London has effectively been subject to a biblical deluge. Following extensive descriptions of the rampant flora and nonhuman fauna that evolve to inhabit this inexplicably changed ecosystem, the novel goes on to present the British Isles as now populated largely by descendants of the lower classes. By presenting the nation in a feral state of mutual aggression, Jeffries's aim, John Plotz has proposed, was to present a post-Darwinian picture of "endlessly looping venality."[20] The return to a brutal state of nature here witnesses political structures reimagined from a foundation of violence. As in Hobbes, that entails a state of continued conflict: the war of all against all. *News from Nowhere* imagines an altogether gentler world. But Morris took unlikely and illuminating consolation from reading Jeffries's novel. The picture of "barbarism once more flooding the world" in *After London* had the desirable result, Morris wrote, of unleashing "real passions and feelings, however rudimentary" in the place of "our wretched hypocrisies."[21]

The contested terrain depicted in *After London* helps to underscore the radicality of the changed world imagined in *News from Nowhere*. That radicalism has both environmental and interpersonal dimensions, although this ultimately proves to be a distinction rejected by Morris. The natural disaster portrayed by Jeffries's novel, in Morris's account, effects a return of human society to a less coddled and conditioned state. Morris's socialism challenged the distinction between "nature" and human nature. As his comments on the unleashing of "real passions" suggest, Morris saw *After London* breaking open a falsely settled view of human nature. *News from Nowhere* similarly deconstructs the relationship between society and individuals and the resulting conceptions of who and what we are. The people in "Nowhere" display no underlying greed, selfishness, or acquisitiveness, all traits that are created, the novel posits, by industrial capitalism. The transformation of the built environment similarly reverses the degraded state of human nature, supplying Morris's vision of a changed society with a wider ecological dimension. Heightened sensitivity to the effects of a carbon-based economy, in turn, brings out a further layer to the novel's critique of capitalist modernity: the toll on the environment.

In *News from Nowhere*, England returns to a condition closer to the rhythms of the preindustrial world. "Nowhere" may look like a rolling back of human society to a less developed, more primitive state. But Morris's novel thereby plants the seeds for an alternative future, within the here and now. We may find one point of analogy in the 2020 shutdown of the global economy. In much the same way that Covid briefly gave rise to empty streets and hazeless skies, Guest's arrival in "Nowhere" takes him to a world without the smog, bustle, and churning traffic of modern London. Writing in July 2020, Lawrence Wright wondered whether "the glorious experience of living with less pollution, however momentary, will linger in our consciousness as an achievable destiny – and as a reminder that major transformations are possible."[22] Empty streets and hazeless skies endure, in Wright's speculative hopes for the future, as the perceptual residues of an experience that will prove to have enclosed a vision of a possible future – what we might, adapting Emily Rohrbach, call a reverse poetics of anticipation, in which we strive to return to a future we have already seen.[23] Morris's novel similarly lodges its luminously rendered scenes in Guest's baffled mind with the hopes of their having a similar lingering influence in the reader's sensorium.

These changes come together with transformed interpersonal arrangements. Guest's confusion at society's changed mores is a source of the book's charm and humor. But Morris also subtly elaborates a *new* account of human nature in the process. The changed world of *News from Nowhere* includes, as I have noted, a wholesale reworking of human society. Those changes include the eradication of politics as such. Where *The Last Man*, as we will see in Chapter 4, used England's conversion to a republic to make an oblique reflection on the political situation in Shelley's present, Morris (who claimed to despise the very word "politics") is more forthright. The House of Commons remains in operation, we learn, but as a storage house for manure – less a jab at worthless politicians than the even more damning suggestion that the building has finally rendered itself *useful*. The people of "Nowhere" have no need of politics. They settle disputes through rational if heated conversation and resolve interpersonal conflicts without the interference of the law. (There is no need for divorce because there was never marriage to begin with.) Yet this does not, crucially, amount to a world in which the final form of politics has been decided, nor the permanent settling of contention. This remains a world, as Morris had written of *After London*, of "real passions." Replacing the entrenched corruption of political and associated institutions with a society organized around collective well-being allows the inevitable differences between people to find other outlets and resolutions.

Guest experiences some of the same disorientation experienced by Gulliver. But he does not experience the sudden disappearance of politics and other institutions of governance as a disruptive break. Morris's utopia is characterized by gentleness. Society returns to the nature-inspired rhythms of agriculture, craft work, laboring by hand, and a world no longer harried by the remorseless pace and grinding toil of modern life. That can look like a retreat to the past. Guest at first thinks he has retreated several centuries *backward* in time rather than advancing forward. The architecture and design featured in the book, like the art of the Pre-Raphaelites and Morris's wider circle, recall an archaic medieval past. But *News from Nowhere* instills these premodern tableaus with an urgent modernity. This unmodernized, decarbonized society materializes not as one of privation. The novel instead presents the unfurling experience of a rich, engrossingly rendered world (albeit one that seems, at times, to have a sunnier climate than nineteenth-century England). Morris's fully worked-out vision comes to seem, like the allegorical dream world of Bunyan's *Pilgrim's Progress*, more real than reality itself. At the same time, the book also unfolds as the series of leisurely speculations suggested by its subtitle: "An Epoch of Rest, Being Some Chapters From a Utopian Romance."

Morris thus supplies the world imagined by *News from Nowhere* with countervailing movements. A meandering retreat through an idyllic, archaic-feeling England, the book also fast-forwards to a serene and eminently graspable (if not readily attainable) socialist future. The bearing of these scenes upon contemporary political debate was, accordingly, both direct and indirect, partial and all-encompassing. The novel includes diegetic dialogues and essays on human nature, education, and the motivations behind work, love, and anger. But the book and its political message do not stand or fall based on whether we decide to pursue the socialist agenda these interjections none-too-subtly outline. The novel also works in more subtle and insidious ways to dislodge and supplant things as they are. Morris may not have expected modern society to revert to a state analogous to the premodern past, giving up private property and consumerism for shared ownership and wageless work. Nor, presumably, did he expect that the use of coal would simply cease. But much as vines work their way around the edifices of half-ruined buildings and the roots of trees work, over long expanses of time, to dislodge man-made structures, so the political possibilities elaborated by Morris work their way into the mind of Guest and the book's reader, gradually eroding resistance and taking root in the cracks. The serene and bucolic world imagined by *News from Nowhere* thereby impresses upon the political present, whose seemingly fixed institutions, the book suggests, can be uprooted and returned to the earth.

Explosive Change: Apocalyptic Politics and the Early Romantic Age

Morris wrote at the *fin de siècle*, the cultural moment that saw Oscar Wilde's embrace of a decadent socialism together with a wider sense that the world, from France to Russia, was on the brink of change.[24] The events that bring the world of *News from Nowhere* into being include violence. Morris alludes to the bloody repression of an actual nineteenth-century protest in "How the Change Came," where he explains that London's Leicester Square was the site of a prospectively violent revolution. Without erasing the presence of this imagined violence, which echoes those recent events in that same location, *News from Nowhere* ameliorates any sense of rupture through its elastic, interlooping time frames and emphasis on gradual, natural processes. The scenes of former violence are now healed, overgrown by trees, much as the grimy, crowded world of London has been returned to a replenished natural state. As with the multifaceted rupture imagined by Swift, the subtle uprooting emphasized by Morris found parallels, this chapter will go on to show, in the late Romantic age, where newly sharpened concerns with the end of the world converged with diverse currents of change, political and otherwise. Those developments took shape, however, in the shadow of the French Revolution, whose explosive change shaped new visions of the end of politics.

The events set in motion on July 14, 1789, were experienced as both cataclysmic and regenerative. Cast as a world-shattering disaster by conservative opponents such as Edmund Burke, the fall of the *ancien régime* constituted a glorious triumph for revolutionary sympathizers – the birth of a new world. In addition to a permanent break with the past, the French Revolution marked the seeming onset of inevitable change, if not instantaneous utopia: not only the end of politics as formerly organized but the end of politics as such. Godwinian theories of perfectibility imagined a world with no further need for government, in which rational public conversation rendered existing institutions obsolete. Those theories had plebeian counterparts. Jon Mee notes that the idea of "an endpoint when all debate and discussion would cease" frequently featured in the rhetoric of popular radicalism.[25] But visions of perfected governance and democratic consensus also came together with more incendiary visions of revolutionary change. They were coupled, moreover, with the pursuit of other worlds and lands altogether, as with schemes to escape Europe for the Americas that sought to create a new society from the ground up within supposedly vacant space and exploratory voyages to the South Seas.[26]

Explosive change was idealized by some early Romantics. But images of sudden, fiery conflagration were also readily narratable as descents into chaos, casting demands for sudden transformation as the flipside of a Hobbesian scene of terror. An image from "The Life of William Cobbett, Written by Himself" (1809), a sequence of satirical prints by James Gillray, depicts radical politics through the lens of these revolutionary polarities (Figure 3). In England, the "Jacobin" threat became identified with popular radicalism. Cobbett was at the forefront of the emergent movement that demanded political and economic recognition for what would come to be known as the English working class. "The Life of William Cobbett, Written by Himself" depicts the political firebrand and journalist at work on his biography, recalling a period when he "was yet hesitating between a Radical-Reform and a Revolution." The print casts his *Political Register* as a dangerously incendiary work. With that publication, the print has Cobbett admit, "the fabrick of my visionary greatness vanished," and these "Schemes for my Country's good perished by the blaze of my own Candles!" The print depicts Cobbett, "surrounded by flames and beset by ghosts," starting back in his chair, "overturning his writing-table," and "dropping his pen." Behind his right shoulder is "a black replica of himself"; over that shadow's shoulder leans the Devil, while, still further behind, "the Bats and Harpies of Revolution" hide their heads "in the gloom of night." The unleashing of a hellish conflagration, by way of Cobbett's protodemocratic politics, has its origins in the demonic associated (by way of the Devil's "bonnet rouge") with the French Revolution.

Gillray's print presents a not-so-quietly damning view of radical politics. But the sequence and shape of its narrative prove more challenging to determine. At the level of allegory, the print implies that Cobbett has sold his soul to the (French) Devil, who has returned to claim his due. The print, in turn, proposes, on the plane of historical events, that the radical agitation and uncompromising demands advanced in Cobbett's writing will lead to a dire outcome, if not outright disaster. These narratives converge, confusedly, in the issues of the *Political Register* "already blazing" on the table. Three other copies are in front of him, one alluding to the "Hell-Fire-War in Spain" and others featuring a "Plan for to Hang up all the Public Robbers without Judge or Jury," "Hints on ye Rights of Napoleon the Great to the Throne of Great Britain," and an attack on the Jubilee ("a Damned Ministerial Humbug upon the country"). Further issues address the "Stupidity of the Whigs," "Bank Notes our Ruin," and the "Blasted Ignorance of Ministry," while others cite demands for "New

The Life of WILLIAM-COBBETT, *written by himself.*

Figure 3   James Gillray, "The Life of William Cobbett, Written by Himself [No. 8]" (1809). BM 1868,0808.7868. © The Trustees of the British Museum.

Parliamentary Reform" and the "Necessity of a new Party." The point here is clear. Cobbett's dogmatic strain of popular radicalism, building upon revolutionary fervor and antiestablishment feeling, promises to consume the country in hellish chaos of the kind predicted in *A Leaf from the Future History of England* (where Cobbett enters power only to himself face execution under a tyrannical emperor). Whether Cobbett's writings provide the incendiary spark or fan existing flames becomes irrelevant. The presence of eternal hellfire makes these blazes perpetual and self-replenishing. At the same time, the print builds upon the dire reputation of Napoleon as the new avatar of revolutionary terror, slaughter, and tyranny. By adding figures from recent and contemporary radicalism to the mix, the print taints them all with the same brush. As with the *Leaf from the Future History of England*, the only alternative is to step outside contention altogether, retreating from reformist politics of any stripe into reaction and counterrevolution. Anything else spells the end of the world, beginning with the end of politics.

The use of apocalyptic rhetoric was widespread in the Romantic period. The depiction of Cobbett surrounded by flames vividly imagines radical change as prospective destruction. But apocalypse also acquired more positive inflections, tied to millenarian visions of the future, in which this world gives way to another, perfected universe. The destruction of the existing world might be considered a necessary and even an invigorating prospect, whether the cleansing fire deemed necessary for altered perception in Blake's engravings or the pulling down of the past and accompanying ascent of the people. That vision of revolution found one afterlife in the Marxism of Rosa Luxemburg, who advocated for "catastrophe" as the necessary precondition for meaningful change. At its most extreme, the apocalyptic rhetoric of the revolutionary age amounted to a promise of reinvention: the hope of quite literally making the world anew. But the prospect of the end of politics not only gave way, with the onset of terror and war, to visions of chaos and destruction; the disappointment of revolutionary hopes also gave way to new ways of viewing the world, including the natural world, as such.

For William Wordsworth, the descent of the French Revolution into factionalism and bloodshed represented a personal cataclysm. *The Prelude* described the early 1790s as a blissful "dawn" – a "very heaven" for the young. Wordsworth had a "fundamentally different" understanding of apocalypse to his "millenarian contemporaries" during his period.[27] He also had a subtly different understanding of utopia. His visions of another world did not take shape, he wrote in the same section of *The Prelude*, "in Utopia – subterranean fields," or "some secreted island, heaven knows where," but *here*, "in the very world, which is the world / Of all of us."[28] Wordsworth's blank-verse treatment of the "Growth of a Poet's Mind" narrated the collapse of those expectations – and with them, the poet's hopes for the future. Wordsworth found solace, as "Lines Written a Few Miles above Tintern Abbey" records, in visiting and revisiting natural scenes. From one perspective, this was (as we say when we pick ourselves up again after disappointment) not the end of the world. But from another perspective, the failure of the French Revolution was shattering, a loss that reverberated throughout his subsequent writings and that shaped his mature poetic philosophy.[29] Wordsworth overcame despair through recourse to the "Imagination," a poetic faculty that found its home in an idealized "Nature" that extended beyond his local surroundings or even the natural world to quasi-divine superintendence of human development and society. The loss of political hope for Wordsworth witnessed the implosion of his almost-realized hopes for this world ("the very world, which is the world / Of all of us"). His pursuit of recompense issued in another "apocalypse": the apotheosis of Nature, wrenched out of time, so as to become a new world in its own right. While they parted ways from Wordsworth, his late Romantic successors followed his example in making encounters with the natural world both a substitute for and complex double of new political worlds.

For Geoffrey Hartman, Wordsworthian "apocalypse" saw nature sub-sumed within individualized perception, a version of what Keats would term the "egotistical sublime." In seeking to "cast out nature" and achieve "an unmediated contact with the principle of things," the mind sought out "the inauguration of a totally new epoch." M. H. Abrams, for his part, criticized those who used the term apocalypse "loosely" to mean "any sudden and visionary revelation, or any event of violent and large-scale destruction – or even anything which is very drastic." Abrams sought instead to "restrict 'apocalypse' to the sense used in Biblical commentary, where it signifies a vision in which the old world is replaced by a new and better world."[30] But just as Wordsworth was "deeply suspicious of allegor-ical language," Jonathan Roberts observes, he was also "deeply suspicious of allegorical apocalypse as a deterministic embrace of purificatory vio-lence." In such "moment[s] of revelation" as his encounter with "Black drizzling crags that spake . . . As if a voice were in them," Roberts proposes Wordsworth found a means to "forestall the possibility of his apocalypse being read allegorically."[31] Those haunting and uncanny encounters with the natural world offer a further way to connect Wordsworth with his successors, despite growing political differences.

Shelley's narrator alludes to "Tintern Abbey" in the opening paragraph of *The Last Man*. "In my boyish days, she was the universe to me," Lionel Verney writes, echoing Wordsworth (who recalls "the coarser pleasures" of his "boyish days" in his poem on revisiting the banks of the River Wye). "When I stood on my native hills," Lionel continues, "and saw plain and mountain stretch out to the utmost limits of my vision, speckled by the dwellings of my countrymen, and subdued to fertility by their labours, the earth's very centre was fixed for me in that spot, and the rest of her orb was as a fable, to have forgotten which would have cost neither my imagination nor understanding an effort" (*LM*, 7). The vision of the natural world in Shelley's novel acquires complex political and economic meanings. But while they reached different conclusions about their implications, Shelley and her contemporaries shared Wordsworth's interest in revelatory encounters with fields, trees, rocks, and chasms. In *The Last Man*, Wordsworth finds a fellow spirit, of sorts, in Adrian, an idealist based on Percy Shelley. The horizons of politics and thinking about the planet more widely had begun to undergo dramatic shifts. Adrian's utopianism acquires fleeting currency, but only once the plague takes hold and the landscape starts to be littered with bodies. Like his poetic precursor, Adrian finds solace from his earlier political disappointment by imagining conversations with the rocks.

Politics and the "End of the World" in the Late Romantic Age

For the writers examined in this book, the French Revolution had echoed down through subsequent decades. Millenarian hopes, revolutionary ideals, and cataclysmic breaks with the past gave way to the repression of the Napoleonic age and a general darkening of political moods.[32] Wordsworth had imagined poetry as a means of overcoming both personal and political disenchantment. But Byron – favoring no such sublimation – gave in to biting cynicism. *Childe Harold's Pilgrimage* used the contorted growth of a poetic mind to chronicle Europe's descent into cycles of repression and violence, presented as accreting experiences of bitterness and loss. Revolutionary hopes, meanwhile, migrated to or issued from other geographic arenas including Greece and South America, further scrambling the relationship between revolutionary change and the political spectrum (as so-called Liberal Toryism, for example, made support for South American independence compatible with economic imperialism).

Published the same year as the first cantos of *Childe Harold's Pilgrimage*, Anna Letitia Barbauld's *Eighteen Hundred and Eleven* scrutinizes the same war-torn world surveyed by Byron's hero, imagining future visitors to a ruined London. Barbauld's poem might seem to mark the decline of Europe and the birth of a new world order, with one home in the Americas. But as Jessie Reeder has argued, the poem stages the formal incompatibility of political independence and economic progress.[33] Byron provided his own spins on this conjuncture, presenting a "new" world that had itself grown old.[34]

Revolution had not, of course, meant only one thing during the early Romantic age. But the early nineteenth century witnessed an array of new vectors for change, from Greece to Venezuela. The prospect of sudden rupture and political upheaval, welcome or otherwise, increasingly contended, moreover, with other kinds of evolution and transformation. The growing sway of popular movements challenged existing institutions, calling the status of elite political men, the next chapter will show, newly into question. The early nineteenth century witnessed, at the same time, economic malaise and accompanying distress. The death of proreform protestors at the hands of armed cavalry on August 16, 1819, echoed like a thunderclap through the country. But some saw the Peterloo massacre as a kind of end point, the terminus for certain vectors of political hope. In his *Masque of Anarchy*, Percy Shelley heralded the rising of the masses after being trampled down by poverty and state power. That poem (intended for a book of songs, but not published for over a decade) can be cast as an unconvincing rallying cry, composed from a detached retreat. But as Amanda Jo Goldstein has compellingly shown, the poem also goes beyond the terms of revolutionary politics and prophesized futures, casting the violence as "an event in natural history" while "obsessively fretting the question of how the material evidence of the political clash . . . is absorbed and recirculated through atmospheric, geologic, and metabolic cycles." In weaving between assemblages of atoms and gatherings of people, Goldstein strenuously argues, the poem imagines new agencies materializing in tandem with a dynamic understanding of the natural world.[35]

The natural world gave rise to its own visions of sweeping change, beginning with man-made effects upon the global environment – which created "Nature" anew. Late Romantic writers lived through the escalation of coal-fueled industrial production. They accordingly witnessed firsthand the onset of the fossil-fuel usage responsible for the current climate crisis (and, in some accounts, the start date of the "Anthropocene").[36] By the time Shelley wrote *The Last Man*, England was alone responsible for the majority of the world's carbon emissions.[37] As Andreas Malm has demonstrated, contemporaries were acutely aware of the damaging consequences of steam power for the laboring classes and urban environments, as well as the wider toll of colonial extraction regimes. The darkening of skies following the eruption of Mount Tambora supplied an ominous double for these developments, troubling the distinctions between nature and society, material forces and human agency.[38] Some writers went further still, voicing fears that man (specifically European man) was unalterably deforming the global environment, expanding Swiftian appeals to the despoiling influence of the species into claims about man's permanent damage to the planet. This emphasis on damage coupled with visions of decline. Romantic-era writers in the wake of Malthus contemplated the demise of the human species through starvation or illness while, at the same time, countenancing the end of the planet, whether through erupting volcanos or shifting shorelines.

These reflections were supplied with added meanings and resonance by recent discoveries in geology and the fossil record. Georges Cuvier advanced the hypothesis that a series of "catastrophes" had destroyed existing species, transforming the face of the earth. In earlier versions of his studies, Melissa Bailes notes, Cuvier, in turn, suggested the possibility of "*future* revolutions of the earth, implicitly forecasting the extinction of present species, including humanity."[39] As Martin Rudwick has demonstrated, in the definitive account of these theories and their European circulation, contemporary geohistorical discoveries showed that "the earth had had a highly eventful *history*, passing through many different and distinctive phases, long before the present world came into existence." All of that "complex and eventful geohistory" – which included evidence of floods spanning the globe – "had preceded not only the earliest written records of human history but the human species itself." Those discoveries amounted to "a story of a long and complex sequence of Worlds before Adam" that radically revised the time frames for human life on the planet.[40] At the same time, they amounted to nothing less than the claim that the world had ended several times before.

These visions of catastrophe acquired varied and uncertain political meanings. Late Romantic writers built upon post-1789 visions of violent collapse and sudden change. As the Wordsworthian valences of *The Last Man* show, they expanded upon the compensatory visions of personal and natural apocalypse that followed from leaving political hopes behind. But they were also newly equipped, by recent upheavals and contemporary theories, to imagine a series of *new* worlds following this one. That included worlds in which man had no place. Rudwick frames his studies of the transformed conceptions of time made available by stratigraphic discoveries in the early nineteenth century with the words of Cuvier, whose discoveries promised radically expanded knowledge "beyond the limits of direct human experience." "Would it not be glorious," Cuvier had asked, for geologists to "burst the limits of time," just as astronomers had "burst the limits of space?" He thereby pointed to "the extension of reliable human knowledge in both dimensions, beyond the limits of direct human experience." Astronomers, "although physically confined to one small planet," had already "learned to calculate the motions of the whole solar system, and were even reaching beyond it to the stars in the inconceivable vastness of deep space." In the same way, geologists, "although physically confined to the present moment, could hope to penetrate back into the inconceivable vastness of deep time."[41] Cuvier's "catastrophism" supplied new resonance to prospective and actual endings, extending their significance beyond the time of mankind altogether.

Byron followed these discussions in some detail. He preceded his biblical drama *Cain* with a note stating that he had "partly adopted in this poem the notion of Cuvier, that the world had been destroyed several times before the creation of man."[42] "Derived from the different strata and the bones of enormous and unknown animals found in them," this "speculation," Byron went on, was "not contrary to the Mosaic account, but rather confirms it; as no human bones have yet been discovered in those strata, although those of many known animals are found near the remains of the unknown."[43] This was, in one sense, an orthodox explanation. But in the dramatic action of *Cain*, that "speculation" has disturbing implications. Lucifer taunts Cain with claims about the earlier generations of beings whose existence thereby serves to challenge man's supremacy. The Devil's assertion that the world before Adam was "peopled by rational beings much more intelligent than man," a prefatory note confirmed, was "a poetical fiction to help him to make out his case." But Byron also pointed to its disturbing implications for his newly vulnerable protagonist. In bringing now extinct species, as demonstrated by the fossil record, together with evidence that the planet had undergone transformations (that "the world had been destroyed several times"), Byron called the status of *man* pointedly into question.

Byron echoed these insights elsewhere. In one reported conversation, he expanded their implications from individual anguish to the fate of the species. Those remarks began with reflections on new energy regimes: "Where shall we set bounds to the power of steam? Who shall say, 'Thus far shalt thou go, and no farther?' We are at present in the infancy of science. Do you imagine that, in former stages of this planet, wiser creatures than ourselves did not exist?" In these same remarks, he identified the "fable of Prometheus" as a forerunner to carbon-fueled power and speculated about air and even space travel ("I suppose we shall soon travel by air-vessels; make air instead of sea voyages; and at length find our way to the moon"). Anticipating current proposals to use technology to save the world from climate disaster, Byron looked back at Cuvier when he speculated that "when a comet shall approach this globe to destroy it, *as it often has been and will be destroyed*," men will "tear rocks from their foundations by means of steam, and hurl mountains, as the giants are said to have done, against the flaming mass."[44] These statements amplify and expand upon apocalyptic rhetoric in ways not conceivable prior to the late Romantic age. They unseat mankind's eminence, by suggesting the presence of earlier races of intelligent creatures. At the same time, they look ahead, to the prospective end of the species.

In *The Last Man*, Shelley invoked the end of the world in multiple registers. The sun inexplicably becomes a "black orb," and England experiences failed crops, "devastating storms," flooding, and a year without winter (inverting the 1816 "Year Without a Summer"). At the cliffs of Dover, the characters contemplate meteors leading to a tidal wave. These latter visions, Bailes suggests, allude to the "flood that, according to numerous geologists, caused the last revolution and extinction of various species" and that had resulted from "a comet's passage close enough to the earth to produce enormous tidal waves that engulfed the continents." Yet none of these prospective threats (all of which portend, in some sense, the end of the world) have lasting consequences. As such, Bailes deftly proposes, Shelley builds "suspense and anticipation for an expected apocalypse, only immediately to quell it." Verney dreams that the ocean, "breaking its bounds," will carry away "the fixed continent and deep rooted mountains, together with the streams I loved, the woods, and the flocks." That image, Bailes suggests, invokes Cuvier's "grand theory of past catastrophes" only to resist its pull, retracting the possibility of an added layer to this human crisis. In *The Last Man*, Shelley thus rejected both the "biblically and geologically founded deluge of the past as a possibility for the future destruction of humanity."[45] She similarly backed away from the portents of darkened skies, instead making the plague the origin for what she terms the "last year of the world."

Byron's "Darkness" presents the most extreme vision of world-ending in the works of both writers. In addition to invoking the "Year Without a Summer," Byron's poem acquires deepened meaning in relation to what Rudwick terms the "inconceivable vastness of deep time." But while "Darkness" purports to depict the extinction of light, life, and hope, the poem also has more ambiguous resonances. In imagining the end of the world, Byron also imagines the end of politics. In the process, the poem's "darkness visible" offers glimpses of the other worlds that might take shape in the wreckage. The world imagined by "Darkness" is, in a word, bleak. The "bright sun" has been "extinguish'd" and stars "wander darkling in the eternal space," while the "icy earth" swings "blind and blackening in the moonless air."[46] "Morn came, and went – and came, and brought no day" (6) – a line whose stilted progress replicates disorientated adjustment to a world where time no longer has formal markers. This evacuation of existing categories expands to the hollowing-out of society and collapse of all expectations. Men "forgot their passions" as "all hearts" are "chill'd into a selfish prayer for light" (9). The "palaces of crowned kings" and their "thrones" are "burnt for beacons" while forests are "set on fire" (with dubious relief experienced only by those who live in the "eye" of volcanos) (10–11, 19, 16–17). In a sense, the world has stopped, its movements suspended. But those movements are, in fact, turned against themselves, repurposed in the service of the self-consuming vortex that "the world" has become.[47] With the sun dead and human action reduced to a "prayer for light," the natural world must be consumed by the need for heat. A world increasingly driven by carbon-fueled manufacture and trade must now use itself up for bare survival, leaving "cities . . . consumed" (13). And yet, in rendering the pull toward inertia and extinction, Byron presents a dynamic world picture. By spelling out the consequences of the sun's death, "Darkness" supplies – like a film played in reverse or a photographic negative – a mirror image of the world that has been lost. Beyond its stunning pyrotechnics ("crackling trunks / Extinguish'd with a crash" [20–1]) and gruesome tableaus, "Darkness" captures the motion of a dynamic, interdependent universe. At the point when the movements of that world are suspended, before turning inward or ceasing entirely, tremors of alternative possibility and even other worlds become discernible in the shadows.

"Darkness" sees the world degenerate into brute survival and wild, animal madness. But the poem does not depict the bare life constituted through its exclusion from sovereign protection, nor does it show man reverting to a Hobbesian state of nature. In both cases, the sovereign political sphere to which those conditions are opposed simply does not exist. This is not only a world outside politics and law, but a world *without* politics and law. Man is reduced to an animal condition here. But in that process of stripping away, *contra* Hobbes, "War ... for a moment was no more" (38). That fleeting pause in the cycle of violence offers a flickering glimpse of an alternative. To be sure, violence continues, deepening this nightmarish vision. But Byron uses this fantasy of the world reaching its end – in which "all earth was but one thought – and that was death" (42) – to ask what might take shape between the end of politics and the end of the world. The moment in which men "forget their passions" marks a complex site of forgetting and resetting (exemplified in the later vignette in which two enemies survive but no longer recognize one another). Even in imagining the brutal stripping away of human society to a barren anti-"state of nature" – in which "nature," self-consumed, turns in upon itself – Byron offers suggestive glimpses of other worlds in the embers of this one, even as that world, paradoxically, no longer exists. Byron's vision of the end of the world, the opening line tells us, comes from "a dream, which was not all a dream" (1). The line may suggest that its catastrophe does not only belong to the realm of dystopian fantasy: it could happen here. But it might equally suggest that a darkly nightmarish vision is *not all* the poem presents.

The remainder of this book shows how visions of the end of the world can be both politically generative and aesthetically resonant. I conclude here by asking what glimmers of possibility emerge from Byron's aestheticized treatment of a faded planet whose waning light casts the "pall of a past world" on a sky where the remaining stars "wander ... Rayless, and pathless" (30, 3–4). These desolate scenes and ending worlds resonate with indeterminate significance, if not potential. Indeed, the final, irrecoverable end of the world – without the viable prospect of escape to another world – might provide a strange kind of pleasure, even consolation. "Darkness" employs some of the same acoustic patterning that David James has discussed under the banner of "critical solace," describing men "in the dread / Of this their desolation," who "fed / Their funeral piles with fuel" (7–8, 27–8). The forgotten or evacuated world of the poem also makes contact with more recent fictional worlds, including the eerily barren terrain of dystopian and science fiction. Those oddly calming scenes of spinning outward into the void or looking out at the nothingness of a desolate shoreline parallel the strangely placid scenes that conclude "Darkness," in which ships bob "on the abyss without a surge" in tideless waters after the "moon their mistress" has expired (78–9).[48] The following chapters turn to political activity and debate, revealing how reflection on endings intersected in the works of Byron, Shelley, and their circle with political developments on the ground. But literature, "Darkness" lets us see, creates its own worlds, allowing us to look beyond politics to other circles, expanding and echoing, rippling and converging, amidst the closing of some horizons and opening of new ones.

CHAPTER 2

The Last Whigs

"What a ministry – Lord Liverpool has a fit and goes out." Thus John Cam Hobhouse, reformist MP for the borough of Westminster, began an 1827 letter to radical organizer Francis Place referring to the departing prime minister. Hobhouse went on to catalogue the ailments that had recently incapacitated, or killed, various members of the Tory government, making his letter more like "a hospital return," he wryly noted, "than a list of cabinet ministers." Place replied in a state of simulated agitation. He echoed Hobhouse's remarks about a vulnerable ministry afflicted by a wave of illness and misfortune. But his letter amplified them into exclamations about the future of the government and the fate of the country: "What a Ministry! aye! What a government!! What a nation!!! what a state of Society!!!!" Place's mock-hysteria aside, this death and decline was, from his perspective, congruent with a wider shift. The "old vulgar delusions," he noted approvingly, were coming to an end. With the dissolution of the existing political establishment, there would be "no 'Man of the People'" any longer, only the people, the soon-to-be-enfranchised demos, themselves.[1]

The ranks of political men were dwindling. "Name if you can ten men so circumstanced as to be likely to be called to govern the country who are at all qualified for the office," Place challenged, responding to the recent deaths in the parliamentary ranks. He went on to describe a transformation in which these were minor casualties. "All things" were "looking to one point ... all moving slowly yet simultaneously on a grand scale." "Government men and would be Government men" were "piddling about trifles, laughing or scoffing at the 'march of intellect,' without being able to understand the great moral and intellectual changes which have taken place and are continually taking place, and what overjoys me is, that they cannot be stopped."[2] Politics had fundamentally changed, Place claimed, and parties were in decline. Even populist figureheads like those of previous generations (Place cited John Wilkes and "Charley" Fox) could no longer answer the purpose of "the people." By contrast with the latter half of the eighteenth century, there was now a "public" – "not a good public certainly," Place hastened to emphasize, "but one which will in time become good." There were now "much more clever men." But even they were outstripped by the "reasoning part of the community." The French Revolution still animated this expanded new body politic with progressive hopes: "I mean by the observing reasoning portion of them, the so called 'Incorrigible Jacobins' – the Radicals – the stigmatized people who are fast going before their leaders."[3]

In the early decades of the nineteenth century, political identities and institutions faced various challenges, including from Bentham's theories, Catholic emancipation, and the renewal of antislavery organizing. Equally important, from Place's perspective, was the incipient mass politics that promised to swallow up individual leaders into the body of "the people." These various developments would eventually converge around a new figure: the liberal politician, whose reason instrumentalized new governing principles and thereby anchored revised understandings of party politics, global trade, imperial rule, and public opinion. The transition into liberalism – and the reinvention of nineteenth-century partisanship around Liberals and Conservatives – was a complex process that took shape over multiple decades. I engage these shifts in this chapter by way of their consequences for one long-standing political grouping, the Whigs, in the decades leading up to the 1832 Reform Act.[4] The demands for radical reform that gathered steam during the early nineteenth century posed seemingly existential challenges to the Whigs as a force within national political life. The more canny wing of the party reached accommodations with brewing demands for expanded suffrage (and shifted ground, less decisively, around growing demands to abolish slavery).[5] But the Whigs did not go gently, and the party cast a long shadow forward into the Victorian age.

The Whigs were not at the foreground of national politics in the period I consider here. But they continued to summon complex attachments. These spectral hopes and fraying ties were telling in their own way, as a measure of what was at stake in brewing political changes. The prospect of the "Last Whigs" offered a means of reflecting upon the sense of ending, both personal and political, with which the swirling developments alluded to by Place were imbued. Hobhouse forged his political identity, this chapter will show, in the eroding middle ground between the "Whigs" and "the people," bringing into focus contradictions attending the shift into a new era of liberal politics. Byron, by contrast, remained firmly attached to eminent Whigs from a rapidly fading past. Those identifications, inextricable from his self-conception as an author and public figure, converged with poetic meditations upon impermanence and faded potential as his attachment gave way to detachment and the presumption of elevated standing gave way to erosion and loss. Together, the personal reflections and private writings of both men – including their correspondence with each other – reveal how partisan identities and political orientations enfolded multiple relationships to historical time and political futurity.

Hobhouse, in my account here, looks ahead to the ascent of liberalism and "liberal" subjectivity. As Peter Mandler has observed, "liberal" tendencies were already discernible in Whig politics during the early nineteenth century.[6] At the same time, Mandler notes, the aristocratic Whigs, remaining adaptable, exerted a vital influence on the reign of Victoria. Combining a distinctive cultural style with seeming responsiveness to popular demands, they fleetingly served to bolster an alternative vision of the political future with one foot in the political past. But that rapprochement with the country took shape in the context of radical failure, including the faltering emergence of Chartism, the steady ascent of political Liberalism, and new ideas about society, the economy, and the body politic. In the pre-Reform period that I address here, backward-facing appeals to the Whigs imagined alternative futures to those bound up with political modernization. Where Hobhouse can be viewed as, in some sense, an early liberal politician, Byron, by contrast, staked his claim as the last Whig (or rather, the first of the last Whigs). As this chapter shows, those identities were forged in response to a unique moment of ferment and transition. Their appeals to modernizing roles and vanishing pasts acquired added resonance, moreover, in the context of the endings emphasized in Place's letter. Before turning to Hobhouse and Byron directly, I consider some of the tangled historical legacies bound up with "Whig" identity and show how the fallout of the French Revolution brought internal fractures within the Whigs to breaking point. I begin by asking how political parties – like families and workplaces – enfold multiple temporalities and unresolved conflicts.

Crowded Out: The Whigs and "the People"

In seeking to form "an impression of historical time in everyday life," Reinhart Koselleck proposes that we may look, above all, to "the successive generations in family or in working life." Families and professional environments have a privileged status, for Koselleck, as sites where "different spaces of experience overlap and perspectives of the future intersect, *inclusive of all the conflicts with which they are invested.*"[7] Historical time, in Koselleck's account, takes shape in, and as the relationship between, different temporalities. The family dinner table or the workplace conference room present scenarios in which mutually entangled relationships to the past and their attendant "conflicts" become apparent (and, we might add, with an eye on the academic department meeting, inescapable). We may say much the same for political parties. Parties share features with both families and professional organizations as intergenerational groupings in which individuals shape the course of their lives. With their ties to aristocratic lineages, great houses, and early populisms, the Whigs in particular can be understood as the locus of "overlap[ping]" and "intersect-[ing]" ambitions and orientations. Far from undermining their status as a political party, that multiplicity was constitutive of their identity *as* a party.

Who the "First Whigs" were is "a question notoriously hard to resolve," J. G. A. Pocock writes, with an eye on the English Commonwealth and its republican heirs.[8] The Whig party had its nominal point of origin in the 1680s as supporters of the Earl of Shaftesbury in the Exclusion Crisis (rendered by John Dryden as a fiendish rebellion in *Absalom and Achitophel*). Multiple varieties of Whiggism, in Pocock's phrase, were at play over the course of the long eighteenth century, from the aristocratic patronage regime (or "Whig oligarchy") of the early eighteenth century to various strains of radical, antiestablishment, and heterodox opposition. Swift, as we have seen, deplored the effects of the 1688 Revolution and despised the Hanoverian monarchs who succeeded Queen Anne. But both supporters and detractors of prime minister Robert Walpole, the political bogeyman of the early Hanoverian age, claimed the "Whig" label. The opposition to Walpole mobilized so-called radical Whig arguments. An expansive version of that "Patriot" ideology helped, in turn, to drive unrest in the American colonies.[9]

In mid-eighteenth-century England, "nearly all the political world" was "Whig," Mandler writes, in the broad sense of "supporting a balanced constitution and a reasonably tolerant Protestant Establishment." Whig governments were "broad-bottom coalitions, embracing a wide variety of connections." But there was another entity, *the* Whigs, a high-aristocratic collection of families "generally older and wealthier than the average landed clan," who viewed themselves as "politically separate and distinct."[10] While he did not share this background, Edmund Burke came to be seen as an exemplar of opposition politics who famously

defended the Marquess of Rockingham's "Whig" connection. But the
Irish-born statesman was also an outlier, combining support for elements
of the landed elite with qualified appeals to public opinion and popular
support. Even fairly narrow accounts of eighteenth-century "Whig" politics, this brief sketch makes clear, include a tangle of lineages, beliefs,
political groupings, and attitudes toward "the people" and revolutionary
change.

   In ideological terms, parties can only accommodate so much dissension.
The French Revolution, a radical break, promised to split the party
permanently. In his *Appeal from the New to the Old Whigs* (1791), Burke
sought to repair the breach between factions. Aside from his association
with a culture of fashionable indulgence, Charles James Fox became the
figurehead for a more spirited, public-facing version of Whiggism. Fox also
recognized a version of popular sovereignty. The breach between Burke
and Fox, which included spectacularly dramatic and emotional scenes in
the House of Commons, came to stand in for a larger divide. Burke
invoked the 1688 Revolution as an argument in favor of constitutional
stability. But revolution, in the eyes of Fox's more radical followers, ought
to comprise a break with the past. The conflicting views and incommensurate perspectives internal to the Whigs – as they are internal, I suggest, to
any political party – could not withstand this kind of conceptual break.
The French Revolution introduced altogether new visions of the political
future, moreover, pushing beyond the populism courted by Fox or the
"people" that Burke imagined as a bulwark against new visions of mass
politics and democratic change.

   When Byron met Hobhouse at the Cambridge University "Whig
Club," that name indicated commitment to the principles of the 1688
Revolution. But two decades after the fall of the Bastille, "Whig" suggested
attachments to an antiquated-seeming past as much as any commitment to
progressive change in the present. Byron was no fan of the "rabble" and
frequently cast the demos as a bloodthirsty Jacobin mob. "I am not
democrat enough to like a tyranny of blackguards," he wrote to
Hobhouse in October 1819. But in that letter, he also contemplated
a return to frontline political activity: "If there is to be a scene in
England to which all seems approaching – by the violence of the political
parties – you will probably see me in England in the next spring." He
nevertheless made a telling addition: "I have not yet decided the part
I ought to take."[11] Byron has been attached, with greater and lesser specificity, to the Whigs, in particular to the Foxite Whigs and Holland House.[12]
As I have argued elsewhere, Byron maintained an active desire to return

and take some "part" in politics from his exile abroad, an attachment to political engagement from within his estranged state that informed his identity as a public figure and the political stances adopted within his writings.[13] Revisiting Byron's various plans to engage in political activity – in England and beyond – can help us to acquire a fuller understanding of available partisan roles within this period and thereby to pose wide-ranging questions about "Whig" identity and the changing physiognomy of politics as a whole. I pay particular attention here to the textual figures that Byron and his political circle constructed: how they presented their political roles to themselves and to each other. But beyond helping to illuminate literary writings by Byron and his circle, these engagements with the roles available to political men comprise powerful meditations on political change in their own right. Especially critical to the changing status of political men were the challenges posed by an increasingly restive populace and its real or imagined threats to established political structures. We find one guide to these political changes in private diaries and anonymous pamphlets written by Hobhouse (the former collected and published by his daughter later in the Victorian age). Beginning with his Westminster election campaigns, Hobhouse was forced to engage with remnants of the aristocratic Whig elite and faced the prospect of a renovated future for the party; he also navigated the rapidly shifting fault lines of popular radicalism and reformist politics. Byron, by contrast, became preoccupied with a rapidly fading Whig past.

In an 1829 letter, Place described the "posture of things in England" to Hobhouse. There was "some contention between Brunswickers and anti-Brunswickers," he wrote, employing a derisive name for the Hanoverian monarchy. But this was of "little moment," as party names "now go for little." The cause, Place went on to explain, was a kind of mass political homicide. Catholic emancipation, passed that same year, created irreparable fractures within the Tory party. But the borough of Westminster, Place announced, had "killed the Whigs as a party ... and Canning shouted the requiem, 'Ribbons and Rubbish – favours at their heads and brickbats at their tails'" (an allusion to a notorious speech by the Tory statesman George Canning to which I return below).[14] The newer generation of the Whig party represented by Sir John Russell would be crucial to the passage of Reform. But parliamentary matters now had "very little place" for Place, who "really [did] not know how the parliament can be of any use to the people at present." In a letter to Hobhouse the following year, he made a still more shocking claim: that members of parliament all deserved to be hanged. Place's letter underscores the distance traveled from the political environment in previous decades when that statement would have been tantamount to treason. Beyond matters of context or temperament, Place's remarks also point to changing conceptions of the body politic and the emerging trajectory of radical politics. Together, these changes (which would converge in the Reform Bill of 1832 and feed into Chartism) substituted new conceptions of the political nation for the world of elite political men, while looking to fantasies about overthrowing the ruling classes *tout court*. These trends were already in motion earlier in the decade, when the anchoring role of individual political men was under increasingly evident strain.

"Parliament positively dissolves on Tuesday next," Hobhouse wrote to Byron in June 1818, "and our world here is more mad and silly than ever."[15] The same letter described a situation of continuing political corruption, lamenting that 6,000 guineas could now be paid to acquire a seat.[16] These allusions to reformist complaints and necessary structural change coupled with partisan enmity. Hobhouse went on to register his antipathies toward the Tory elite, promising to transmit critical remarks on the Duke of Wellington, together with a recently circulated letter attacking Canning, "which made a monstrous noise this session."[17] He went on to update the exiled poet about the political situation on the ground. Douglas Kinnaird, a mutual friend from the Cambridge Whig Club, had been "put in nomination" for Westminster, opposed by Henry Hunt and Major John Cartwright (the veteran radical briefly profiled in Hazlitt's *Spirit of the Age*). Amidst references to various acquaintances about town, Hobhouse noted that the "glorious" Sir Francis Burdett, another radical stalwart profiled by Hazlitt, had "commend[ed] himself" to the poet. The letter concluded by noting that Byron was longed for by his various political associates in London, with a parting plea – "Devil go wid ye – why dont ye come among us" – that recalled his observations elsewhere that Byron would be an asset to "Reform."[18]

Hobhouse skirted the edges of Holland House, the aristocratic retreat and refuge of Whig magnates (where Byron had launched his short-lived dalliance with parliamentary politics). He ultimately turned to Westminster, the London borough whose "popular elections" were notorious nationwide thanks to unique political procedures that enfranchised more male residents to create one of the most expansive electorates in the country. The efforts by the Westminster Committee to maintain a steering role in the borough's politics nonetheless met with resistance on the ground: the inchoate legacies of popular radicalism and the growing demands of an unpredictable, rowdy body of "electors."[19] Hobhouse sought to convince Byron that his recent activity was broadly sympathetic with their past. Yet his political career parted ways with those earlier commitments. Turning away from quasi-aristocratic visions of elite political leadership, Hobhouse became inseparable, in Byron's eyes, from the unruly contours of the "rabble." Although he emphasized his distance from the radical fringes, the Whig circles at Holland House saw him as part of that dangerous world. Hobhouse thereby occupied a paradoxical role: the Whigs thought of him as a radical, yet he continued to be viewed as an establishment Whig by "the more perspicacious" members of the radical side.[20]

These fractures surfaced throughout Hobhouse's correspondence with Byron, issuing in fireworks on the page. Reading the various stances adopted in their writings shows both men engaging critically with this shifting political terrain. These personas were forged in relation to available roles, in both parliamentary and extraparliamentary contexts. But they were also, I propose, complex *textual* productions developed in (at times antagonistic) dialogue with each other. Byron shared much of Hobhouse's antipathy toward the Tory establishment and controversial repressive measures. Yet he was equally capable of siding with the more liberal wing of the Tory side over more progressive, reformist causes. The emerging division between Byron and Hobhouse was symptomatic of larger shifts. As Burke had intuited, the middle ground was shifting: there was shrinking terrain between the respective extremes of the counterrevolutionary establishment and the burgeoning radical cause. Hobhouse's parliamentary career took shape amidst a growing cleavage, within the Whigs, between the aristocratic establishment and the so-called radical Whigs and philosophical reformers. Efforts to preserve the Whig cause for a future generation thus coincided with the prospective disappearance of the party. Hobhouse's efforts to reconcile "the people" with "the Whigs," carving out a political role amidst the noise created by contending factions, left him occupying a hollowed-out space redolent of absences that would continue to unsettle the psychology of liberal politics.

Two weeks prior to describing the "mad and silly" political landscape to Byron, Hobhouse returned home to discover two letters: one from Burdett and one from Bentham.[21] Alongside recognition for Hobhouse's illustrative notes to *Childe Harold's Pilgrimage*, the two men praised him for the semipublic letter addressed to Canning (which he had mentioned to Byron as having made a "monstrous noise" that session). Hobhouse was, in fact, the veiled author of this printed missive, which had – as Hobhouse noted to Byron, without noting his role as its creator – "completely silenced G. C. who has never been heard to joke since." The letters from Bentham and

Burdett posed a pointed question. The Westminster Committee were to approach him as a possible candidate for election, but first they wanted to know whether Hobhouse was in favor of "annual parliaments and universal suffrage," issues that became a litmus test for reformist candidates.[22] Hobhouse planned to "write something by way of speech, with opinions, &c., and an attempt to reconcile *the people and the Whigs*."[23] In the first instance, he experienced affective overload: unable fully to digest the contents of these letters, he and Kinnaird "went together to the Crown and Anchor – great crowd, but no crowding. No Whigs there."

These remarks evoke a rapidly evolving political landscape. The Crown and Anchor tavern would have a key role, we will see, in Hobhouse's future election campaign. Here, his account of that venue suggests a harmonious model for social and political organization – "great crowd, but no crowding" – in tandem with a conspicuous political absence: "No Whigs." Hobhouse claimed to have eschewed his earlier identity. "I have left off my wig and my Whig principles together," he told Byron in September 1818. If he did have a seat in parliament, he continued, "I should have abjured them both by throwing the former on the table as Burke did his dagger."[24] This overdetermined reference to Burke's 1791 famous gesture rejecting Fox in the Commons, which replaces Burke's gothic dagger with a more bathetic metonym, conspicuously protested too much: one can, after all, fairly easily put a hairpiece back on again. Alongside these efforts to distance himself from the Whigs, with whom he remained on "uneasy terms,"[25] Hobhouse expressed similar wariness about the wider populace. When at the hustings for his election campaign the following year, Hobhouse claimed that he was well received by the multitude (who greeted the other candidate with shouts of "No Whig!"). Yet he also dreaded the hissing of the mob, or being shouted at by its members, indicating his disquiet with the changing terrain of reformist politics. Those anxieties around his capacity to maintain an autonomous public role and the pressures exerted by the wider body politic find a spatial analogue in his remarks about the Crown and Anchor. But in any case, the placid scene of "great crowds" but "no crowding" that Hobhouse described proved fleeting. This sense of calm contrasted especially sharply, as the concluding part of this section will go on to show, with his subsequent account of the disturbance at that same venue following the ensuing election.

The spaces associated with popular radicalism operated in dynamic interchange with print culture and wider circuits of conversational exchange. Complicating stereotypes of "alehouse politicians" and rowdy drinking houses, Jon Mee emphasizes the sophisticated combinations of semidomestic intimacy, sociable exchange, and contentious debate

embraced by members of the London Corresponding Society (and affili-
ates including William Godwin) during the 1790s in line with its reformist
agenda and improving ethos.[26] Hobhouse's accounts of the Crown and
Anchor, at a later moment of "Reform" and in the context of local
Westminster political contests, contribute to an expanded, more deeply
textured history of the spatial coordinates of popular radical activity. They
are particularly illuminating in sonic terms. Accounts of the tavern capture
in microcosm the practical and conceptual pressures upon the spaces of
political activity as they converged around the precarious figures of individual men (in ways already apparent from Hobhouse's anxieties at being
hissed at from crowds when on the hustings). With Hobhouse's eventual
election campaign, these various fault lines became apparent in his account
of the postelection "chairing" of Burdett in a lavish coach at Hyde Park
Corner, which culminated in noisy scenes at the Crown and Anchor.

The ceremonial "chairing" had passed without disturbance: "so large
and orderly a crowd were never before assembled in London," Hobhouse
assured Byron.[27] But a procession had continued on to the tavern, where
matters became notably less organized. The "disturbance" at the Crown
and Anchor began, Hobhouse wrote in his diary, as soon as Burdett and his
friends entered, with cries of "Burdett for ever!" and "Damn the
Committee!" There was no dinner, which had been part of the problem.
But someone had also "got up and told Burdett *'he was but a man'"* and "all
was uproar." Following efforts to laugh off the interruptions and an
attempted speech by Kinnaird, Hobhouse "got on the table" to make
a "short loud appeal to the crowd." Hobhouse noted that the *Times* had
reported his improvised remarks. They had come there, he stated, "to
commemorate an event which he hoped would often recur, of electing the
great man in the chair as their representative because, by fatal experience,
they had found that he was *the only man whom they could trust*." Politicians,
he more darkly noted, were sources of disease to the people. Describing the
crowd, to laughter, as an "assembly of Jacobins" – a term of "no consequence" that he "seldom heard ... applied except to the enemies of
corruption" – Hobhouse concluded with toasts to various causes. These
interventions, "strange to say," his journal account continued, had the
"desired effect": "the noise subsided ... music was introduced – the toasts
proceeded. Burdett's health was drunk – then Kinnaird's – then mine ...
No-one was heard afterwards, and soon Burdett and his party went
away."[28] All was harmony. But in contrast with the placid atmosphere of
his earlier visit, the Crown and Anchor had become an altogether more
contested, volatile space. The self-regulated "crowd, but no crowding" had

been overwhelmed by clashes between themselves, divided political representatives and a rowdy group, whom Hobhouse, half-jokingly, termed an "assembly of Jacobins." That scene focalized a larger predicament. In his subsequent election campaigns, Hobhouse would need to quell the "noise" unleashed by his prospective supporters, while remaining "but a man" speaking to men.

Hardened Politicians: Hobhouse's *Letter to Canning*

The tensions on display in the disturbance at the Crown and Anchor came into sharper focus as Hobhouse entered more directly into political campaigning. "The Whigs are down for ever," he wrote to Byron, claiming that the parliamentary opposition were "the laughter of all England in four and twenty hours" after failing to attack a government measure.[29] Canning, meanwhile, was in the ascendant. Hobhouse's political rival was an adept with crowds. The future Tory prime minister had made a "glorious speech," Hobhouse noted to Byron with begrudging admiration, in which he mocked the recent challenges faced by Whig candidates at the Westminster election. This was the same speech to which Place would allude a decade later, in the letter cited above claiming that the Westminster Committee had "killed" the Whigs as a party. Place expanded Canning's mockery of the failed election campaigns into a wider critique of both parties, which he sought to consign to the dustbin of history. But in the moment, Canning's charges demanded a more nuanced response. In his *Letter to Canning*, Hobhouse would stake out his own position as a reformist candidate, between the people and the Whigs, implacably opposed to the Tory establishment.

The Whigs talked of their popularity, Canning noted, but clashed with the crowds. "I am myself supposed to partake of the unpopularity attached to ministers," his speech continued, cranking up the sarcasm, "but I have at least stood the ordeal of a contested election without such *embarrassing marks of affection* as overwhelmed the Whigs at Westminster ... these favorites of the people [were] covered with ribbons and rubbish, with laurels on their heads ... obliged to shelter themselves from *their surprising popularity* behind a troop of his Majesty's life guards; whilst the hero of their triumph was fain to prefer a file of grenadiers to the usual suite of a successful candidate!"[30] Hobhouse quoted Canning at length in his letter to Byron. The speech saw an undeniably smug Canning ("the scoundrel," Hobhouse fumed) deride his opponents for the drubbing they had faced in the Westminster election, turning their pursuit of popular success back against them with derisory, ironic references to their *popularity* and the people's *affections*. The garlanding of the successful candidates with ribbons and other trappings (the kind of "buff and blue" regalia that Byron appreciated) had been replaced with jeering and attacks, leaving the Whigs on the defensive. Since then, Hobhouse informed Byron, they had "become sulky, and begin now to complain of the new House of Commons just as much as they did of the old one: so that I should not wonder if they were obliged to come to the Reformers at last."[31]

In his 1827 letter, Place would visualize the detritus of elections being swept away altogether, as "the people" and the "march of intellect" led the country into a new future. In the meantime, Hobhouse needed to grapple with the demands of being a parliamentary candidate. The fractures running through his political role can be discerned in the *Letter to Canning*. Among its other explosive charges, this quasi-public missive attacked Canning for his disdainful treatment of an older radical. Writing anonymously, Hobhouse warned Canning that "not an echo of those shouts of laughter, which hailed your jests upon rebellious old age and traitorous disease, not an echo has been lost in the wide circumference of the British Islands":

> Those shouts still ring in our ears: they will never die away as long as the day of retribution is deferred; they will never die away until we are finally extirpated by your triumph, or you are annihilated by our indignation. Do not flatter yourself, that by securing the connivance of Parliament, you are safe from all national censure. *Parliament does not represent the feelings any more than the interests of the British nation.* It would be an insult upon the character of this great, this glorious people, to suppose that their representatives were sent to the House of Commons to encourage this hardened ferocity of a hardened politician. The nobler portion of the nation are certainly no members of either House: the better educated, and the more wealthy, at least the more independent, are to be found without the walls of Parliament. You are (and what dishonest man is not?) an enemy to Reform. But you shall be told, Sir, that the extreme necessity of Reform, and of choosing our representatives from some other classes of society, was never so decidedly shown as in the reception of your speech.[32]

Hobhouse mounted a scathing attack here on a loftily detached political establishment drawn from the elite "classes" of society. Assuring Canning that his derision would not be forgotten ("not an echo of those shouts of laughter . . . not an echo has been lost"), Hobhouse skillfully shaped his mockery into a portent of their future "annihilat[ion]" at the polls. Canning had attacked a vulnerable old man. But those "shouts of laughter," Hobhouse claimed, would "never die away," until one side or the other was extinguished. This incendiary epistle became its own extra-parliamentary echo chamber, in which Canning's remarks, reverberating across the kingdom, returned to haunt him. Yet, aside from the righteously Percy-Shelleyan cast taken by these portents (which "still ring in our ears"), this was hardly a statement of revolutionary intent. Hobhouse maintained that "hardened politician[s]" should be replaced from the "nobler" side of the people and some "other classes" of society. His observations that "the better educated, and the more wealthy, at least the more independent, are to be found without the walls of Parliament" were hardly suggestive of social levelling. Hobhouse looked squarely ahead, here, to the liberalism of the mid-nineteenth century. But at this moment, he occupied a confused, contradictory space that located him, in turn, within a fractured, even impossible role. The subsequent ascent of his own political career saw him navigate these various factions into eventual electoral success (leading to his eventual appointment, under Melbourne, in Queen Victoria's inaugural ministry). But these episodes also point to a precarious political figure and the complex absence at its heart, which took shape around his only partial detachment from the spectral figure of the "Whig" politician.

That disjuncture became explicit in his textual persona. In the letter to Byron that described the raucous scenes at the Crown and Anchor, Hobhouse downplayed the unruly atmosphere. That redaction of events extended, in turn, to a kind of self-censorship: Hobhouse did not include mention of his conciliatory speech to the crowd in the account sent to Byron. By contrast, although he touted the *Letter to Canning* to Byron, he did not mention his own authorship. At a remove from this work, in the spectral role of its unidentifiable author – which he elsewhere compared to the anonymous satirist "Junius" – Hobhouse could avoid the contradictions of his own lived experience. Just as he erased his own assertive presence in organizing the crowd and ultimate failure to contain its quasi-"Jacobin" energies, he erased his own authorship and its role in expanding the orbit of his political agency (even as he also noted the efficacy of the publication to Byron). These contradictions risked making Hobhouse's critique against Canning redound on his own head. The *Letter to Canning* accused its subject of being closed off to the demands of the people. Yet the audience that confronted Hobhouse, amidst the bustling scenes at the Crown and Anchor, could advance the same critique. They could equally accuse him, that is to say, of belonging to a sealed-off elite, as a semi-"hardened" politician in his own right. His unease with the noise of this group (and elsewhere with "hissing" crowds) suggests discomfort with the growing role of the masses in politics per se. Hobhouse had sought to contain these emerging tensions by accommodating them within the trappings of existing roles, embodying the paradoxical position of radical, reformer, and Whig, all at once. At the same time, he sought to reconcile them, into a vision of a future political leader presiding over a harmonized polity, anchored by a familiar kind of political man.

Despite being caught between available political roles in his own moment, Hobhouse acquired clarity in at least one respect: he limned the contours of a newly respectable kind of middle-class politician. That did not mean greater receptivity to democratic demands. On the contrary, his arguments for broadening the base of the electorate and regularizing the practice of elections were accompanied by vocal suspicion about expanding the franchise too far.[33] There was therefore a great irony in the attacks he received from Byron. Far from identifying with the rabble, Hobhouse remained highly invested in a sense of propriety. He spoke about the "beautiful and orderly" scenes comprising "immense crowds, well-dressed and decent" at political events.[34] He noted to Byron which politicians did and did not wear hats. Where Hobhouse looked squarely ahead to the politics of mid-Victorian Britain, Byron remained animated by contending impulses. Both men remained wary of what Hobhouse – in the same letter that deplored the "unclean animals" sullying the edges of politics – termed the "preachers of the mobocracy to come."[35] The poet remained invested, for his part, in whatever oppositional possibilities remained available within the Whig role, even and perhaps especially as that position ceased to be a viable one.

Byron's Whig Detachment

Before his final departure from England, Byron had an extended flirtation with Whig politics.[36] Byron's fleeting involvement with the political scenes of fashionable London was bound up with another contemporary phenomenon: dandyism. In 1821, he reflected upon that attachment in "Detached Thoughts," a collection of journal entries. "I liked the Dandies," Byron wrote, adding that "though I gave up the business early, I had a tinge of Dandyism in my minority, and probably retained enough of it, to conciliate the great ones."[37] In a posthumously published compilation of Byron's conversation during his final years, Edward Trelawny described his continuing ties to this earlier identity as tantamount to belonging to the end of a race:

> The character he most commonly appeared in was of the free and easy sort, such as had been in vogue when he was in London, and George IV was

Regent; and his talk was seasoned with anecdotes of the great actors on and off the stage, boxers, gamblers, duelists, drunkards, etc., appropriately garnished with the slang and scandal of that day. Such things had all been in fashion, and were at that time considered accomplishments by gentlemen; and of this tribe of Mohawks the Prince Regent was the chief, and allowed to be the most perfect specimen. Byron, *not knowing that this tribe was extinct,* still prided himself on having belonged to it; of nothing was he more indignant, than of being treated as a man of letters, instead of as a lord and a man of fashion.[38]

Byron made further reflections upon dandyism in "Detached Thoughts." Aside from references to notorious dandy Beau Brummell, that fragmentary commentary included appreciation for gambling, boxing, and the wider rough-and-tumble of the age. But while qualifying Trelawny's characteristically embellished assertion about his dandyism (claiming to have only had a "tinge" of the dandy in his youth), his comments leave us with questions about what, precisely, Byron's attachments were. The sense of a receding past with tenuous links to the present surfaces in Trelawny's claim (albeit without, in that case, granting Byron any self-awareness) about the poet representing the last man at the end of the race.[39] That sense of "lastness" could also carry a sharper edge. The reference to the lost "tribe of Mohawks" was mirrored, with an altogether different inflection, in suggestions made to Hobhouse that if Byron had been there he would "scalp" his enemies, casting him at once as an atavistic figure and also a lone avenger, in whom the apparently vanished past comes back to life. But fuller attention to the meditative tenor of "Detached Thoughts" reveals distinctive ways of thinking about loss that complicate the relationship between the past and the present, framing vanished political possibility in relation to an indeterminate future.

Byron remained wedded to an elite, aristocratic model of political leadership. That identification intersected with his self-conception as a lord, shaping a sense that he was above the commercial marketplace (in addition to having a literal birthright that, among other things, permitted him to take a seat in parliament). *Don Juan* mobilized a satirical persona around the Whig "buff and blue," together with some sharp-edged attacks on Tory elites. But the ascent of post-Waterloo Toryism also gave rise in Byron to acute nostalgia for the Whigs. "Detached Thoughts" folded these attachments into layered, personalized reflections on the past. In tandem with their references to the social whirl and decadent excess associated with Regency culture, Byron focused on specific political figures, whom he measured against his unfulfilled "Ideal of an Orator" (*DT,* 5 [610]), including "old Courtenay" (*DT*, 1 [608]) and the speechmaking of prominent Whigs and Tories, such as Canning ("sometimes very like [an Orator]," *DT*, 5 [610]). Byron's recollections of attending parliament come together with his own experience giving speeches in the House of Lords. But relatively straightforward instances of biographical and political-historical accounting quickly become infused with a poignant sense of loss given added significance by flickering glimpses of continuity. In such remarks as "[Lyttleton] is still alive, I believe," Byron combines a simultaneous note of passing away with lingering presence.

The older Whig generations have a special role in "Detached Thoughts." Fox appears as "a debater, which to me seems as different from an Orator as an Improvisatore or a versifier from a poet" (*DT*, 5 [610]). Byron's reflections upon Richard Brinsley Sheridan turn an elegiac gaze on the late statesman and playwright. But those reflections on Sheridan, who had been dead since 1816, also loop back into vivid recollection, as Byron interrupts himself: "No, it was not the last time: the last time was at Douglas K[innair]d's. I have met him in all places and parties – at Whitehall with the Melbournes, at the Marquis of Tavistock's . . . in short, in most kinds of company, and always found him very convivial and delightful" (*DT*, 9 [612]). Byron here makes use of the present perfect tense ("I have met him") in such a way that makes the past continuous with the present; he found Sheridan delightful company in the past, but in saying he has "always found him" that way, he glancingly makes room for the prospect that such company persists. As he turned to other horizons, his various writings from this period confirm, Byron's attention and energies were also oriented toward the domestic political arena, animating these reflections on the past in relation to the political present.

Byron's levels of political commitment, his attachment to his aristocratic title, and the changing geographic horizons of his engagement with "politics" remain contested.[40] The Whigs, the later cantos of *Don Juan* bemoaned, seemed destined to be perpetually out of place. But whatever its real-world implications, Byron's attachment to the Whig party remained a constant. In his 1820 poem on the death of George III, that attachment spanned both terrestrial and celestial domains.[41] "Detached Thoughts," composed in the same period, turned to a vanished past in relation to an empty-seeming future. Byron recalled his own political speechmaking and the times he witnessed that of his Whig idols, reflecting in the process upon the disappearing prospects for oratory. David Francis Taylor has helpfully examined the tension between Byron's "investment" in parliamentary speechmaking as "an effective cultural and political force" and his "concomitant awareness that even the greatest speech is an event that can never fully be recovered or repeated."[42] In "Detached Thoughts," reflections on ephemerality meld with wide-ranging meditations on loss and identity. In bringing these insights together with reflections on his literary and political influences, Byron located politics at the heart of a fuller reckoning with his changing affective investments and imagined future vistas. "Detached Thoughts," as that title suggests, comprised a series of disconnected journal entries. Yet this extended piece of writing, whose entries Byron numbered and titled, also comprised an extended meditation upon *detachment* as such.

Byron wrote his *Monody on the Death of the Right Honourable R. B. Sheridan* soon after his 1816 departure from England (in the same concentrated period of composition that produced "Darkness"). This poetic tribute to the recently deceased politician and playwright casts light on Byron's continued Whig attachments and their bearing on his continued interests in politics. At the same time, the *Monody* occupies a space of ambiguous detachment, complicating the relationship between faded potential and future possibility. In "Detached Thoughts," Byron recalled his time in the elder statesman's company, mourning his loss while locating Sheridan alongside the great orators of the age. The *Monody* invokes Sheridan's oratorical gifts and literary talents, stressing his forceful interventions in politics:

> A mighty Spirit is eclipsed – a Power
> Hath passed from day to darkness – to whose hour
> Of light no likeness is bequeathed – no name,
> Focus at once of all the rays of Fame!
> The flash of wit – the bright Intelligence,
> The beam of Song – the blaze of Eloquence,
> Set with their Sun – but still have left behind
> The enduring produce of immortal Mind,
> Fruits of a genial morn, and glorious Noon,
> A deathless part of him who died too soon.[43]

These lines, cut with dashes, capture Sheridan's verbal swordplay in and beyond the Commons ("flash of wit"; "blaze of Eloquence"). They confirm Sheridan's status as a "mighty Spirit," whose "deathless" gifts and contributions persist in his writings.[44] At the same time, the jagged meter ("a Power / Hath passed . . . Focus . . . of fame") looks ahead to the switchblade reversals of Byron's later satires (as well as Percy Shelley's "Ozymandias," whose line breaks mark the fall of ages). But while these are apparently the first lines Byron wrote – in a poem that he claimed to compose in a tempest of feeling – they do not appear at the beginning of the published poem. The opening lines of the *Monody* have a subdued mood, lulling the reader into a state of becalmed acceptance. They also mark the dawn, soon after Byron had parted from England for the last time, of a new aesthetic register:

> When the last sunshine of expiring Day
> In Summer's twilight weeps itself away,
> Who hath not felt the softness of the hour
> Sink on the heart, as Dew along the flower?
> With a pure feeling which absorbs and awes
> While Nature makes that melancholy pause,
> Her breathing moment on the bridge where Time
> Of Light and Darkness forms an Arch sublime; –
> Who hath not shared that calm, so still and deep,
> The voiceless thought which would not speak but weep?
> A holy concord – and a bright regret,
> A glorious sympathy with Suns that set?
>
> (1–12)

The poem goes on to locate the reader within a tightly specified time and place: a landscape still drenched in sun ("Summer's day declines along the hills" [19–20]) but marked by the impending loss noted in the poem's opening lines on the expiring sunlight. These opening lines also describe a temporal space: a "melancholy pause" in which "Time" still bridges light and darkness. The *Monody* duly proceeds to its laments for Sheridan, wallowing not in "harsh Sorrow, but a tenderer woe . . . A sweet dejection – a transparent tear," all shed without shame by those left below (13, 16).

Byron proceeds to enumerate the toll of Sheridan's passing, in the dynamic lines about his "bright spirit." But the introductory lines that frame that portrait infuse this pointed loss with a sense of lingering potential, supplementing the aggressive, assertive movement of the later lines with a warm, throbbing tenderness. In the poem's opening, the sunlight, crucially, has *not* yet passed away. The arresting tone (whereby Byron sounds not unlike Wordsworth, for whom "setting suns" belonged to a poetics of both personal loss and immanent transcendence) gives way as the poem dwells, instead, upon Sheridan's gifts: his piercing eloquence and dazzling wit. But while "their Sun," Sheridan, has set, the *actual* sun still exists – at least for a time – and it is from within *this* twilight time that the poem catalogues his "sparkling" legacy. Sheridan had left "vanquished Senates" trembling with his thunder (46), and Byron enumerates the influence of his "strength of feeling" upon hearts ("electric – charged with fire from heaven, / Black with the rude collision – inly torn, / By clouds surrounded, and on whirlwinds borne") and minds (through thoughts that have "turned to thunder – scorch, and burst") (34, 89–92, 94). The *Monody* was, in fact, read before performances of Sheridan plays at Drury Lane, and the poem makes a further turn to their "glowing portraits" (51). "Here in their first abode you still may meet," the poem continues, "Bright with the hues of his Promethean heat, / A Halo of the light of other days / Which still the splendour of its orb betrays" (55–8). These deictics accordingly place the published poem within that realm of performance, such that the poem's introductory setting (which is to say its *sun*-setting) comes from a specific source, declaimed by a speaker from the stage.

Returning to public space, with the poem's actual or imagined appearance in the theatre, brings us full circle. Kinnaird and Hobhouse had dispassionately contemplated the future of politics at the uncrowded Crown and Anchor; Byron meditated from abroad upon a lost Whig past, his own as well as that of Sheridan. But in contrast with "Detached Thoughts," the *Monody*, written and performed at the behest of Kinnaird (Byron's banker and the manager of Drury Lane) came from a moment close to Byron's involvement in Whig politics. The poem catalogued and elaborated Sheridan's gifts, including as an author of plays. But that account of Sheridan's power – which Byron, invoking the myth that would prove so generative for him and the Shelleys, termed "Promethean" – had another layer of resonance. The poem locates its tribute within a carefully rendered space of reflection, at the close of one day, but on the threshold of another: a space in which the fullness of that potential and the prospect of its political actualization might yet be felt even as its loss is lamented.[45] In his subsequent writings, Byron would deepen, at once mellowing and darkening, the aesthetic landed upon in this early poem – which recurs in the sun-drenched worlds of *Childe Harold's Pilgrimage* and an array of writings about Promethean gifts and burdens. He would, in turn, raise the political stakes of that aesthetic, locating the setting (or vanishing) sun and expiring (or enduring) gifts on the brink of unknown futures, at the opening onto entirely other worlds. At the same time, he sharpened his understanding of poetry's capacity to pierce the public sphere. When he came to compose the early cantos of *Don Juan*, Byron had not entirely let go of his partisan investments. His factious and contradictory impulses shaped the composition and reception of that poem and had complex afterlives, the next chapter will show, in debates over ending slavery.

CHAPTER 3

Byron, Brougham, and the End of Slavery

At once a "burlesque" of literary forms including the historical novel and a satire of political "bigwigs," *Whitehall* (1827) looked back at early nine-teenth-century London from an imagined future.[1] But in contrast with many accounts of those decades then and since, Irish-born author William Maginn gave the abolition of slavery a crucial role in the politics of the period. The novel imagines a freed Jamaican man (and his enslaved servant) visiting the center of power, where concern about unrest in the West Indies has become palpable. "At that period," the narration states, "the fermentation of popular sentiment in the Antillic Colonies was at its height," while a veteran member of the Admiralty remarks that "the case is plain": "Barbadoes [*sic*], Demerara, Jamaica herself, are on the eve of insurrection!" It was not "from the Caribbean colonies alone that the proud supremacy of the English tyranny was menaced," but also the "millions" agitating nearer home. The chapter detailing these brewing changes has an epigraph from *Childe Harold's Pilgrimage*: "Can tyrants but by tyrants vanquished be, / And freedom find no champion and no child?"[2] Emancipation and Reform were, indeed, on the horizon, as the novel's highly self-conscious narration presciently foresees. But the book also imbues its speculative projections with the clarity of hindsight. The lines quoted in the epigraph are more ambivalent, a tone Byron echoed in *Don Juan*, where the poet welcomed the arrival of some abolitionist reforms to the slave trade but also shrugged that slavery seemed destined to continue "and the thing / Need not seem very wonderful."[3]

The end of slavery was a long time coming. Abolitionist campaigning first gathered steam in the late eighteenth century, driven by a transatlantic network of antislavery activists.[4] But their demands faltered, as the age of revolutions gave way to an era of global warfare and geopolitical complex-ity. The 1807 Slave Trade Act represented a crucial milestone, but was also inadequate. Wilberforce had ended Britain's formal participation in the slave trade; as Byron sarcastically noted in *Don Juan*, he had "at last" made the price of slaves "twice / What 'twas ere Abolition."[5] But the slavery question remained unsettled at the time of the poet's death in 1824. The question was not whether slavery was wrong: the intellectual argument against enslaving human beings for profit had long been lost.[6] Public opinion further hardened against slavery as the years went on, helping to drive new demands, including for emancipation. In 1833, the Slavery Abolition Act formally ended slavery in the British Empire and – following a period of required apprenticeship – freed the enslaved. But we should resist the tendency to pin these developments to a straightforward progress narrative. Even nuanced accounts risk falling prey to a teleological, Whiggish tendency to see abolition as inevitable, as though the end of slavery were somehow preordained. But the record reveals no such thing.[7] The brutal toll of enslavement continued for decades beyond the formal end of the slave trade. Evolving political-economic logics and emerging visions of imperial governance – including calls for "amelioration" – found new ways of taking control over and reproducing Black lives.[8] Fresh arguments and rhetorical strategies emerged in the late Romantic age, seeking to create momentum for ending slavery outright. But this second wave of abolitionist campaigning faced a new challenge: how to imagine slavery's end.

That ending could be cast in peaceful terms, with slavery disappearing at a stroke or gradually withering away to nothing. Ending slavery was also cast as a dramatic act of leveling, accompanied by the frisson of revolution (and the very real prospect of violent upheaval). In both cases, the difficulties associated with imagining an end to slavery coupled with the challenge of foreseeing what might come next. Enslaved persons were not always present within, let alone central to, discussions of the postslavery future. The economic thought of Adam Smith was predicated upon the undoing of a larger imperial polity, in which, Christopher Taylor argues, enslaved people found fraught kinds of belonging. That tightly-knit sovereign whole gave way, Taylor demonstrates, to a free-trade economy that consigned the formerly enslaved to abandonment and neglect.[9] As this chapter will go on to show, the recalcitrant presence of formerly enslaved persons, building upon a deep history of contestation and resistance, troubled the newly circumscribed British polity during the transition into the Victorian age. This chapter's main aim is to reexamine slavery's sidelined role during the "Age of Reform." I use the case of Henry Brougham to show how demands for the immediate end of slavery – while largely excluded from reformist politics in this period – played an awkwardly disruptive role in the domestic arena. Parliamentary debates over emancipation in the 1820s failed to reconcile calls for ending slavery with plausible visions of the future. As such, I propose, they imagined a world in which slavery would, effectively, never end – or a future in which the presently enslaved had no place. But they did so, this chapter demonstrates, amidst contested affective terrain.

Debates about the pace and practicality of ending slavery summoned a lot of feelings, including lofty humanitarian sentiments, appeals to benevolent stewardship, and hopes of personal and national salvation. But the affective contours of the antislavery cause were also jagged and uncertain, including impatient agitation and swelling anger as well as, in the colonies, prospective discontent and violent resistance. As antislavery debate in England continued through the 1820s and into the 1830s, the cause "attracted young men and women, many of whom were impatient with the caution of their parliamentary champions."[10] Wilberforce and other abolitionist MPs were shocked in 1830, for example, when a proposed motion for the immediate end of slavery from the floor of an antislavery meeting was "overwhelmingly carried."[11] The momentum for ending slavery was further accelerated by threats of resistance from the enslaved. But these demands for rapid change faced considerable challenges. Calls for immediate emancipation were held back by appeals to gradualism. Wilberforce and his peers expressed sympathy with the proslavery elite, especially around fears of enslaved resistance. The abolition movement, not unlike the reform movement, remained divided between radicals and moderates, ardent reformers and defenders of the status quo. Those fractures gave rise to competing visions of the future, bound up with various kinds of feeling.

Brougham became a prominent advocate for abolition and emancipation, building upon a career-spanning concern with the realities of a global economy anchored by bound labor. Writing in the *Edinburgh Review* about Morris Birkbeck's *Notes on a Journey in America*, Brougham spoke in detail about the evils of slavery in the United States and the still-more desperate situation in the West Indies.[12] Brougham also had a reputation for drama. He was incendiary, unpredictable, and arguably even unstable. Beyond idiosyncrasies of personal character, his career points to fissures within the abolition movement. Brougham leaned into his reputation as a political firebrand possessed of radical, potentially dangerous enthusiasm. His interventions thus underscored the tension between gradualist measures and calls for immediate emancipation. Echoing the anti-imperialism of Edmund Burke, Brougham called attention to the false distance between "domestic" matters and supposedly distant colonial affairs. In addition to the changing contours of abolitionist campaigning, his career points to buried fault lines in existing accounts of the wider period. There were points of connection between the respective movements for abolition and parliamentary reform and even greater overlap between the public mobilization driving these issues. But Brougham underscores the core *disjuncture*. At the same time, he points to parliament's distance, on both issues, from volatile energies from below. His case thus calls for renewed attention to the vectors and intensities of political feeling in the Late Romantic period. With the transition into the early Victorian age, this chapter will go on to show, Brougham remained a disruptive figure. The postemancipation moment was one of imperial reconfiguration. Brougham destabilized efforts to secure a new national mood of equipoise and emotional restraint with stubborn reminders of an unsettled past and slavery's unfinished business.

Byron was concerned with the political status of his writings and meditated on his relationship to fading remnants of the "Whig" past. The analogy between literary and political spheres also functions in the other direction. Brougham gave speeches in parliament "with the design of . . . exciting a sensation throughout the country."[13] He had claims to being, in some respects, a literary figure. The scrutiny received by Brougham's interventions, as with that attracted by Byron's published writings and literary persona, points not only to the interplay and overlap between literature and politics but also to the ways in which both men became legible within the wider affective public sphere. That sphere, crucially, had transatlantic and imperial dimensions. Examining colonial trials for "disaffection," Tanya Agathocleous has shown how wayward impulses and dissident sympathies were profiled and policed.[14] Those late nineteenth-century trials imputed recalcitrant, "disaffected" feeling to Indian subjects and proceeded with legal codification and harsh penalties. The racialization of British subjecthood, discourse, and affect in the late Victorian age represented a considerable advance upon the period I examine here, when prosecution and censorship were more limited to unlucky radicals and daring publishers. But concerns about "sedition" did not end in England.

In September 1819, a month after the Peterloo massacre saw a proreform meeting descend into state-sponsored violence, an article headlined "Seditious Meeting" appeared in Demerara's *Royal Gazette* newspaper. The article cited alarmed commentary from England about swelling popular demands for "Annual Parliaments, Universal Suffrage and Election by Ballot" and expressed particular concern about female reformers, who had made "public exhibition of their shamelessness and unwomanly depravity" (seeking to instill "deep-rooted abhorrence of tyranny" into the "minds of their offspring").[15] Reprinted in the West Indies, these anxieties about disloyalty and affective excess were made legible in relation to fears about "sedition" among the enslaved, tying proreform energies in England together with rumbling discontents on and around the plantations. The enslaved were subject to horrendous violence and retribution for even the perception of disloyalty. But their actual and prospective resistance also played an important role in shaping the volatile affective terrain I return to view in this chapter. Expressions of "Romantic" feeling or incitements of political "sensation," that is to say, were not limited to the vocal contributions of literary and political men in the domestic arena. They also emerged, by way of the colonies, as Black resistance.

During this inchoate moment of domestic unrest and imperial transition, feeling took on a complex – and complexly racialized – charge. Displays of "excessive" feeling thus acquired multifaceted, unpredictable significance. While not codified and surveilled to the same degree as at the height of the late Victorian British Empire, feeling was closely scrutinized during the late Romantic age. But what Maginn's novel referred to as "the fermentation of popular sentiment" could, at this moment of heated feeling and fluid change, move the needle. As historians have recently emphasized, developments on the ground in the "new sugar frontier" had an important and neglected influence on "metropolitan sympathies" – as was also the case, in more explosive fashion, for a spate of violent uprisings from Demerara in 1823 to Jamaica in 1831.[16] As the campaign to abolish slavery entered its final phases, the contrarian sentiments attributed to Brougham collided, spectacularly, with popular feeling from below and resistance from the enslaved. The end of slavery thus remained an explosive issue, and these conjunctures of charged feeling served as forceful challenges, I propose, to plainly fantastical visions of slavery peacefully ceasing and passing away. Byron had, by that point, been dead for several years. But the kinds of feeling invested in his personas and animated by his poetry outlived him. They found a complex double in Brougham, whose affective excesses unsettled the transition to a new phase of imperial control with contested visions of the worlds to come.

Byron and Brougham: Opposites Attract

Hazlitt presented a characteristically counterintuitive portrait of Wilberforce in *The Spirit of the Age*. Deeming the abolitionist leader "specious, persuasive, familiar, silver-tongued … amiable, charitable, conscientious, pious, loyal, humane, tractable to power, accessible to popularity, honouring the king, and no less charmed with the homage of his fellow-citizens," Hazlitt went on to describe the peculiar contradictions that resulted from these efforts at appearing *too* virtuous:

> Loyalty, patriotism, friendship, humanity, are all virtues, but may they not sometimes clash? By being unwilling to forego the praise due to any, we may forfeit the reputation of all; and, instead of uniting the suffrages of the whole world in our favour, we may end in becoming a sort of by-word for affectation, cant, hollow professions, trimming, fickleness, and effeminate imbecility.[17]

In seeking to elicit the approval of all, Wilberforce papered over his competing motivations. In the process, he brought to light his affected goodness and dubious sincerity. That core of "cant" made his a hollow virtue.

Eric Williams's seminal study *Capitalism and Slavery* (1944) was also concerned with insincerity. Ending slavery, in Williams's accounting, was driven by self-interested considerations: slavery was no longer profitable, making abolition expedient.[18] At the same time, Williams offered probing – at times excoriating – analysis of the competing and confused motivations of the abolition movement, including their affective contours. In parallel with Hazlitt's suspicions about his self-serving humanitarianism, Williams dismissed Wilberforce for his "sentimentality."[19] But rather than merely discounting the role of emotive abolitionist campaigning, Williams carefully differentiated between its respective wings. Abolitionists in parliament, for all their rhetoric, were mealy-mouthed, advocating for tightly circumscribed reforms. Williams pointedly called out the shortcomings of the evangelicals in parliament, who offered further evidence that prudent calculation, including at the level of sympathy, was the core motive for ending slavery; he gestured, at the same time, to the potency of the popular movement, whose demands for drastic change were sidelined by Wilberforce and his peers. The frequently acerbic tone of *Capitalism and Slavery* underscores the affective layer of this analysis. Williams advanced not only a tactical and political objection to Wilberforce, but a stylistic one.

Hazlitt's portrait of Wilberforce's hypocrisy and Williams's remarks on the self-serving tendencies of the evangelical movement were echoed by Byron. His positive remarks elsewhere notwithstanding, the poet disliked Wilberforce's proselytizing and distrusted his motivations, describing him to Hobhouse as a "canting . . . son of a bitch."[20] Byron, for his own part, was not particularly interested in opposing slavery. In this, he resembled many of his Whig contemporaries. Charles James Fox had been a noted abolitionist. But divisions within the party – and growing conflict with France, including in the West Indies – blunted Whig advocacy for the antislavery cause. In Brougham, however, Byron had a complex double in debates over abolition. In tandem with his growing role in parliamentary reform, Brougham became a prominent advocate for abolition and emancipation. As the result of his vigorous engagement with these causes, he developed a reputation for "zeal." That reputation was, I will suggest, a Byronic one. Brougham had features in common with the poet, from his lordly bearing to his rebellious public persona. The two men clashed, at times spectacularly. Byron's poetic attacks on his excessive feeling and wayward sympathies crystallized accusations leveled at Brougham throughout a career that saw him labeled "dissatisfied, restless, independent, and ungovernable."[21] *Don Juan* became a critical site at which these parallels were worked out.

My purpose here in connecting Brougham and Byron is not to trace any direct relationships or lines of influence. Byron helped to popularize ideas of the "Satanic" rebel that closely parallel those attached to Brougham. But this chapter does not set out to make the case that poetry shaped perceptions of the politician. Nor, despite their personal connections, does my claim that Brougham became a "Byronic" figure depend upon any direct links with the poet (although it certainly does not preclude them). Attending to poetry and parliamentary debate during the late Romantic age – and to the wider affective public sphere in which both literature and politics took shape – I approach the case of Brougham both in its specificity and for its wider resonance, as an event within a larger media ecosystem. Like Byron, Brougham was among the figures profiled in *The Spirit of the Age*. But he shared more in common with the rebellious, impetuous poet than with the glibly self-assured figure of Wilberforce. Beyond an accident of history, the complex doubling of the two men points to the continued interchange between literary and political realms in the late Romantic age. Brougham allows us, in turn, to trace the changing political valences of excessive, "Romantic" feeling beyond Byron's lifetime and into a new age.

Byron did not like Brougham.[22] A lawyer, Brougham had represented Byron's wife in their public separation. He was also a founding contributor to the *Edinburgh Review*, the Whiggish publication on which Byron had turned his ire in the early satire *English Bards, Scotch Reviewers*. In Canto x of *Don Juan*, Byron recalled his animus toward Brougham with comments on the legal profession:

> A legal broom's a moral chimney-sweeper,
> And that's the reason he himself's so dirty:
> The endless soot bestows a tint far deeper
> Than can be hid by altering his shirt; he
> Retains the sable stains of the dark creeper.

(x.15)

Byron punned here on the pronunciation of Brougham's name – "pronounced Broom in the south," he wrote in the notes to *English Bards* – casting legal work as "endless soot" whose "sable stains" had not only soiled his shirt but marked his skin. Brougham's critics would employ similar imagery to capture his brushes with a dirty rabble. The association with coal-tinged blackness would, in turn, acquire racialized meanings, as this chapter will go on to show.[23] *Don Juan* reveals how the "tint" associated with Brougham's actions was bound up with claims about his character. This poetic attack had an unpublished precursor. Byron's complexly entangled personal, temperamental, and political critiques of Brougham made their mark more obviously on his earliest drafts for *Don Juan*, underscoring the complex and shifting status of both politician and poem in the evolving affective public sphere.

In his drafts for the opening cantos of *Don Juan*, Byron set out to settle various scores. The poem's unpublished "Dedication" condemned the controversial Tory foreign secretary Viscount Castlereagh and the poet laureate Robert Southey, whom Byron despised for his hypocritical pieties and about-face on his earlier radical sympathies. In manuscript, Byron made some further, seemingly more light-hearted attacks. That included a rather tasteless stanza about the recent suicide of MP Sir Samuel Romilly. Byron used Romilly's death to undercut pious truisms with a parenthetical reminder of chaotic worldly realities: "One sad example more that 'all is vanity,' – / (The jury brought their verdict in 'insanity')."[24] Moving beyond personal invective allowed Byron to expand the poem's historical and political horizons.[25] The later cantos of the poem extended that reckoning, this book's Coda will show, to the prospect of the world ending. In his drafts of the poem's opening cantos, by contrast, Byron's writing remained riven by partisan animus. While the poem ultimately stabilized around a stance of self-assured urbanity, its tone and Byron's poetic persona during these early phases of composition were considerably less stable.

Even after Byron parted ways from politics in England, his poetry remained animated by factious energies and a spirit of contention.[26] Brougham helped to reanimate these political energies, summoning Byron's anger (along with the incoherence that often accompanied his anger). Even more, arguably, than Byron's other satirical targets in *Don Juan*, Brougham thus became a complex foil for the poet. In stanzas drafted for the poem's opening canto, Byron attacked Brougham's political opportunism, describing an unpredictable, self-defeating, inconsistent personality (traits that the poet, to some extent, shared). That critique also had a political dimension. At a time when the Whigs, as Byron had lamented, lacked orators, Brougham came to be known as a feisty public speaker (as Shelley confirmed when she cited his recent debate when asking for Hobhouse's assistance to attend the House of Commons). His articles, similarly, were characterized by an "iconoclastic, lively, and sometimes abusive style."[27] Brougham nonetheless remained at a complex remove from the Whig establishment, keeping a foot in popular politics. Although well placed to join the party elite, he was equally successful in cultivating an outsider platform; alternating between these poles, he alienated moderates while also disappointing the Westminster radicals.[28] That vacillation was bound up with a reputation for emotional excess and volatility.

Byron had his own storms of fervent political feeling, not least in the three speeches he gave to the House of Lords, which included a fiery oration in support of the "Luddite" frame-breakers. Even after his exile, Byron's poetry continued to lash out at, and more subtly critique the nation and political system he had left behind. The attacks on Castlereagh and Southey in the unpublished "Dedication" to *Don Juan* frame the poem around his principled antagonism toward the Tory elite and its literary enablers. Describing these and other attacks as "good, simple, savage verse," Byron pointed to the political impulses and personal animosities that were seemingly excised from, but that survived underneath and alongside, his writing of *Don Juan*.[29] We encounter further evidence of Byron's attitudes toward – and continued investment in – politics from the body of the drafted opening canto. Even more, in some ways, than the "Dedication" (whose nonpublication became prudent), the rejected stanzas on Brougham offer insight into the developing method of Byron's poem, including warring impulses that were ultimately submerged with the growing ambitions for the new work.

Byron's personal antipathy against Brougham triggered political invective. In a series of *ottava rima* stanzas, the poet mounted a withering critique of Brougham's repeated attempts to engage in politics. A legal advocate for Leigh Hunt and Queen Caroline, in addition to Byron's wife, Brougham sought to navigate between his establishment aspirations, on the one hand, and his courting of crowds, on the other. After the loss of backing from one patron, for example, Brougham had "flirted" with the radicals, before returning to the Whigs.[30] These abrupt swings and slippery attachments provoked Byron's poetic attack. In an accompanying note, he summarized what he saw as a disreputable career. "Distrusted by the democracy – disliked by the Whigs – and detested by the Tories," Brougham was "too much of a lawyer for the people – and too much of a demagogue for Parliament." As an orator, his performances for various audiences undid themselves: he was too corrupt to be popular, too scheming to be widely trusted. Brougham was, Byron concluded, the "outcast of all parties."[31] His attack in verse similarly described a politically evasive, hypocritical, shape-shifting figure. A "Tory by nurture, Whig by circumstance," Brougham was, also, "A Democrat some once or twice a year" (17–18).

Taken as a whole, the rejected "Brougham stanzas" expand Byron's scattered critiques into a full-blown character assassination. It was a pity, the poem remarks, with an eye on the sultry world of Juan's seductions, that they did not have a lawyer like Brougham in Spain:

> Famous for always talking and neer fighting,
> For calling names and taking them again,
> For blustering, bungling, trimming, wrangling, writing,
> Groping all paths to power, and all in vain,
> Losing elections, character, and temper,
> A foolish clever fellow – 'Idem semper'!
> . . .
> The People's Sycophant, the Prince's foe
> And serving him in the more by being so.
>
> (3–8, 15–16)

These lines, as Peter Cochran has noted, follow the example of Dryden's attacks on greasy politicians in *Absalom and Achitophel*, as well as Pope's withering character sketches.[32] They present Brougham as a figure endlessly divided against himself, "losing elections, character and temper, / A foolish clever fellow." In the accompanying note, Byron tied Brougham's innate corruptibility with his unreliability. He was "a speaker upon all questions," whose "support has become alike formidable to all his enemies – (for he has no friends)" and whose "vote can only be valuable when accompanied by his silence." That damning verdict was echoed in the stanzas. But Byron's pointed critique in the prose note, with "silence" as its resonant last word, contrasted with its poetic counterpart, which remained animated by a restless energy.

The stanzas do not quite work. They lack the kind of dynamic, dialectical through-lines demonstrated by Hazlitt's essays. As poetry, the heaped-up insults overwhelm the *ottava rima* stanza, their pummeling excess better suited to Popean couplets. Byron's dissatisfaction is suggested by his repeated writing and rewriting of some lines (and presumably contributed to the eventual decision not to include the stanzas in the poem).[33] That excess also threatens to break down the divide between the two men, as the inconsistency attributed to Brougham resurfaces as the restless energy of Byron's poetry. Byron remains in danger of protesting too much, unconsciously registering his own political contradictions. Accusing Brougham of "blustering," "bungling," and "groping all paths to power," he risks both trying too hard and going too far, letting his feelings become entangled with the poem, "losing" his "temper." Hobhouse made that fear explicit when he reviewed the draft of the poem's opening canto, warning that Byron had let animus get "mixed up with the whole poem." He employed the same phrasing as he instructed Byron that if he became "mixed up" ("as you inevitably will be") "with the character or the adventures or the turn of thinking and acting recommended by the poem," he would lose "the fame attached to the supposed former delineation" of his "sublime & pathetic feeling." What was admirable in Childe Harold would not be acceptable in the "Rake Juan."[34] The poem would, steered by Hobhouse and other factors, pursue other trajectories. Byron would ultimately hone his "savage" verse into more pointed critiques, while adopting a more glib, aloof vantage point. But the restless energies that became "mixed up" with the early phases of the poem continued to be attached to his public persona and poetic reputation.

The contradictory impulses identified in (and mirrored by) Byron's poetry surfaced throughout Brougham's subsequent political career. His vigorous support for reform made him a lightning rod for conservative criticism. His swerves into popular politics, meanwhile, fueled his reputation for waywardness and volatility. That reputation became even more pertinent to his involvement in abolition. At the level of national debate, reform and abolition were separate issues. But these vectors of Brougham's political energies became inseparable, not least after he was elected "with the help of his anti-slavery reputation" and then used that platform to "campaign flamboyantly for parliamentary reform."[35] The entangling of those causes further compounded Brougham's conflicted reputation, as his often-vocal interventions led to continued clashes with his contemporaries.

As such, I will now go on to show, he underscores the ways that feeling was mobilized in and around debates about the ending of slavery. Emancipation would prove compatible with the transition to a new era in the British Empire. But Brougham helped to keep alternative prospects alive, interrupting the seamless passage between eras and the assimilation of abolition to a larger national narrative and imperialist logic. Before turning directly to the vexed moment of emancipation, I examine parliamentary debate during the preceding decade. The prospect of a peaceful end to slavery, debates in parliament make clear, was an illusory and dubious one, predicated upon the disappearance of enslaved and formerly enslaved people from view. But Brougham's disruptiveness, incongruence, and refusal to pipe down – precisely the features that Byron had, in self-implicating fashion, satirized – helped to upset that premise from the outset.

The Ends of Slavery

Brougham's association with abolition went back to the outset of his political career. He garnered acclaim for his *Inquiry into the Colonial Policy of the European Powers* (1803), which attracted Wilberforce's approval for its criticism of slavery. In his first major parliamentary speech, Brougham lamented the failure of the 1807 Act to secure a full global ban, calling out lax or absent enforcement and painting emotive scenes of severed communities. Whatever their success in helping to extinguish the remaining slave trade, these sentimentalized appeals had little meaning for those already born into the slave societies of the Caribbean. As debate shifted to existing communities of enslaved people, a new set of arguments and rhetorical strategies became necessary. Those calling for immediate emancipation had to contend with a pervasive emphasis – both from those who ostensibly supported abolition and those who were invested in slavery's perhaps permanent continuation – upon amelioration. Whether or not those advocating for these mitigating reforms also supported abolition was, in some respects, moot.[36] Evading the prospect of sudden, "revolutionary" breaks and dangerously innovative "experiments," their proposals for improving slavery effectively dodged the issue, avoiding the need to ask what it would mean for slavery to end. This explicit and effective advocacy for delay meant that the transition beyond slavery was pushed into an ever-receding future. Calls for the abolition of slavery in the British Empire had thus reached an impasse, caught between competing visions of the better world to come and the incompatibility of those future horizons with a present that seemed destined to continue.

Slavery, some abolitionists vaguely conjectured, would simply come to a peaceful end. They conjured images, in turn, of an almost pastoral future, in which forced toil in unbearable conditions gave way, somehow, to the free labor of an emancipated rural peasantry. In addition to retarding reformist measures, those bucolic visions of postslavery worlds had a further consequence: making existing enslaved persons disappear. Those visions of freshly dawning futures effectively razed the terrain on which slavery had taken place, supplanting the realities of brutal work camps with images of unspoiled islands.[37] But these images were not uncontested. Female-led organizing and strategic interventions in print culture – as illustrated by the publication and reception of Mary Prince's *History* (1831) – helped to keep the violent realities of slavery and the erased humanity of enslaved persons in view. Brougham, for his part, served as a powerful conduit for those energies in parliament, challenging harmonious and quiescent visions of slavery's ending. His interventions would help, in turn, to return the recalcitrant presence of the enslaved to view.

The antislavery movement "occupied a different terrain" to proreform politics during the pre-1832 period (even as abolitionist campaigns "often shadowed or paralleled the surges of radical politics"). The ending of slavery was also cast as a "self-contained measure," with some abolitionist leaders viewing their cause as "standing above politics and the quarrel of interests."[38] Although the abolitionists in parliament made common cause with the Whigs, these were ultimately distinct groups (mirrored by a complex assemblage of government elites, proslavery Tories, and West Indian plantation owners).[39] Debates on abolition and reform, while in some cases gathering momentum from each other, were also liable to pass like ships in the night. Sir Thomas Fowell Buxton – Wilberforce's successor as the head of the abolitionists in the Commons – remained wary, for his part, about debates over parliamentary reform and the end-times atmosphere they portended. "Storms seem gathering in every direction," he wrote in 1831, with an eye on working-class reform riots and a cholera epidemic, "and the tempest may soon brake upon my own house."[40] In presenting abolition on their own narrow terms, its parliamentary supporters blunted wider antislavery demands. But their economizing fueled a backlash. The reticence of Wilberforce and Buxton helped give rise to a "radical anti-slavery current" that "distrusted" their "timid proposals" as well as the "deceptively accommodating response of the government." As much as abolition represented a self-contained measure, the feelings summoned by slavery portended significant upset, as the storm clouds of resistance began to gather at home and abroad.

Although fears of enslaved resistance persisted among white planters and metropolitan elites, the prospect that enslaved people would form their own communities was less pronounced in the second decade of the nineteenth century than in the wake of the French Revolution. But the prospect that slavery could continue unchanged had similarly begun to recede from view. Debates over emancipation were thus concerned less with whether slavery needed to be reformed than with how and when. The question of pace acquired special salience. The founding in 1823 of the Society for the Mitigation and Gradual Abolition of Slavery Throughout the British Dominions marked a critical shift. But as its name confirmed, that organization favored a combination of going slow and drawing out. The Society's members were not, moreover, "endeavouring to rouse indignation against particular acts of extraordinary cruelty, or to hold up to merited reprehension individuals notorious for their crimes" a published "Prospectus" noted. They were "only exhibiting a just picture of the nature and obvious tendencies of Slavery itself, wheresoever and by whomsoever practiced." But the Society also had a new end in mind. They had too readily believed that, with the ban on the slave trade, slavery would "undergo a gradual, but rapid mitigation, until it had ceased to reproach our free institutions and our Christian profession, and was no longer known but as a foul blot in our past history." The failure to reach that goal led to a pointed demand: the "gradual and final extinction, in all parts of the British Dominions, of a system which is at war with every principle of religion and morality, and outrages every benevolent feeling."[41]

In a debate on May 15, 1823, Buxton stated the aims of the newly founded Anti-Slavery Society in the House of Commons. Their object, Buxton informed the chamber, echoing the published prospectus, was "nothing less than the extinction of Slavery – in nothing less than the whole of the British dominions." But he reaffirmed the commitment to going slow. The Society and its members did not seek the "rapid termination of that state – not the sudden emancipation of the Negro." Buxton was not suggesting a dramatic, cataclysmic break. He was not, in fact, suggesting much of a break at all – "nothing rapid, nothing abrupt, nothing bearing any feature of violence." Instead, he imagined a gradual fading away. Slavery, he feared, "will never be abolished: it will never be destroyed." Instead, he went on, "it will subside; it will decline; it will expire; it will, as it were, burn itself down into its socket and go out." The abolitionists would not seek "to cut down slavery, in the full maturity of its vigour." Rather, Buxton went on, as though channeling Keats's nightingale, they would "leave it gently to decay – slowly, silently, imperceptibly, to die away, and to be forgotten."[42] Elsewhere, Buxton was more aggressive and sarcastic, instructing his peers to "screw from your Slave all that his bones and his muscle will yield you." But the harsh irony here gave way to the same pacifying register: "only stop there; and, when every Slave now living shall have found repose in the grave, then let it be said, that the country is satiated with Slavery, and has done with it for ever."[43]

The countervailing movements associated with these various calls for ending slavery converged around one word: "extinction." Buxton informed the Commons that the Anti-Slavery Society sought slavery's "gradual and final extinction." In the years following the passage of emancipation, Buxton became involved in a global movement to ensure the "extinction" of slavery and to promote the "civilization" of Africans. As that pairing makes clear, these aspirations had dubious implications for those whose lives and civilization were in question. The "extinction" of slavery was predicated, to some degree, upon the presently enslaved disappearing from view. Buxton made that premise all but explicit in the image of "every Slave now living" having "repose in the grave." In practice, allowing slavery to "die away, and to be forgotten" would entail the neglect and abandonment of formerly enslaved people.[44] Buxton's subsequent coupling of abolition with missionary efforts situates the extinguishing of slavery next to imperialist endeavors that sought to remake – if not replace – colonized peoples in the name of an emergent civilizing mission. That supposed regeneration, in tandem with calls for the final "extinction" of slavery, helps bring out more fully that word's resonances. While not yet carrying its Darwinist meanings, "extinction" suggests environments cleared of existing populations, communities wiped clean of existing practices, living individuals swept into a buried past.

In the event, slavery dragged on, disastrously, for another decade. The founding of the Anti-Slavery Society in 1823 helped to set the agenda for ending slavery outright. But its emphasis on mitigation also helps to explain why emancipation was some time coming. The rhetorical posture of calm was a strategic one, as was the casting of slavery as a "blot" (that might, in a Popean rhyme supplied by Buxton's remarks, simply be "forgot[ten]"). But that left the question of just how, exactly, slavery was to end. In the same May 1823 debate, George Canning presented an authoritative voice in favor of delay. Addressing the Commons in response to Buxton, Canning situated himself within the by-now familiarly doubled rhetoric, seeking an end without rupture, dissolution without disaster. Yet his comments also highlighted the incompatibility between some antislavery demands and political stability. Canning did not want slavery to "continue indefinitely." It was emphatically *not* "a system to be carefully preserved and cherished." But the time was not yet ripe for doing away with the institution. He elaborated:

> I think the House will be of my opinion that at this time of day we must consider property as the creature of law; and that, when law has sanctioned any particular species of property, *we cannot legislate in this House as if we were legislating for a new world*, the surface of which was totally clear from the obstruction of antecedent claims and obligations.[45]

For Canning, the stability of the world was upheld by the rule of law (and the guarantee of property, as law's "creature"). Ending slavery would thus amount to the end of the world.

Brougham was an exception to this mood of quiescence and stasis. Where Buxton had been conciliatory and Canning had invoked quasi-Burkean stability and continuity, Brougham was recalcitrant when he rose to address parliament in the same debate. He acknowledged that he was keeping his fellow members from their beds but, while now late at night, he could not "leave the question to be finally disposed of" without having his say. This emphasis on disrupted rest gave way to expressions of sheer impatience. Buxton had pointed to earlier abolition measures put forward by Pitt, Dundas, and Burke ("the least addicted to change," Brougham wryly noted of the latter).[46] But simply making more demands for better treatment was not enough: resolutions of the same kind, he reminded his peers, had been moved in 1797 and again in 1816, "calling upon the Prince Regent, in the strongest terms, to recommend to the local authorities in the colonies to carry into effect every measure which might tend to promote the moral and religious improvement, as well as the comfort and happiness, of the Negroes." Twenty-six years had gone by since the resolutions first passed by Fox and his contemporaries, "and where were the benefits, the visible effects, of these Addresses to be found?" They were, "in fact, *not one step more advanced in the great work of improvement* than we were before."[47]

Brougham called attention to the endless deferrals that accompanied ameliorationist measures – and the hollowing out of the forward movement implied by "*the great work of improvement*." But he was not able to propose a viable alternative. While he called attention to continued suffering and voiced pent-up frustration, he could not offer a way beyond the impasse. The deadlock was broken by energies from below. The Anti-Slavery Society remained in favor of going slow. But its founding helped renew interest in the wider cause, including revived popular support. In response to wider public agitation, some "within the respectable ranks of organised abolitionism" took up "the call for immediate emancipation, without compensation to the slave-owners." This turn toward greater urgency coupled with a newly aggressive tone from domestic campaigners. The anonymous 1824 pamphlet *Immediate Not Gradual Emancipation* was followed by "a stream of antislavery writings imbued with a vehemence and intransigence lacking in parliamentary abolitionism."[48] Much of this new antislavery writing was the work of women, attracting Wilberforce's paternalist displeasure. Buxton sought to draw a line, dividing his work in parliament from what he termed "popular feeling." But Brougham, for his part, remained a moving target. He did not identify fully with the evangelicals, just as he kept his distance from the Whig reformers. Yet he remained at an unstable, volatile remove from popular activity. The tensions surrounding debates over ending slavery thus became legible in his public figure, which hovered at a remove from organized abolition and popular organizing while remaining animated by his own uniquely disaffected energies.

Brougham, Political Zeal, and Black Resistance

On April 15, 1831, Buxton addressed the House of Commons. Amplifying his statements from the previous decade, he now called outright for slavery's immediate "extinction."[49] His speech pursued various tacks. The "whole slave-population" of Britain's West Indian possessions, Buxton stated, was in "a miserable condition" and the enslaved were depressed. The "whole system" was "so destructive" to their "moral and physical welfare," he concluded, that it ought "to be abolished." But while he gestured at specific examples of "oppression and cruelty," he did so, he hastened to add, "without the slightest feeling of hostility" toward those who generated their wealth and status from Caribbean slavery "and without the slightest disposition to cast reproach upon them." He distanced himself, moreover, from domestic agitation and unrest from below, denying that the "strength" of the case for ending slavery had anything to do with "popular feeling." Buxton voiced his sympathy for slave owners who faced financial ruin from the passage of abolition without compensation. But he also underscored the haunting realities of slavery's culture of decline and death, bringing renewed attention to mortality rates together with a gruesome image. The enslaved were, he asserted, said to be dying off "like rotten sheep."[50]

Emancipation came two years later. But we ought to be hesitant about chalking up the end of slavery as a further victory for the "Age of Reform." While abolition was mixed up with other causes at the level of popular debate, parliamentarians approached the end of slavery as a specific legislative measure rather than as part of a wider reformist agenda. Crucially, moreover, the impetus for ending slavery came, to some degree, from beyond parliament – and outside the British Isles. Reports of antislavery debates and accounts of proposed legislation made their way to the West Indies, where they were eagerly taken up by those whose lives they most urgently affected. But the enslaved not only echoed existing demands. They transformed them, taking the matter of abolition into their own hands. Following the formation of the Anti-Slavery Society in 1823, news had traveled to the West Indies that lawmakers in London were proposing measures to ameliorate slavery. Enslaved people in Demerara responded to these rumors by demanding their own freedom. Aside from representing a material threat to slaveowners, their demands were coded as a marked intensification of feeling. While "several hundreds of the rebels" had been killed, one soldier wrote of the ensuing uprising, "*their revolutionary feelings do not subside*; and from the arrangement going forward, and the military they have to contend with, very serious mortality must ensue." "So much," he concluded, "for the propriety and policy of Mr. Buxton's motion."[51]

The rebellion in Demerara was experienced not only as a militaristic disturbance, but an affective one.[52] Resistance by the enslaved made a profound imprint, in turn, upon the affective public sphere in Britain, injecting new levels of urgency into domestic debate. Beyond the "alarm" promoted by accounts of bloodcurdling violence and specters of earlier uprisings, this included more subtle and deep-rooted kinds of disruption and unease. That sense of affective disturbance persisted, I will now go on to suggest, beyond the passage of the 1833 Act. Abolition may have been presented as a relatively self-contained reformist measure. But emancipation was also congruent with a larger process of "imperial reorientation" that would help to consolidate a new phase of the British Empire and free trade.[53] Feeling took on special importance at the point of transition between the late Romantic age and the Victorian era, not least in the sentimental nationalism that adhered to the demure young queen. Brougham's persona acquired a doubly transformed significance in this environment. The statesman was not only cast as a vigorous political debater, at odds with new kinds of stability and decorum. He was also seen to bear a deeper stain, as a diabolical rebel whose actions and emotions associated him, in the public imagination, with intemperate popular demands and Black resistance.

We can begin to discern this reputation in a pamphlet that featured extended extracts from Brougham's writings and speeches. Despite its apparently neutral guise, *Opinions of Henry Brougham, Esq. on Negro Slavery* (1830) sought to humiliate the statesman by circulating evidence of his earlier support for the colonial system. "A public man never exhibits stronger proof of vigour of understanding and honesty of purpose," its preface stated, "than when he risks his popularity for the sake of enforcing opinions of which he has previously been the zealous opponent." This apparent defense of Brougham's reversals was, in fact, an attack on flagrant inconsistency. Brougham "*was* the unpopular advocate" of the existing colonial system – which included slavery – "not because he thought it was just, but because he thought it was inevitable." He had "*now* become the passionate agitator of *immediate emancipation*" who talked of "'*plucking up the plant of West Indian Slavery by the roots, and brandishing it in triumph over the heads of the tyrants.*'" Brougham had, the pamphlet claimed, voiced his support for the wider colonial system. He had now, with the zeal of the convert, become a "passionate" advocate for what the pamphlet cast as violent and sudden uprooting: "*immediate emancipation*."[54] Those seeking a "dispassionate consideration of the West Indian question," the preface to *Opinions* stated, "cannot but feel that the opinions of such a man as Henry Brougham must always deserve the attention of the thinking part of mankind."

Dispassionately considered, Brougham's recent "zeal" could only appear at odds with his earlier support for the empire, making him at once a hypocrite and a hothead. "Whether the disposition to deal savagely with any grievances, however great, involving the destruction of long-established interests, is such as to create confidence in the leader of a party or the head of a government," the author sarcastically added – implying that such a violent "disposition" was far from desirable in politics – could be left "to the cooler reflection of those who watch the times, and have any thing to lose." The "more limited object, at present in view" was "to oppose the calm and reasonable grounds on which the former opinions of Mr. Brougham on the subject of Negro Slavery were founded, against the ravings which have marked his career as candidate for the representation of Yorkshire." Brougham thus found himself in a double bind. His "dispassionate" views included qualified support for the wider colonial system. But his more recent statements undermined themselves with their own passion. As with Byron's attacks on Brougham's demagoguery, *Opinions* tied those "ravings" directly to his courting of popular constituencies and support for heterodox causes. The claims about Brougham dealing "savagely" with proslavery interests inflected references to his "zeal" and "passionate" agitation, in turn, with the added suggestion of ruthlessness and primitive violence.

These personal attacks gave way to a wider reflection on competing imperial systems, including their governing of enslaved subjects. *Opinions of Henry Brougham* began with a quotation from *Inquiry into the Colonial Policy of the European Powers*, Brougham's 1803 account of the colonial system. That quotation appears in the pamphlet as follows:

> It may fairly be assumed, as a general principle, that a multitude collected at random from various savage nations, and habituated to no subordination but that of domestic slavery, are totally unfit for uniting in the relations of regular government, or being suddenly moulded into one system of artificial society. In fact, the sudden formation of a political body has always been found the most arduous achievement in the art of governing.

The quoted extract suggests that enslaved Africans (from "savage nations") were "unfit" for "regular government." But *Opinions* made two crucial changes to the original text. The passage as quoted there omitted a clause from the end of the first sentence, which went on to claim that this "unfit" state was the case "more especially after living for a series of years in a state of tumult and disorder, unnatural even to barbarians." While doubling down on claims about supposed African primitiveness, that clause attributed some of the energies animating enslaved peoples to a wider global condition: the age of revolutions. More significantly, the second sentence in the quoted extract rewrote the original text, displacing the context and distorting the intended meaning. "In fact," the extract in *Opinions* read, "the sudden formation of a political body has always been found the most *arduous achievement* in the art of governing." "In the most polished states," the original passage read, "the sudden and violent dissolution of an established government has a strong tendency to produce disunion," recalling "the alarm excited in the earlier stages of the French Revolution." Brougham's *Inquiry* went on to discuss the challenges associated with forming a new polity in language that recalled conflicts ranging from the English Civil War to recent upheaval in Europe. As such, he tied prospective resistance by the enslaved (cast in *Opinions* as failed attempts to form a new "political body") to the wider processes of political "dissolution" and "disunion" entirely proper to a continued age of revolution and upheaval.

The deployment of Brougham's remarks was strategic. In much the same way that constitutional reform was cast as a prospective source of national unraveling, Brougham's remarks were deployed to suggest the unfitness of the enslaved to their own freedom, underscoring the "arduous" work and likely disaster associated with organizing politics in their interest (let alone with creating a new "political body" with their lives at its center). In his reference to the wider age of revolutions, Brougham had "the sudden and violent dissolution" of governments in the "polished states" of Europe in mind. His original remarks also had a further context: the founding of Haiti. The prospect of the enslaved rising up to overthrow their enslavers represented a cataclysmic prospect for Britain and the wider European imperial system. But in the intervening decades, a different array of prospects for the future had taken hold. As debate shifted from whether slavery would end to when and how, the emphasis was no longer on preservation at all costs. Indeed, violent rebellion from the enslaved could be invoked as a further justification *for* reform, as a means to prevent the enslaved taking matters into their own hands. Abolitionists could now point to the need to amend the status quo as a means of avoiding the anarchy of revolution. But traces of earlier fears about the dramatic change resulting from enslaved resistance persisted, not least in the breathless reporting of actual and prospective slave revolts.

By the time of the 1833 Slavery Abolition Act, emancipation had come, in some respects, to appear convenient. Ending slavery, once conceived of as the end of the world, became a newly tolerable prospect. Those with a property interest in the enslaved were to receive financial redress, with substantial compensation for the owners of slaves and plantations.[55] Emancipation also created readily exploitable sources of labor, as the formerly enslaved entered into a required period of apprenticeship that allowed the planter elite to benefit from their labor (without any longer needing to be responsible, however minimally, for their welfare). But while marking the shift into a newly liberalized era of modern empire and free trade, this transition and its implications for formerly enslaved people were not uncontested. Apprenticeship, in particular, became a renewed point of contention. Deemed little better than slavery, the proposed measures gave rise to vocal opposition and activism that succeeded in reducing the required period to five years. Resistance from the enslaved had helped to jolt the elite into the final stages of emancipation; recalcitrance around apprenticeship now challenged efforts to naturalize continued exploitation, in the face of slavery's supposed "extinction" and disappearance. Although the causes of reform and abolition were separate at the level of parliamentary debate, they remained aligned at the level of popular challenges. That alignment intensified as a newly circumscribed understanding of the national polity took hold, in tandem with growing imperial ambition.

The Reform Act helped to clear the way for the Slavery Abolition Act the following year, eradicating the West India interest in parliament. But matters become more complicated when we return to view the role of popular energies and unrest from below in the respective causes, including violent resistance.[56] These various oppositional energies and their unpredictable, inchoate character can be discerned in an 1833 print, "The Reform Bill's First Step Amongst His Political Frankensteins" (Figure 4). "Reform" appears here as a creaking giant with a devilish visage, bearing a crate of captive "Conservative" men on his back.[57] That monstrous figure has issued, in a cloud of black smoke, from a room identified as "Laboratory 1832." Alongside a figure trumpeting "Free Trade," the dark plumes of noxious smoke feature the labels "Rotten Boro[ugh]s" and "Abolition of Slavery." At the level of chronology, the print assembles a causal

Figure 4 John Orlando Parry, "The Reform Bill's First Step Amongst His Political Frankensteins" (1833). BM 1868,0808.9475. © The Trustees of the British Museum.

connection – albeit a loose one – between long-standing corruption, the abolition of slavery, and the appearance of the Reform Act. That legislation, cast as a terrifying monster in its own right, issues further demands here, liable to take on monstrous lives of their own: "His Political Frankensteins." But the print not only emphasizes the unintended consequences of passing Reform. The black smoke that trails in the monstrous creation's wake suggests that the Reform Act was *itself* the product of dangerously swirling energies and dark arts.

"The Reform Bill's First Step Amongst His Political Frankensteins" offers one example of how abolition and reform were imagined in tandem. Brougham offers another, as a rare figure who had made the connection between ending slavery and reforming parliament explicit throughout his career. He continued to be tarnished by his vigorous participation on both fronts. In the years leading up to the Reform Act, Brougham entered high politics as Lord Chancellor, attracting mockery for this ascent into the establishment. But with the transition into the Victorian era, he became an outcast once again. Deemed too rebellious for the post-Reform government, he returned to the front lines of abolition, where he became a strenuous advocate for ending apprenticeship. In March 1838, large meetings devoted to that cause were held, with Brougham in the chair. Hobhouse was appalled by what he viewed as Brougham's naked hostility against the Cabinet. The "invective" addressed toward ministers at the antislavery meeting was "boundless," he railed, claiming that his former rival had "outlied himself." Brougham had also written a "violent letter" addressed "to the Delegates of the Emancipators of the Blacks," denouncing the government as "an ephemeral power, supported only by Court favor" and promising, a scandalized Hobhouse recounted, "to assist in getting rid of us on his return." Another statesman, amplifying Hobhouse's claims that Brougham's conduct was promoted by "personal and party motives," accused him of displaying a "wickedness of which the world hitherto found no example."[58] Expelled like Lucifer from the angelic corridors of power, wearing the metaphorical mark of Cain, Brougham now added to his Byronic reputation for inconsistency the poet's devilish reputation for rebellion and eternal resistance.

The black marks against Brougham took on further guises in a series of interrelated prints from the immediate post-Reform period. In two of these images, Brougham appears as a darkened presence, estranged from the Whig ministry, at the edges of politics. In a print following his appointment as Lord Chancellor in the lead-up to the Reform Act, Brougham appears in dark robes and with a charcoal black face as "A Select Specimen of the Black Style." A further image depicts Brougham with the same dark coloring, this time as a mangy four-legged creature posed proudly like a lion in Trafalgar Square above a caption identifying this strange animal as "A Black Sheep. Not Exhibited in the Zoological Gardens." Brougham's contrarian reputation was not only accentuated in these visual depictions. It was also explicitly racialized, as becomes clear when we locate these images in relation to a further print from the same artist in which Brougham appears as Othello, suffocating a piece of legislation. I noted above that the pronunciation of Brougham's name allowed critics including Byron to suggest that his reputation was tarnished by his connection with popular causes. The use of a darkened pigment to depict Brougham in these images made that marking literal through the employment of actual and effective blackface.[59] The significance of these images went beyond personal attacks on Brougham's political positions or even parliamentary politics as such, however. The charcoal coloring used to mark his alienation from the circles of power also functioned metonymically to invoke actual enslaved people, animating Brougham's Byronic reputation for rebellion and recalcitrance in relation to actual and imagined Blackness.

In 1838, a further image by the same artist depicted the government at the point of transition into a new era. "The Royal Cosset" (Figure 5) portrays the monarch as a shepherdess tending to her ministry, a gaggle of sheep. Victoria had been crowned the previous year, at the tender age of eighteen. In the print, Melbourne – also known as William *Lamb* – receives food from the angelic young queen, while Hobhouse, Russell, and other Cabinet members identifiable by their uncannily human faces line up behind him. Brougham, however, appears outside the flock, at the far right of the image. Facing the other way, he announces his refusal to "gloze" or flatter the young monarch. His alienation from the circles of power has a further visual dimension, which recalls the earlier images. With a darkened countenance and a grizzled expression, Brougham is the black sheep. The image makes the same use of effective blackface as the earlier cluster of images. But in this image, intriguingly, Brougham may not be alone. At the far left appears a further dark-visaged sheep with its back to the viewer, proximate to (but also obscured by) a patch of darkness that opens beneath the monarch's ivory hand. "The Royal Cosset," which appeared at the moment of vocal debates over apprenticeship, alluded to Brougham's continued refusal to pipe down or be quiet. But the print also presented a more unsettled vision. The presence of the "black sheep" – in fact, there are two – makes this image legible in terms of another group that were, as the trope requires, simultaneously included in and excluded from

Figure 5   John ("HB") Doyle, "The Royal Cosset" (1838). NPG D41450. © National Portrait Gallery, London.

belonging in the family. Taken as a proxy for formerly enslaved West Indians, the black sheep, singular and plural, serve as stand-ins for Black subjects in the wider British imperial polity from which they have been cast out and excluded: a reminder of their unassimilated presence and unsilenced demands.

Vincent Brown has powerfully discussed the shifting significance attached to slave mortality in debates over abolition and emancipation. When Buxton spoke to a parliamentary committee in 1832, Brown writes, he "folded a generic argument, about the immorality that caused demographic deterioration, into what seemed a scientific truism." Buxton thus justified his argument, Brown concludes, "in terms appropriate to an age in which the influence of sentimental rhetoric was yielding to bureaucratic rationality."[60] The distance from the first attempts to introduce slave registries supplied these empirical appeals with added significance and affective impact. Abolitionists registered considerable impatience that the facts about slave mortality had been so well known, for so long. The numbing persistence of this knowledge helped drive new proposals. But rather than the incendiary demands channeled by Brougham and others, Buxton conjured newly morbid images of death and decline, coupled with dark scenes of depression, misery, and devastation. This image suggests another view. In contrast with the "rotten sheep" that Buxton tied to the death-driven governance of the slave economy, the black sheep of this image unsettled and complicated the casting of the enslaved as an immiserated population, preserving a note of recalcitrance and defiance.[61] The threat of violent resistance from the enslaved jolted the elite into enacting emancipation. But in subtly insistent ways, these images point to the unsettled dynamics that persisted beyond the ending of slavery, in which lives for which Britain had been responsible (and which the imperial polity had effectively abandoned to death, Taylor argues, in favor of a free-trade economy) rose up with reminders of their existence. That dynamic finds a further parallel, beyond the debates and figures I have addressed here, in the novels of Mary Shelley.

Recent commentaries have discussed Frankenstein's creature in relation to the figure of the subaltern and refugee, as well as the enslaved (picking up, in the latter case, upon the monster's self-description as a "slave").[62] The 1833 "Political Frankensteins" print tied the Reform Act to abolitionist demands, thereby linking both causes to inchoate popular energies (including, obliquely, enslaved resistance) and their unforeseen consequences. We find a further guide to the relationship between Frankenstein and slavery by looking ahead to The Last Man, a novel whose concerns with the eventual extinction of a dwindling population expose and expand upon the submerged thematic importance attached to these questions in Frankenstein. The dilemma faced by Britain's imperial administrators in the early nineteenth century was, scaled up, analogous to that faced by Victor Frankenstein as he confronted the product of his own fiendish experiment. In the place of a single, abandoned individual was an unwanted population. The practice of slavery revolved in direct and literal ways around the dynamics represented in the two novels: the creation of life and the exposure of an entire population to death.[63]

Frankenstein was tied, throughout the nineteenth century, to mass politics in England and Ireland. The Frankenstein myth provided Victorian novelists with a prototype for failures of social responsibility and their tipping over into worker unrest. "If the capitalists truly cannot shake off the terrifying power which they have brought into being (and since they live off its labour, they cannot)," Chris Baldick summarizes, "then they are saddled, like Victor Frankenstein, with a threatening monster who will never leave them in peace."[64] The monster serves here as a potent figure for the native proletariat created by the "terrifying power" of capitalism. But slaves had been created in ways that went beyond the figure of the domestic worker. In their continued support for the owners and drivers of slaves, Britain's rulers were complicit with a system that had overtaken the biopolitical functions of managing life and death. That dynamic was further compounded as plantation management became more explicitly geared around reproducing an already existing enslaved population. The nation and its elites, that is to say, presided over a system that had helped to create a population the nation was not willing to support and sustain. Britain had produced new lives that were consigned from natality to a life of neglect and suffering – in effect, abandoned at birth.

The debate over ending slavery in the years following Byron's death saw England confront the question of what to do with those lives. When they spoke about the enslaved peacefully disappearing or becoming a rural peasantry, abolitionists gave little indication of how such a world might come into being beyond vague and wistful appeals to a space outside history – and unrealizable within established geography. With the eventual passage of emancipation came the effective ending of one side of the empire, as another set of imperial ambitions emerged, focused on the Indian subcontinent. But the transitional period examined in this chapter witnessed, for a short window, other horizons, as a further detail from parliamentary debate makes clear. Responding in 1831 to Buxton's allusions to the mortality rate in the Caribbean, one unscrupulous supporter of the West India interest claimed that excess deaths were attributable to the climate. But that climate, another MP objected, had not prevented another singular occurrence: the emergence of the Haitian freedom fighter Toussaint Louverture.[65] The Americas remained a site for imagining clean slates and open horizons, often predicated upon the erasure of existing populations. But the "New World" was also the source of unpredictable eruptions and volatile energies. Haiti introduced altogether new modalities and praxes for freedom and emancipation.[66] Byron deemed Bolívar and other revolutionaries as fierce as their earthquakes and hurricanes.[67] Those energies were felt, in turn, back in England, as the enslaved made their imprint known, in large ways and small, upon the affective public sphere. While the voices of Mary Prince and other Black Atlantic authors carried unmistakable urgency and ringing insistence, incorporating the West Indies within the wider imperial polity reminds us that the entire cultural-affective field was organized in racial

terms. In the figures adopted by Brougham, zealous feeling and diabolical rebellion took on distinctly Byronic guises. Whether and to
what extent his recalcitrance intersected with Black resistance is a more
challenging question, this chapter has set out to demonstrate, but no
less important to a reckoning with the changing ends of politics
between the late Romantic age and the new Victorian world.

CHAPTER 4

"Crowns in the Dust"
The Ends of Politics in The Last Man

"The last man!" Mary Shelley wrote in her journal for May 1824. "Yes I may well describe that solitary being's feelings, feeling myself as the last relic of a beloved race, my companions extinct before me."[1] Shelley experienced a terrible catalogue of loss over her lifetime, beginning a few days after her birth with the death of her mother Mary Wollstonecraft. The death by drowning in 1822 of her husband Percy provides an obvious reference point for her remarks identifying with the "last man," the end point of "a beloved race," others "extinct" before her. But the significance of Shelley's identification with the "last man" – and its relevance to her subsequent novel of that title – only emerges fully when we take account of another pivotal figure from Shelley's life and the late Romantic age. Byron had died the previous month, but at the time of her journal entry, Shelley believed he was still alive. Learning soon thereafter of his death in Greece afforded an opportunity to expand her personal reflections upon loss (which now included Byron, whose corpse she visited during the composition of the novel)[2] into a wide-ranging meditation upon ending lines and dying races.

In *The Last Man*, Barbara Johnson proposed, Shelley sought to paint her mourning on a "universal scale."[3] In this chapter, I argue that the novel brought Shelley's personal grief and her expansive philosophical reflections together with politics. The argument proceeds in two parts. In the first half of this chapter, I show how the figure of Lord Raymond – addressed here in comparison with George Eliot's imagining of a Byronic politician forty years later – emerges as an early locus for political hopes in the novel, before the unwinding of institutions and the death of mankind render any hopes for the political future moot. The second half of the chapter draws the novel's early focus on politics together with its ever-more evacuated landscapes to tender a politically inflected reading of the *The Last Man* as a whole. I place special emphasis on two marginal figures – the narrator Lionel Verney and his sister Perdita – and attend closely to the resonance of the novel's barren terrain with political appeals to the "state of nature" (including the ways that the Americas became an explicit locus for those questions). Johnson offers a sophisticated account of how Shelley's disavowed autobiography became a means of brokering the connection between last men (or women) and humanity as such. More recent readings have used Shelley's novel to further problematize universal narratives, including the very status of the human. By restoring politics to the picture, I return to view a critical missing step within these discussions while also highlighting a kind of breaking point. Shelley may have sought to imagine an alternative kind of political community. But while the novel strains toward more universal concerns – or seeks to deconstruct them – it ultimately marks the failure to imagine a world beyond politics, or a life beyond species. Accounts of the novel that seek to read alternative futures out from the book's fractured community risk neglecting the extent to which those futures take shape against the backdrop of haunting losses, even as those losses occasion their own resonant absences.

Approached with an eye on biography, the foundation of Shelley's novel in grief may seem self-evident. The subject of the *Last Man* is "personal loss," Anne McWhir writes, "and its emotional focus is sometimes painfully intimate and confessional."[4] The emphasis on loss in *The Last Man* finds one obvious locus in Percy Shelley, whose heart Shelley reportedly kept in her writing desk.[5] The novel's introduction, in which an ungendered narrator and companion visit the cave of the Sibyl, describes an actual trip conducted by the Shelleys. That poetic appeal to a "matchless companion" now "lost" drapes their severed partnership in the lightest of fictional veils. But that notoriously obscure preface also initiates the novel's concern with the transfiguring of identities, by way of uncertain voices, into new entities and echoing absences.[6] The book proper opens with plot and character dynamics that multiply (and, to some degree, scramble) the personal reference points from Shelley's life. Those character dynamics take shape in dialogue with Godwinian political theory and contemporary radicalism, as well as more faintly discerned protofeminist and quasi-democratic impulses. This delicately crafted web of allusions to Shelley's contemporary moment intersects, in turn, with the novel's myriad scenes of individual and collective loss. The novel's interest in the future of politics, I propose, thus intervenes between its biographical matrix and the imagined end of the species. In its later volumes, the book leaves politics behind. But even these evacuated scenes have uncanny political significance. The concern with the changing ends of politics throughout *The Last Man* thus weaves together the particular and acutely personal with the general and universal, making this richly layered and densely allusive novel resonate with hitherto-neglected significance.[7]

On a quiet evening in the second half of the twenty-first century, politics in England ceases. "Every thing in the constitution" of the newly formed republic, we learn in volume one of *The Last Man*, "had been regulated for the better preservation of peace." On the last day of an election for the executive role of Lord Protector, "two candidates only were allowed to remain; and to obviate, if possible, the last struggle between these, a bribe was offered to him who should voluntarily resign his pretensions; a place of great emolument and honour was given him, and his success facilitated at a future election" (*LM*, 101). When a series of evening debates fails to clinch success for either candidate – the aggressive populist Ryland or the Byronic aristocrat Raymond – the night finally arrives "when parliament, which had so long delayed its choice, must decide: as the hour of twelve passed, and the new day began, it was by virtue of the constitution dissolved, its power *extinct*" (*LM*, 99, emphasis added). This dissolution proves temporary. Yet this concluding "*extinct*," like the subsequent reference to the "*last* struggle" between candidates, takes on special gravity in a narrative ultimately concerned with the extinction of the human species, providing what we might term an anticipatory echo of the greater loss to come.

Whatever we conclude about Shelley's own politics, the respective ends imagined in *The Last Man* – of politics and human life, the republic and the species, the governed population and the populated planet – resonate suggestively with each other. That conjuncture appears at once ominous and oddly harmonious. Yet the reference to parliament becoming "extinct" at this stage in the novel carries a muted force whose full impact only becomes apparent over the course of the book as a whole. In this first half of the chapter, I set out to recover the importance of the novel's Byronic presences, which I discuss in relation to counterparts from the late Romantic and Victorian ages. That means taking seriously Shelley's speculations about what Byron's return to politics – albeit in an imagined twenty-first-century future – might have looked like. While I am not concerned with factually determining what role in politics Byron might have taken had he returned to England, reflections upon that question, including Byron's own private meditations, have important analytical value, both in locating the poet and his writings within a dynamic field of political position-taking and in illuminating his wider political and literary reputation. Locating Byron in relation to contemporary politics clarifies what was and was not possible at this moment and the alternative itineraries Byron helped to make imaginable, in and beyond his lifetime.

Alongside Shelley's immediately posthumous depiction of Byron in *The Last Man*, I examine George Eliot's later fictional reimagining of his life in *Felix Holt* (1866). Byron permitted both novelists to assess changing political horizons. Eliot cast a critical eye on his oppositional (and "revolutionary") commitments by locating them in an England where the 1832 Reform Act had already taken place. By contrast, *The Last Man* sought to reconfigure and thereby overcome the political divisions and impasses of her own moment. These attempts to reimagine the ends of politics, this chapter will argue, were bound up with her reimagining of Byron. The character of Lord Raymond in *The Last Man* thus provides a window not only onto Byron's politics, but those of Shelley herself.[8]

In her 1982 essay "My Monster/My Self," Johnson proposed that Frankenstein's monster can be seen as "a figure for autobiography as such."[9] *Frankenstein*, in Judith Butler's lucid summary, might thus "in some sense be Mary Shelley's autobiographical work" even as it is "not quite sufficient to say either that the monster reflects Mary Shelley in some mimetic way or that it provides an eloquent metaphor for her private feelings about herself."[10] In what follows, I bring the insights of Johnson's pathbreaking essay on *Frankenstein* (crystallized in the assertion that "autobiography would appear to constitute itself as in some way a repression of autobiography")[11] together with her earlier essay on *The Last Man*, in which she meditates upon the human(ist) limits of Shelley's novel. This discussion also further extends the scope of my account of Byron and politics to include his developing reputation and fictional representations of "Byronic" figures. These aims coincide. The figure cut by Raymond in *The Last Man* provides an illuminating commentary upon the imagined political roles available to the poet and those around him, while also figuring possibilities foreclosed to Shelley herself. The representation of Raymond, that is to say, belongs to Shelley's own political biography. We may say much the same for *The Last Man* as a whole.

Byronic Presences in *The Last Man*

Early glimpses of a Byronic figure appear in the opening pages of *The Last Man*. Narrator Lionel Verney begins his tale with the story of his father. A fixture at court and close friend to the heir to the throne, the senior Verney is a bright spirit with a sparkling wit. But he is also dissipated and reckless. The future monarch's marriage – to a "haughty princess of Austria" (*LM*, 8) – leaves this former intimate out in the cold. After gambling away the remains of his fortune, he flees for the hills: "Ask where now was this favourite of fashion, this companion of the noble, this excelling beam, which gilt with alien splendour the assemblies of the courtly and the gay – you heard that he was under a cloud, *a lost man*" (*LM*, 9, emphasis added). The sad story concludes when Verney's father dies in debt, leaving his family destitute. This brief episode introduces Lionel's humble background – the death of his mother, a poor cottager, leaves him an "unprotected orphan" – and establishes his ties to the royal family and his burning resentment at their treatment of his father. At the same time, the fate of Lionel's father underscores the "evanescence" of popularity and the fleeting nature of life. *The Last Man* will extend this concern with worldly vanity to the level of the species and planet. But this brief narrative about passing fame also encodes more specific references to Byron and to a "Byronic" world of dazzling glitz, reckless profligacy, and lonely skulking figures (although Lionel's father more closely resembles Byron's wastrel father than the poet himself). Byron's proximity to the dandies and Regency glamor overwhelmed his Victorian reputation and allowed the poet himself the occasion for elegiac reflections on lost personal and political potential. In Shelley's novel, this "lost man" similarly anticipates the novel's *last* man and the multilayered significance with which the story imbues that figure.

Lord Raymond is the novel's most obviously Byronic presence. We first encounter Raymond – the "sole remnant of a noble but impoverished family" (*LM*, 30) – as a revolutionary fighter in the continued struggle for Greek independence, where he is hailed as the "darling hero" of that "rising people" (*LM*, 31). Raymond is "supremely handsome" and "honey-tongued," but also inconsistent and conflicted, at once seeking and shunning ambition and eminence (*LM*, 30–1). He first appears in the novel as a foil to Adrian, the son of the deposed king. Adrian is intensely empathic, with an expressive countenance: tall, slim, with silken hair and an excess of sensibility (*LM*, 19). He is also a visionary, whose philosophical reading and emancipatory impulses lead him to lofty hopes for mankind. Most strikingly, for a former heir to the throne, he becomes a principled republican. His benevolent conduct and poetic rhapsodies on goodness win Lionel's affection, despite his initial disdain – based upon their treatment of his father – for the royal family. Raymond, by contrast, displays pride, resentment, and emotional volatility. Drawn back to his claim to nobility, he wavers between calls to reestablish monarchy and pursuit of further democracy, winning over former "royalists" to his middling course. His pursuit of a mythical "kingship" and ambition to unite crowns builds upon his earlier success in Greece, where his victory in battle locates him above those locally who "might rank higher in title and ceremony." "When he appeared," we learn, "whole towns poured forth their population to meet him; new songs were adapted to their national airs, whose themes were his glory, valor, and munificence" (*LM*, 31).

The relationship between Adrian and Raymond has a clear basis in the friendship between Percy Shelley and Byron.[12] For now, we may simply note that the political orientations of the two men correspond broadly with their real-life counterparts: vocally republican and airily utopian in the case of Shelley, a more unstable combination of prejudice in favor of patrician rule and sympathy for oppressed foreign peoples in the case of Byron. But these relatively straightforward correspondences acquire added complications when these characters become caught up in *actual* political activity. Adrian's mother, the "haughty" defender of a reactionary monarchy, pushes for her son to reclaim the throne. Raymond, a close associate of the deposed monarchy with an elite background of his own, becomes a more plausible contender for the vacant position of Lord Protector. He contends for power, as we have seen, with Ryland, the leader of the "popular party." As the novel progresses, these men become more closely identified with the respective constituencies of "royalists," "aristocrats," and "democrats." At the same time, their respective characters, *as* characters, come into sharper focus, further muddying their basis in biography. Their political significance shifts and broadens, that is to say, as their relationship to real-life figures becomes at once more focused and more narrow, complicating easy conclusions about where our sympathies, personal and political, are meant to lie. Where we might have expected clear sympathy for Percy Shelley, the novel is far from endorsing his idealistic political platform. Raymond, meanwhile, with his volatile impulses and overweening ambition, presents a less obviously appealing figure. But in political terms, he achieves notable success.

The political "crisis" in the novel's opening volume gives way to the temporary government shutdown that renders parliament "extinct." The ensuing contest circles around Raymond and Ryland, whose respective parties correspond with growing cleavages in the English body politic during the 1820s. At the same time, these two men are characters in their own right. Ryland, leader of the popular party, is "a hard-headed man, and in his way eloquent" (*LM*, 42). Although Ryland has been identified with William Cobbett, with whom he shares a propensity for antimetropolitan rancor, he also shares an elite background with Henry "Orator" Hunt.[13] Early on in the novel, Ryland brings a bill "making it treason to endeavour to change the present state of the English government and the standing laws of the republic," displaying his dogged dedication to following through on the country's new commitment to postmonarchical governance (*LM*, 42). Raymond proves more sympathetic to the return of royal power and more at ease with elite leadership. He succeeds in eventually bending support away from Ryland, painting visions of the "splendour of a kingdom, in opposition to the commercial spirit of republicanism" and advancing agendas for national reform and regeneration. More significantly for his political role, he garners followers by way of his own claims to eloquence and oratory: through the "flow of language and graceful turns of expression, the wit and easy raillery that gave vigour and influence to his speech" (*LM*, 47).

The depiction of Raymond in *The Last Man* repeatedly signals Byron's tempestuous, rebelliousness, and passion; these combine to create his infectious charisma and brooding appeal. Yet while duly noting these parallels, critics have not noted the ways this portrait goes beyond simple personal resemblance. Shelley not only invokes Byron here: she reworks and rewrites key aspects of his biography. The deepening of the novel's political plot further bends away from the facts of Byron's life. The depiction of Raymond draws upon existing images of the poet, including his passionate intensity and volatile, even reckless temperament. But Shelley also *reimagines* the recently deceased poet as a galvanizing political presence, fusing together selected aspects of his biography with imaginative reflections upon the political figure he might have come to represent had he lived and returned to England. In particular, the book vindicates Byron's speculations about his unactualized potential as a political orator. This Byronic figure was not, however, divorced from biography; these aspects of her portrait acquire added interest through Shelley's personal observations and investments. But rather than the incidental product of *roman-à-clef* eventually displaced as the action of the novel takes hold, Shelley's portrait was constructed, I contend, with a view to the specific contours of the figure Byron cut in politics, both in tandem with his literary reputation and as a constitutive dimension of his public identity.

Shelley's novel reincarnates Byron within a fictional world and an imagined future. *The Last Man* was thus doubly removed from the political situation on the ground in the 1820s. The novel take place in a chivalric, timeless-feeling England reminiscent of early nineteenth-century romances and historical fiction, including that of Walter Scott. At the same time, the novel imports Byron into a future where some measure of reform has already taken place. These complex displacements, I would suggest, enhance rather than dilute the novel's political potency. *The Last Man* features detailed accounts of the machinations between aristocratic and democratic factions, the latter characterized as "reformers" (*LM*, 38). Shelley thus invoked, even as she reworked, the political fault lines of her own moment. At the same time, she deepened her portrait of Raymond, imagined both as a Byronic adventurer and an idealized "politician." The "sole remnant" of a dwindling line of nobles, Raymond brings Byron's self-mythology together with his premature death, supplying him with a resonant "lastness." Yet while Shelley could have cast Byron as a partisan relic or political dinosaur, she instead charged his reanimated figure with political significance and potential. That becomes clear by comparing Raymond with George Eliot's imagining of an aspiring Byronic politician half a century later, in the middle of the Victorian age and at another moment of reform.

His Master's Voice: The Byronic Politician after Reform

Byron's biographer Leslie Marchand offers perhaps the most compelling summary of Byron's political views when he notes that, while Byron "often spoke sympathetically of the frame-breakers or other insurrectionists among the people," he "always envisioned himself and others of his class as men on horseback leading and directing a rebellion which would lead to a new government by gentlemen of liberal sympathies."[14] That assessment encloses speculation about what role Byron might have taken had he returned to England. But the image of the poet lording over the people while mounted on horseback also raises more questions than answers. Byron *had* planned to return to England in 1819, after recent events inflamed his excitement. But what "part" Byron planned to take upon his projected return remained (and remains) something of an open question. The following year, rumors circulated about a letter in which, from one summary, Byron stated that "if the radicals only made a little progress & showed some real force he would hasten over & get on horseback to head them."[15] But Byron was at a remove from the moderate, respectable faces of reform while expressing vocal antipathy toward popular radicalism. It was not clear, moreover, that he would have aligned with a government led, in Marchand's words, by "gentlemen of liberal sympathies," nor what, exactly, that would have meant at the time.

During the same period, perceptions of Byron's politics became further complicated – and, to some degree, clouded – by his wider reputation, bound up with a, by then, fading, aristocratic political elite and the heights of Regency glitz and excess. Those associations were cemented posthumously with the appearance of figures based on the poet in the "silver-fork" novels of the 1820s and 1830s.[16] Those books took a certain delight in conjuring the high-society drama and fashionable swirl of Regency society. But in the process, Andrew Elfenbein has argued, they sought to consign the Regency to a vanished past (albeit a vividly reimagined one). In using Byron's dandyism to consign him to a former, faded age, these books sought to purge the present, Elfenbein argues, of his corrupting influence. As the late Romantic age gave way to the Victorian era, increasing moralism and shifting political norms solidified his reputation along narrow lines. Interest in his life and works further narrowed to his time as one of the darlings of fashionable Whig society, while his supposed irreligiosity and well-documented transgressions made him an archetypal sinner. As Tom Mole has demonstrated, the anthologized and excerpted selections from Byron's writings – crucial to the developing web of reception that mediated Romantic writing in the Victorian age – led later readers to a partial view of Byron's writings and poetic themes. The evangelical preacher Charles Haddon Spurgeon, for one, discouraged what he termed "men of the Byronic type" from emulating the poet.[17] Other Victorians, including the Brontës, eagerly embraced Byron's darker sides. But for George Eliot, Byron's received biography and this culturally brokered mediation of his writings proved doubly damning.

"Byron and his poetry" came to seem "more and more repugnant" to Eliot, even as the poet remained ("like all of us sinners") "deeply pitiable."[18] She joined with her Victorian precursors in reanimating Byronic figures in her fiction. Although written in the second half of the nineteenth century, *Felix Holt* takes place in the immediate aftermath of the 1832 Reform Act. In Harold Transome, Eliot imagined a version of Byron returning to England and used this homecoming to comment upon his unsuitability to the political world set into motion following his death. Expanding suffrage, Reform had also created wholly new parliamentary constituencies in burgeoning industrial areas. Eliot wrote at a time in which a further wave of reformist debates were taking shape. In returning to this earlier moment, she made its emerging political fault lines intelligible in the terms of her own present (and even directly applicable to then-current debates about a mass electorate and enlightened public opinion). The depiction of a character informed by Byron as an out-of-date, corrupted figure, overly attached to his elite role even as he indulged fantasies about revolution overseas, thus served double duty. In the first instance, hearkening back to his ever-more belated figure sounded the final death knell for a political world organized around a certain kind of man. At the same time, the unflattering picture of the general political scene suggested a pathway beyond the corrupting dynamics of that world into a Liberal future.

Felix Holt begins with Harold's return to England following his travels in present-day Greece and Turkey (where Byron had conducted the adventurous early travels recorded in *Childe Harold's Pilgrimage* and echoed in his final journeys). Returning to his family home in the English town of Treby Magna, Harold announces his plans to stand for election. But he proceeds to upset expectations. In a surprise reversal of his aristocratic family's Tory loyalties, Harold plans to harness the existing support for Whig candidates by campaigning under the banner of "the radicals." For his mother, this betrayal of the family pedigree becomes a grave concern. More broadly, his melding of a Tory lineage with a rowdy, crowd-stirring populism represents a dangerous monstrosity. Drawing a contrast with holding such "opinions" during his foreign travels, his mother implores Harold to consider how "putting up as a Radical will affect your position here, and the position of your family." With equal disdain for English women as for the local elite, Harold does not particularly care what others think. In response to his mother's fears, he scoffs that whenever a "man goes to the East, people seem to think he gets turned into something like the one-eyed calendar in the 'Arabian Nights'" and proceeds with his plan regardless. Felix Holt, the admirable "Radical" of the novel's subtitle, emerges as his foil: rational, dispassionate, and connected with an unthreatening Nonconformist religious tradition.

Eliot identifies Harold with Byron through his personal traits, including none-too-flattering depictions of his reckless opportunism, disregard for women, and verbal and physical excess (like Byron, he struggles with his weight). Eliot had recently impugned Byron's life and writings as "repugnant" in the letter quoted above (p. 115). In *Felix Holt*, the appearance of his poetry in the hands of heroine Esther Lyon provides an occasion to condemn Byronic heroes. Byron is described as a "worldly and vain writer" by Esther's father, a Dissenting minister. Felix describes Byron as "a misanthropic debauchee . . . whose notion of a hero was that he should disorder his stomach and despair mankind" and whose characters are "paltry puppets pulled by strings of lust and pride." These character assassinations rebound upon Harold and are further compounded by his eastern travels. Beyond traversing some of the same landscapes as the late poet, Harold also becomes associated, as the remarks on the *Arabian Nights* make clear, with monstrous excesses at home and abroad. In a version of what Gerard Cohen-Vrignaud has termed "Radical Orientalism," the novel exploits an imagined fusion between a threatening, Orientalized zone beyond England's shores and inchoate democratic demands closer to home. But in contrast with radical deployments of supposed Eastern indulgence to unsettle emerging norms, Eliot emphasizes the need to purge politics of these wayward and threatening influences.[19]

Beyond a mere character type, Harold accordingly becomes a figure for the distorting influences of an archaic past as they fuse with the intemperate "Radical" demands of the present: a dangerous combination. Eliot emphasizes the corrupting influences of his personal character as they shape the two faces of his political identity, looking at once to a bankrupt English tradition and a formless, timeless East. Yet this was, ultimately, a mid-Victorian Byron, mobilizing key features of the poet's identity but ultimately speaking primarily to Eliot's moment. As we have seen, Byron did not live to see the gathering momentum toward the 1832 Reform Bill. While closely attuned to developments within England a decade earlier, he remained at a pronounced remove from both reformist and radical politics. In her depiction of Harold, who "always meant to come back" to England and remained "thoroughly acquainted with English politics" from a distance, Eliot presents an imagined afterlife for the poet, whose return home instantiates a version of his revolutionary entanglements in foreign lands, infusing an aristocratic-led politics with a naked populism (and Orientalizing dissipation). But this was ultimately a fantasy about Eliot's own moment, grounded in a partial and simplified account of the early nineteenth century and channeled through an imagined eastern space in which roving despots meld together with revolutionary freedom fighters.

In *The Last Man*, Shelley also imagined Byron's return to politics in England from exploits abroad. Haughty and ambitious, the "injury" created by some early disappointment had led Raymond to quit England "with a vow not to return, till the good time should arrive, when she might feel the power of him she now despised" (*LM*, 30). As an adventurer in the Greek wars, he becomes the "darling hero" of that people – and will go on to launch a renewed offensive against the supposedly barbarian Turks. Yet he begins, like Byron, the "darling of fame" back home. Tellingly, moreover, he refuses throughout his early Greek exploits to "throw off his allegiance to his native country" (*LM*, 31). But in contrast with Eliot, Shelley does not separate out Byron's political awakening overseas from his ties at home by having one succeed the other. She instead treats his antagonistic relationship to England and his revolutionary activity abroad as two faces of the same political identity. Raymond, in turn, contemplates *returning* to Greece, setting in motion the novel's later volumes. The character of Raymond thus neatly collapses Byron's early travels and his final journey. Where Eliot extended his languorous Eastern voyages and skirmishes with bandits and warlords from youthful travels into early adulthood before having him return to England, Shelley has Raymond live a version of Byron's actual life, then return home again, then return once again to revolutionary war. Throughout, she emphasizes his continuing attachments to the nation of his birth. That includes the ever-present possibility of his return to politics.

Byron and Percy Shelley at the End of the Line

Raymond's initial homecoming in *The Last Man* is a triumphant one. Having come into an "immense fortune in England," he returns "crowned with glory, to receive the meed of honour and distinction before denied to his pretensions" (*LM*, 31). Building upon his wounded pride and volatile impulses, the novel presents Raymond as a multifaceted figure: at once the advocate for royal power in pursuit of his own version of kingship; an imperial adventurer who seeks to unite with the Greeks and govern the whole Earth (beginning with Asia); and a passionate lover willing to abandon everything for love. The international dimensions of his ambition take shape over the subsequent volumes of the novel, where Raymond becomes a complex proxy for the hubris of imperial ambition and an agent in spreading the plague across the world. I conclude my discussion of the novel's Byronic presences by examining how Shelley imagined Byron's return to domestic politics. In Raymond, Shelley reflected upon where the poet might have fitted into England's changing political landscape, refracted by way of an imagined future. At the same time, Raymond was a self-consciously imaginative creation, in which Shelley reflected on the possibilities of moving beyond the limitations both of Byron's warring impulses and of her own divided moment. That reflection was bound up, I propose, with her investments, at once aesthetic and personal, in Byron's poetics.

Eliot joined with other Victorians in presenting Byron as dissolute and morally dubious (if not outright diabolical). *Felix Holt* expanded upon his established political reputation to portray him as an elevated figure: a single, self-aggrandizing man steering radical impulses and an inchoate populace from a lofty remove. *The Last Man* also imagines Byron's return to a country reshaped by reform. Although more obviously true of Eliot's mid-Victorian novel – in which the precarious status of the Transome family and the insecurities of Harold's mother index newly uncertain lines

of social class and inherited status – Shelley also underscored the importance of his elite formation. From "early youth he had considered his
pedigree with complacency," even as he also "bitterly lamented his want
of wealth" (*LM*, 30). His innate, if brittle, sense of his own superiority
grows as the novel progresses. Sent abroad first by slighted pride, he still
feels this earlier rebuff. But these warring impulses galvanize around the
pursuit of supremacy: "Power therefore was the aim of all his endeavours;
aggrandizement the mark at which he for ever shot. In open ambition or
close intrigue, his end was the same – to attain the first station in his own
country" (*LM*, 31).

The Last Man, as we might expect, contains a more detailed reworking of
Byron's biography than Eliot's novel. At the same time, Shelley grants
political success to Raymond, cutting against her nuanced depiction of his
shortcomings. The power vacuum created by the delay in choosing a new
candidate for Lord Protector raises questions about whether Adrian, heir to
the Windsor line, might take up the royal mantle. But while his idealism
makes him the associate of "infinite good," Adrian has no interest in
a public role. Describing himself as a "poor visionary," he notes that he
is not a man fitted to govern nations. As the time comes in which to put his
"theories into practice," he realizes that the visions of his "boyhood" have
faded, leaving him a wan and enervated figure (who is amusingly said by
Raymond, following his retreat back to rural seclusion, to "turn squirrel
again"). Raymond is put forward instead by the circle around the former
monarchy: as an "aspiring noble" who "revived the claim of house of
Windsor to the crown," encircled as he is with the "magic ring of regality"
(*LM*, 31). To follow up on this nomination, it was necessary "to persuade
Raymond to present himself to the electors" against Ryland, the competing
candidate. Raymond, in turn, gives a speech alluding to his "successes in
Greece and favour at home" and speaks of "the state of England; the
necessary measures to be taken to ensure its security, and confirm its
prosperity" (painting a "glowing picture of its present situation"). "As he
spoke," we learn, "every sound was hushed, every thought suspended by
intense attention. His graceful elocution enchained the senses of his
hearers. In some degree also he was fitted to reconcile all parties."

As with Harold in *Felix Holt*, Raymond's life intersects directly with that
of the poet, not least through his connection to Greece. Details from the
complex, layered characterization of Raymond in *The Last Man* were
clearly informed, moreover, by Shelley's own close observation of
Byron's moody tendencies (and her critical evaluation of their consequences, especially for women). An ultimately sympathetic portrait,

Shelley nonetheless presents Raymond's character as "full of contradictions."[20] The emphasis on his "violent" passions and thirst for "self-gratification" draws upon the controversies surrounding Byron's writings and fame. Shelley may also have been seeking to ameliorate these qualities (whose damaging influence on his reputation would still be apparent decades later) and went out of her way to characterize Raymond as a mercurial and appealing figure, even as she emphasized his fatal flaws of honor and pride. Her rendition of Raymond was thus of a piece, we might conjecture, with her own efforts to reckon with Byron's complexities, including as a political thinker and actor. But Shelley also *shaped* these complexities to her own ends. That becomes clear from looking at the distinctions drawn between the central elite male characters, Adrian and Raymond.

In his classic study of Percy Shelley and Byron, Charles E. Robinson attended to the antagonistic "philosophical dialogue" between the two men and traced how their "reciprocal influences" shaped their respective writings. Their "personal friendship and knowledge of each other's work determined that each poet materially affected the 'forms' of the other's work": "more significantly," Robinson maintains, "their philosophical and aesthetic antagonism caused each poet to challenge dialectically the 'spirit' of the other's poetry."[21] While focused on how their poetry staged a dialogic confrontation between two minds (or "spirits"), Robinson also points to the divergent courses taken in their lives, including the contrasting ways that their broadly liberal and humanitarian commitments played out in politics. In an 1812 speech to parliament, for example, Byron addressed the "injustices suffered by the Irish" and "mocked England's oppressive policies" while Shelley, in a contemporary pamphlet, "placed the Irish question in a larger context." Where Byron had, in a pungent speech to the House of Lords, pointed to "past and present injustices," Shelley "expounded his utopian theories of brotherly love, nondefiance, and the necessary supremacy of good" and "prophesied an idyllic future founded on a system of 'wisdom and virtue' that would obviate the need for governmental restrictions."[22] *The Last Man* presented its own vantage point on these various interactions. But in tandem with its reflections on the dialogue between Byron and Percy Shelley – and its author's self-effaced role in that conversation – the novel stages its own complex divides between theory and practice, philosophy and politics.

Raymond and Adrian differ in obvious ways. "No two persons could be more opposite," the narration informs us early in the book. A "man of the world," Raymond looked on the structure of society "as but a part of the machinery which supported the web on which his life was traced": "The earth was spread out as an highway for him; the heavens built up as a canopy for him" (*LM*, 35). Adrian, meanwhile, "felt that he made part of a great whole," owning his affinity not only with mankind, but "all nature." Despite Raymond's professions of friendship, we witness a "spirit of aversion" arise between the two men. Adrian "despised the narrow views of the politician," we learn, while Raymond "held in supreme contempt the benevolent visions of the philanthropist." These dynamics align broadly with those attributed to their real-life counterparts. Byron repeatedly expressed his exasperation at Shelley's idealistic philosophy, particularly his atheism. Where Shelley viewed nature as a source of sympathetic communion and transcendent unity, Byron remained more skeptical. Yet Byron also had measured, even approving responses to his friend's visionary beliefs. "He knew that he could not shake [Shelley's] faith in a doctrine founded upon illusions, by his incredulity: but he listened to him with pleasure ... on account of Shelley's good faith and sincerity of meaning (even as he also used sometimes to exclaim: 'Why Shelley appears to me to be mad with his metaphysics ... what trash is in all these systems!'"[23]

These statements, to which many more could be added, break down divisions between the real-life men. While a clear if complicated dividing line can be established between Byron and Shelley, the relationship between their fictional counterparts accentuates their differences, while developing unique contrasts of its own. The depiction of Raymond, for whom "society" was just one support for the "web on which his life was traced," includes features that Shelley admired in her husband (which are elaborated when Raymond advances his schemes of national improvement). Raymond was not *only* Byron: aspects of the novel's often tender, sympathetic depiction of his character may *also* allude to Percy Shelley. Raymond and these real-life counterparts shift and slide into each other, making the novel's imagining of Byron inextricable from the idealism more commonly attributed to the other poet, the Byronic inseparable from the Shelleyan. Read closely and in dialogue with its various contexts, the novel ultimately reveals the perils of examining its characters in overly narrow biographical terms, seeking a literal one-to-one correspondence. Indeed, the identification of these characters with Byron or Shelley can at times become deeply confused. That does not undermine the importance of biography to the book: this is how fiction-writing works. But we ought therefore to approach these character sketches as multidirectional imaginative portraits even as we *also* acknowledge that these portraits were inevitably the product in part of a creative process that worked through, in both senses, Shelley's own personal attachments.

The political dimension of this personal and imaginative processing comes sharply into focus with the novel's turn toward Raymond as a prospective leader. The depiction of Adrian as a "philanthropist" who despises the "narrow views of the politician" closely fits Percy Shelley. Yet the *conflict* between Byron and Shelley, as reflected in this account of their fictional counterparts, does not apply anywhere near so neatly to the real men. We know that Byron did express contempt for Percy Shelley's "benevolent" visions. Adrian attracts similar suspicion from Raymond. Yet it makes altogether less sense, as this comparison requires, to think about Byron as a narrowly focused "politician" (the label disparagingly applied to Raymond by Adrian). Raymond's self-aggrandizing, imperialistic ambitions cast him at once as "a political man" and a militaristic commander. But the more volatile, skeptical, and detached figure of Byron set him at odds with any stable public role. Both in the structural position he occupies in the novel and in the added details Shelley employs to contour her representation, Raymond takes on a clarity that ultimately detaches him from the poet. His character instead comprises, I want to suggest, an idealized representation of a means by which the divisions surrounding politics might be overcome. As much as Raymond depicts Byron, he also depicts a fantasy of a reimagined "politician." And as much as Raymond galvanizes attention amidst the early political disputes of the novel, he ultimately becomes a means of resolving them, once and for all.

That becomes apparent when we locate the changed political landscape in which Shelley's novel takes place in relation to the rough-and-tumble world of actual politics. *The Last Man* engaged in a multifaceted reflection on the changing ends of governance. With utilitarian calculation and the Americas as conceptual and geographical buffers, the novel gestured toward the outer limits to which such radical ambitions might reach while straining against the recognizable bounds of established, if reformed, political structures. The novel seeks to leave politics behind, while remaining bound, unlike more obviously utopian works, to imaginable versions of what politics *is*. Remaining at the level of politics more narrowly understood, we can now see how the efforts, at least in the early phases of the novel, to resolve these competing demands – of nobility and democracy, the privilege concentrated in some men and independent citizenship for all – converge around Raymond, who vocally expresses his ambition to appear on England's new coinage and to be the "first man in the state" celebrated by his "dutiful subjects" in ballads and the "mumbled devotions" of old women (*LM*, 50). These ambitions are not realized as such. But Raymond does achieve a domineering public role, apparent in the public response to his oratory. That connection becomes secured in a pivotal scene where a speech in which he channels "graceful elocution" into focused attention leads to his being selected as Lord Protector, amidst widespread acclamation.

Parliament threatens to become "extinct," as we saw, following debates over selecting a future leader. This threat of dissolution only proves temporary, given the protections built into the system. These mechanisms for appeasement prove all too successful. "To our extreme surprise," we learn, "when it was moved that we should resolve ourselves into a committee for the election of the Lord Protector, the member who had nominated Ryland, rose and informed us that this candidate had resigned his pretensions" (*LM*, 101). He goes on to describe an at once muted and rhapsodic scene:

> His information was at first received with silence; a confused murmur succeeded; and, when the chairman declared Lord Raymond duly chosen, it amounted to a shout of applause and victory. It seemed as if, far from any dread of defeat even if Mr Ryland had not resigned, every voice would have been united in favour of our candidate. In fact, *now that the idea of contest was dismissed*, all hearts returned to their former respect and admiration of our accomplished friend. Each felt, that England had never seen a Protector so capable of fulfilling the arduous duties of that high office. (*LM*, 102, emphasis added)

The voice of the Sibyl may subsume all the other voices in the novel. But during the political section of *The Last Man*, that role is claimed by a celebrated political man. "Our voice made of many voices, resounded through the chamber," Lionel concludes, "it syllabled the name of Raymond" (*LM*, 102). The "End of History" attendant upon the final resolution of political difference converges here with a vision of the "Last Man." This claim to political success nonetheless acquires complex, even ominous significance as the victory scene witnesses Raymond, who had already united the voices of the crowd, become interpellated into and phantasmatically reproduced by a single resounding "voice" that makes him substance at the level of syllable.

That complexity becomes apparent when we recall that presence here remains shadowed by absence. For all the emphasis here on success, after all, this scene looks ahead to the resonant emptiness of the remainder of the novel, which begins with the unwinding of the so-called political "senate" and other sites of political argument. The scene in which Raymond wins power marks a victory. Yet this scene may also be considered proleptic of future absence: an anticipatory echo of the loss to come, its substance hollowed out by the future presence of absence. The immediacy of enthusiasm here proves transitory. And this scene is followed, in turn, by a strange falling away. Directly afterwards, we learn, the house "dissolved"; the former Protector "gave up" his insignia; Adrian "suddenly disappeared"; and Raymond's supporters were "reduced to our intimate friends merely" as the installed candidate was "conducted ... to the palace of government." Raymond has been fully installed, if not absorbed, into that state structure, a scene followed by his own absence. This momentary quelling of individual political ambition, or at least conflict, comprises an uncanny advance warning of the eventual snuffing out of mankind altogether.

The politics of *The Last Man* as a whole are ultimately quietist – at times quite literally. Shelley silently includes some reforms, such as triennial elections, into the world of her novel. But she mutes the prospect of wider unrest, even as more quietly subversive possibilities persist at the edges. Before turning to Shelley's book as a whole, tarrying a little longer with Raymond will allow me to further substantiate this book's claims about the indebtedness of Shelley's writing to Byron. The novel's investments in political men, capable – if only in temporary and transient fashion – of sustaining alternative futures not only has political implications, but aesthetic ones. *The Last Man* is suffused with allusions to the poetry of Percy Shelley. But the scenes I have addressed here also reveal Shelley's investment in a Byronic poetics. That investment had both personal and poetic dimensions. Raymond sings a "Tyrolese song of liberty" as he mulls his next political moves, in the same exchange where he contemplates his "dutiful subjects" showering him with songs and devotions (*LM*, 49). Shortly after learning of Byron's death, Shelley made a further entry in the journal where she had recently identified with the "last man" and the "last relic" of the race: "Can I forget our evening visits to Diodati," she wrote of Byron, "our excursions on the lake when he sang the Tyrolese hymn – and his voice was harmonized with winds and waves?"[24] Byron's death, I have suggested, helped to galvanize Shelley's plans for *The Last Man*, which she completed in the months following these journal entries. Building upon Shelley's existing identification with the "last man," her novel of that title elaborated the phrase that began her private remarks into a polyphonic meditation upon personal and collective loss.

The death of Byron shortly after Shelley's remarks on the "last man" was a further blow among many. That loss, critics have tended to assume, further underscored the biographical pertinence of her self-identification as the "last relic of a beloved race" and further honed her developing plans for the novel. Yet Shelley's meditations upon the loss of Byron also coupled with her reflection upon wider political changes – from her interest in parliamentary debate to her observation of brewing mobilization for reform – and played a more central role in helping her plans for the novel to coalesce, I have suggested, than critics have appreciated. The implications of reading the novel in these terms are far-reaching and challenge some existing lines of approach. Indeed, *The Last Man*, we might go so far as to claim, took shape only incidentally as a reflection upon the end of the human race. At least in its opening stages, the novel had far more to do with the death of Byron, the "*lost* man" who first appears spectrally behind Lionel's father and who returns to politics only to pass away once again. Reading the novel with this focus in mind does not amount to reading narrowly in terms of Shelley's personal response to Byron's death. But nor should we assume that the outer bounds of that loss can be calculated. That loss became inextricable, I have further argued, from vanishing political possibilities. More particularly, it became bound up, however indirectly, with the disappearance of the Whigs, whose platform was being washed away by the tides of radicalism and reform while facing unnerving challenges from the grating roar of popular political activity. The novel as a whole hardly sounds a ringing endorsement of the antiestablishment republicanism espoused by Shelley's husband and his circle. Raymond instead emerges as a means to reimagine and thereby overcome emerging political divides, whether that amounted to silencing the truly "political" dissent associated with those brewing class divisions or forestalling what Shelley viewed as the dismantling of politics.

In the end, we cannot fully establish the role that Byron played in Shelley's conception and composition of *The Last Man*. But we can and certainly should acknowledge more fully that he provided a crucial foil for the novel's reflections upon politics – and that he was a crucial interlocutor, including posthumously, for its author. Byron's writing played an especially pivotal role, at the same time, in shaping the novel's *own* poetics, the meditative narration whose recurring emphases on plangent loss and echoing absences meld together with its reflections on the changing ends of politics. Shelley's tangled interpersonal relationship with Byron had its own prominent intertextual dimension. Aside from the role that his example played in her emergence as a writer, Shelley had an unsurpassed

endorse the abolition of monarchy. But the antiroyalist sympathies and utopian schemes advanced by Adrian appear in ambivalent terms (not least given Adrian's frail and ineffectual nature and Raymond's quasi-royalism). *The Last Man* does imply some qualified sympathy for the demands of reformers in the 1820s. At the same time, Shelley performs a kind of bait and switch. *The Last Man* opens up wide-ranging questions about political transformation only to narrow their scope by locating them at a pronounced temporal remove, in a future world altogether detached from that of Shelley's present.

In what follows, I ask what we can conclude about the politics of *The Last Man*. At the same time, I show how the novel leaves established formulations of politics (and even the "political") behind, "in the dust." Especially in its attention to Lionel Verney and his sister Perdita, the novel locates high politics in relation to alternative visions of the English nation. The rustic scenes and bucolic retreats inhabited by the Verneys may appear to have little to do with politics, beyond marking its limits and exterior. But their association with scenes not shaped by existing political institutions subtly comments on contemporary debates, impressing on the scenes of politics other possibilities. Without explicitly investing in utopian ideals and the radical tradition, Shelley's novel does, I will propose, stage a complex return to the prepolitical "state of nature." The end of politics, set into motion by the plague, offers glimpses of a desirable rupture with the status quo, including the alternative futures that might come from a return to beginnings. While the book does not get behind any recognizable reformist agenda (bidding an ambiguous "Farewell" to calls for an expanded franchise, collapsed together with the vanity of other human wishes), the dissolution of existing political structures brings into focus idyllic, unspoiled scenes that resonate in complex ways with actual and imagined disruptions to English politics. They find counterparts, in turn, with travels to the ends of the earth and ultimately to other planets – imagined voyages that leave England behind for new worlds altogether.

The ranks of humanity dwindle, over the second and third volumes of *The Last Man*, themselves shadowed by battle and further calamity, to leave a lone survivor: the last man of the novel's title. But these developments are some time coming. The opening volume of Shelley's novel, as we have seen, addresses the personal and political trials of Adrian and Lord Raymond and embroils those characters and narrator Lionel in complex love triangles – with Lionel's sister Perdita, Adrian's sister Idris, and the Greek exile Evadne. Those relationships take shape in the context of political contestation: the factions vying for power following the abolition of England's monarchy. Readers compelled by concerns with the end of the world may be justified in seeing the early portion of the novel as extraneous, even irrelevant. Even some of Shelley's own readers, taking up a book on a then-current theme,[30] were disappointed. But the relationship between these respective stories and the relevance of the disruption of existing political institutions to Shelley's account of the end of the human race was apparent to at least some contemporary readers.

"We have, indeed, at the outset, an indication sufficiently ominous of the approaching dessolution [*sic*] of the world," the *Panoramic Miscellany* noted, "for a king of England, in conformity with the wishes of the people, retires from his throne to make way for the establishment of a republic." That review went on, however, to advance a perhaps unlikely reading of the novel's politics: "Can we wonder at the plague that was to follow, and sweep off all the inhabitants of the earth? The holy salt of royalty removed, what was to preserve the mass from corruption?"[31] We might assume that the wife of Percy Shelley was not particularly sympathetic with this Tory vision of the sustaining power of monarchy (nor with the implied slights here about reform and its degenerating influence). But we can, without adopting its conservative worldview, apply this account meaningfully to the novel. England's conversion from monarchy to republic can be read, in an analogy to the disease that destroys mankind, as having rendered the national government vulnerable to infection (or, adopting the review's term, "corruption"). Viscount Bolingbroke spoke in the eighteenth century about political systems having an inbuilt mortality; Jeremy Bentham, for his part, compared monarchical governments possessed of excess power and maintained by "sinister" prejudice to countries infected by plague.[32] Shelley's novel can be seen, given the republican sympathies trumpeted by her husband and their wider circle, to have replaced an already rotten political system with an improved, idealized alternative, making this conjunction of endings poignantly ironic. The novel may be read as a cautionary tale about the destruction liable to follow from radical political change, but can equally – and more plausibly – be read, in the opposite terms, as the tragic story of mankind's decline made doubly tragic by the optimistic backdrop of continuing reform in an idyllic future not troubled by poverty or evident national distress.

To decide between these options will mean attending to the book in some detail. But we may note at the outset that definitive answers to these questions are purposively withheld. The politics of Shelley's novel remain, I propose, willfully indeterminate.[33] Yet that indeterminacy proves equally important to the book's "politics" as any clear resolution of that question.

The juxtaposition between politics and the plague in *The Last Man*, disruptive of any fixed meaning, creates uncertainty, locating the reader in a space of unresolved questioning: an impasse. The government shutdown that renders parliament "extinct" uncannily anticipates the later plague. These echoes continue. The "crowded senate" (this word echoing contemporary political references, including by Shelley herself, to lofty "senators" removed from popular demands) has a prominent role in the entities to which the novel bids farewell as the plague takes hold. That catalogue underscores the prominence of politics in the novel more widely. The book's depiction of English society centers around elite circles and court intrigue. But the echoing hallways of palaces not only provide an evocative backdrop for the novel's characters: the emptying out of political institutions *also* provides the book with a potent figure for the hollowing out of society more widely. The end of politics thus marks the onset of the end of the world, beginning with the dissolution of human society. These images of evacuated palaces – like the potent image of "crowns in the dust" – resonate with accounts of past dynasties and fallen empires. But Shelley also broadens their implications: this will be the last decline ever.

These are Byronic themes, voiced throughout the poet's early works and echoed in his pungent later writings on post-Napoleonic Europe. Shelley was an ardent reader and transcriber of Byron's writings, especially *Childe Harold's Pilgrimage*. Over the course of *The Last Man*, she develops these themes into a unique set of aesthetic registers. A sense of deep resonance thus comes to surround the available political readings of the novel. Whether or not the relationship between the respective facets of the novel comprises one single process of dissolution, ominously anticipated at the outset, or serves to mark a tragic, ironic contrast, that convergence creates the novel's unique atmospheric texture. That atmosphere was partly "ominous" (in the words of the review quoted above) but was equally characterized by a sense of vacant lightness. The novel's layering of a crumbling past and an uncertain future takes shape amidst serene horizons confronted with a sense of awe, contributing to the novel's spaced-out, almost hallucinogenic atmosphere. At the same time, the book's narrative brings up philosophical quandaries – about completeness without creation, fulfillment without futurity – with a density matched in few other places in English literature beyond *Paradise Lost*.

The indeterminacy of the novel's politics, all of that is to say, remains bound up with its aesthetics. As the book moves away from politics, its polyvalent resonance opens out still further. That layering of significance profoundly complicates our ability to answer some basic questions about the novel's perspectives on monarchy and aristocracy, republicanism and reform, democracy and even early feminism. Establishing the politics of Shelley's novel, beginning with its competing visions of England's new republic, remains challenging (if not altogether ill-advised) for the simple reason that its "politics" take shape at the intersection between competing aesthetic and imaginative vistas, including attachments to politics and the conspicuous absence of politics as such. Either the broad contours of the novel's political investments are obvious, we might conclude, or they become muffled by the layering of imagery and thematics, or they are beside the point of a novel that may have begun with one set of agendas but ended up with bigger fish to fry. But these questions about the novel's implied politics can nonetheless permit us to see how the novel, amidst its other achievements, *also* encloses sharp political critique. That enquiry entails a fuller reevaluation of the novel's carefully layered structure. Fantasies of stepping outside the world of political institutions (and even beyond this world as such) emerge most compellingly by way of the novel's brilliantly inverted return to the "state of nature." The evacuated scenes of the later volumes loop back to earlier concerns signaled by its narrator, a peasant and poacher who skulks the barren edges of the polity, whom Shelley compares to the wolf-suckled founders of Rome.

Shelley was well-versed in political theory, from its classical origins and the English republican tradition to philosophical radicalism and early utilitarianism. In the novel, however, the utopian views and humanist temperament attributed to Adrian – and associated with Percy Shelley – serve, in the first instance, to focalize a clash between theory and practice. "In solitude, and through many wanderings afar from the haunts of men," Adrian "matured his views for the reform of the English government, and the improvement of the people." His visions of "Fertile England" and political brotherhood have an important bearing on the visions of politics presented by the book as a whole. But the emphasis on the workings and mechanics of politics in Shelley's novel forces us to reflect on practice in addition to theory. There may be merit (or at least interest) to Adrian's views. But as a political actor, he is hopeless. As Lionel notes, with more than a hint of possible sarcasm, "it would have been well if he had concealed his sentiments, until he had come into possession of the power which would secure their practical development." Instead, "frank of heart and fearless," Adrian impatiently publishes his intentions of "using his influence to diminish the power of the aristocracy, to effect a greater equalization of wealth and privilege, and to introduce a perfect system of republican governance into England" (*LM*, 34). His "ardour and imprudence," "contempt for the sacredness of authority," and "enthusiasm for good which did not exist" attract mockery and scorn, while the "lofty severity of his moral views" alienates him from the young and inexperienced. Evadne admires his self-assertion but wishes that his will had been "more intelligible to the multitude" (*LM*, 34). Adrian will later ascend to leadership, but only once disease has taken hold and the "multitude" is no longer so numerous.

Raymond, by contrast, steers a successful path to power and public acclaim early on in the book, voicing his commitment to reviving the spirit of monarchy and invoking powerful leaders from Napoleon to Cromwell. Aside from his overweening ambition, Raymond shows an ability to conciliate the public. He also, critically, voices reformist ambitions of his own. After taking power, he finds himself drawn to idealistic visions for the future of the nation: he believes he can cure poverty, reform the nation, make England great again. These ambitions and successes as a politician further undermine the straightforward identification of Raymond with Byron (in ways that do not apply to the identification of Adrian with Percy Shelley). Rather than making him merely the worldly, Byronic foil to Adrian's idealistic systems, Shelley *also* used Raymond to imagine a kind of ideal politician, who combined a version of Byron's persona and ambition, here, with a transformative agenda that ranges from curing national ills to building national galleries and museums. Those futuristic vistas and reformist trajectories become hostages to fortune. The appearance of the plague, coinciding with Raymond's expedition to Greece, dramatically interrupts those plans. But rather than simply switching the focus of the novel, or marking a clear continuation, that shift instead takes shape by way of overlaps of plot and complexly accruing layers of significance.

The Verney siblings, I will go on to show, help to bring that significance into focus. We find further guidance to the politics of *The Last Man* in asking what the novel expressly rejects. That includes, most obviously, the aggressive populism of Raymond's competitor Ryland, who courts the "democratic" faction of the republic. The rancorous leader of the popular party is not only a sourpuss who scowls at his rival's ascent; he is a dangerous demagogue who seeks violently to uproot the peacefully operating English government. Ryland had witnessed, when a young man, the abdication of the king and the amalgamation of the two houses of Lords and Commons. His sympathy for these "popular encroachments" leads him to make "the business of his life to consolidate and encrease them" (*LM*, 45). At first, he is not sorry to see Raymond's lordly machinations draw away some of Adrian's aristocratic partisans. But facing the ascent of Raymond, he concludes that "the thing was now going too far":

> The poorer nobility hailed the return of sovereignty, as an event which would restore them to their power and rights, now lost. The *half extinct spirit of royalty* roused itself in the minds of men; and they, willing slaves, self-constituted subjects, were ready to bend their necks to the yoke. Some erect and manly spirits still remained, pillars of state; but the word republic had grown stale to the vulgar ear; and many – the event would prove whether it was a majority – pined for the tinsel and show of royalty. Ryland was roused to resistance; he asserted that his sufferance alone had permitted the encrease of the party; but the time for indulgence was passed, and with one motion of his arm he would sweep away the cobwebs that blinded his countrymen. (*LM*, 45–6, emphasis added)

The narration's free indirect summary of Ryland's scornful views about the "tinsel and show" of royalty and its paraphrase of his bombastic claims (he will "sweep away the cobwebs that blinded his countrymen") capture his contempt and arrogance. These characterizations come with more than a tinge of distaste, coupled with implied mockery for their staunchly antimonarchical sentiments. When Ryland takes power during the initial phases of the plague, he proves to be a paranoid and ineffective leader. That the novel disapproves of his character more widely becomes still more apparent when he is found dead, in a farmhouse, clutching money: an exposure of hypocritical greed, located in an ironic setting for the gruff man of the working people, as well as a more oblique reference to his failed economic policies.

In the novel's glancing references to the United States, we encounter a more equivocal perspective on popular politics and modern economics. America receives only limited attention in Shelley's novel. But these references provide a further indication of the book's implied endorsement or criticism of political systems, especially those with republican roots and democratic vistas. At a later stage in the novel, once the plague has begun to advance, the narration – looking back at the radical reform advocated by Ryland and the increased role of the masses in politics – ponders whether England might have taken the parallel course pursued by the United States. But this narrative voice, merging with the voice of narrator Lionel, raises skepticism: "Yet could England indeed doff her lordly trappings, and be content with the democratic style of America?" (*LM*, 222). This question couples with a complex, free indirect summary of the worldview put forward by democrats, in which nobility becomes the province of all: "when the

name and title of Englishman was the sole patent of nobility, we should all
be noble." Yet the narration shifts over the course of this same long
paragraph, pivoting from this distanced, possibly even sarcastic, summary
of the populist argument to challenge the Burkean worldview of that still
substantial group in English society who "extolled . . . the Corinthian capital
of polished society" while appealing to "prejudices without number, to old
attachments" and the "young hopes" of those destined to be peers, over and
above what they view as the sullied commercial example of America. The
movement from this skeptically inclined summary of populist views ("Were
the pride of ancestry, the patrician spirit, the gentle courtesies and refined
pursuits, splendid attributes of rank, to be erased among us?" [*LM*, 222]) and
the starkly critical account of the anti-American views of the aristocratic elite
(who "set up as a scarecrow, the spectre of all that was sordid, mechanic and
base in the commercial republics" [*LM*, 222]) induces a kind of whiplash.
But we might equally conclude that the narration here, in an example of the
cultivated indeterminacy I have emphasized, forces the reader to inhabit
a kind of counterpoint. The narration may seem only to come to rest as the
narrative voice shifts *between* one perspective and the other, in the slide
between resisting the earlier view and accepting a not-yet-extreme version of
the latter: "Let not England be so far disgraced, as to have imagined that it
can be without nobles," the passage ambiguously concludes. To the degree
that we can locate Shelley in the narration of *The Last Man*, that voice only
achieves stability in the movement between views, the counterposing of
alternative possibilities.

   The United States, this ambivalence notwithstanding, presents an
important point of analogy for the novel. Both early nineteenth-century
America ("an independent nation with a completely popular government,"
in Brougham's summary)[34] and the novel's depiction of twenty-first-
century England can be seen to present imagined futures for Shelley's
readers. With the exception of the enhanced air balloons that characters
employ for short-haul trips across the British Isles and to the continent, the
futuristic universe of Shelley's novel does not contain science-fiction
elements. The main changes to life in England involve reforms to the
constitution and organization of government, as well as idealized schemes
for national agriculture. The political system presented in Shelley's novel,
in addition to collapsing the two chambers of parliament into one, was in
advance of contemporary England (and, for that matter, England today) in
holding triennial parliaments.[35] That measure was too far even for the
Whig opposition, whose eighteenth-century hegemony was established by
keeping the duration between parliaments at up to seven years. Hobhouse

voiced frustration that even a "pure" Whig administration would never propose triennial parliaments and looked longingly toward the United States. In advance of the 1832 Reform Bill, efforts were made to bypass the House of Lords followed by schemes to pack its benches with newly created peers. The "electors" that Raymond must appease suggest a more democratic franchise, recalling both the kind of popular elections pioneered in the borough of Westminster and the voting procedures of the United States. Although Shelley does not spell out the details, the novel seems to imagine a political system not limited to landowners or those with wealth: a version of the expanded electorate of middle-class men demanded by early nineteenth-century reformers and partially realized at the outset of the next decade. But while the political system of the youthful United States may have provided Shelley with an acceptable analogue for a reformed twenty-first-century England, whether she anticipated (or welcomed) such a prospect for her own lifetime remains unclear. At any rate, there is little indication that votes for women are anywhere on the horizon.

Back to Nature: The Mechanic Class and the Forgotten Sex

Lionel and Perdita are marginal to high politics, but the orphaned Verney siblings become integral to the plot of *The Last Man* as the narrow political dispute spills out onto a larger canvas. Perdita presents an especially important counterpoint to these early scenes as the occupant of a bucolic-seeming realm imagined by her male counterparts as both the outside of politics and the antithesis of the political sphere. When his volatile attachments to politics clash with his no less volatile romantic impulses, Raymond's growing infatuation with Perdita prompts him to make dramatic course corrections. Lionel, for his part, becomes the eventual "last man" of the novel's title, despite being of obscure birth, reaching an unmoored final state that ironically recalls his early circumstances. As such, expanding the novel's range of vision to women and the lower classes, the Verneys eventually help to displace the focus – shared by the elite characters and the novel alike – on political institutions and the trappings of inherited wealth and status. Crucial here are their ways of thinking about the English land and countryside. By the end of the book, their intimate familiarity with rustic landscapes, from flower-surrounded nooks to craggy mountains, has become a shared condition. The same applies for their externality to institutions. Lionel's outsider status appears vividly in the book's opening chapters, which describe his life as a poacher and peasant in the barren northern English countryside, where he has only animals for company. Those scenes provide an anticipatory echo of his isolated condition at the end of the book. Addressed with a view to politics within England, I will suggest, the scenes traversed by Lionel and his sister suggest alternative configurations of things as they are. That includes complex returns to the "state of nature" antecedent to the formation of political institutions and thus to the existence of society as such.

In the opening chapters, Lionel travels to Vienna seeking out a life of "politic intrigue."[36] Called back to England by loyalty to Adrian and the House of Windsor, he conveys his feelings upon arriving home in an expressive apostrophe that pivots away from the cloistered European world he has left behind:

> Farewell to courtly pleasures ... to the maze of passion and folly! All hail, England! Native England, receive thy child! Thou art the scene of all my hopes, the mighty theatre on which is acted the only drama that can, heart and soul, bear me along with it in its development. A voice most irresistible, a power omnipotent, drew me thither. After an absence of two years, I landed on its shores, not daring to make any inquiries, fearful of every remark. (*LM*, 32)

Lionel's return to England has a narrative function: his outside perspective provides a window onto developing intrigues, including Raymond's political ascent and Adrian's nervous breakdown. At the same time, his enchanted perspective on "Native England" and rustic background locate the affairs of court and high politics against a more expansive canvas. Perdita introduces outside perspectives of her own, including alternative spheres to those of elite power. Inhabiting "a little cottage" ("part of Adrian's gift") on the borders of Windsor Forest, her domestic space serves as a kind of microcosm for the alternative worlds in which the Verney siblings operate and which increasingly impress upon and overlap with the worlds of politics.

Lionel's visit to Perdita lets him observe the surrounding countryside. "I had never before been in the neighbourhood of Windsor," he writes, noting that "the fertility and beauty of the country around now struck me with admiration." This admiration increases as he approaches the "antique wood." "The ruins of majestic oaks which had grown, flourished, and decayed during the progress of centuries, marked where the limits of the forest once reached," he remarks, "while the shattered palings and neglected underwood shewed that this part was deserted for the younger plantations, which owed their birth to the beginning of the nineteenth century, and now stood in the pride of maturity" (*LM*, 32). Perdita's "humble dwelling" is in the "skirts of the most ancient portion" of the forest, her cottage "shadowed by the venerable fathers of the forest, under which the deer came to graze, and which for the most part hollow and decayed, formed fantastic groups that contrasted with the regular beauty of the younger trees" (*LM*, 32). The cottage, surrounded by flowers, "seemed to submit to the majesty of nature, and cower amidst the venerable remains of forgotten time." Lionel describes her home as a "fairy retreat," inaccessible to the "noisy contentions of politicians," and later compares Perdita herself to one of Wordsworth's half-forgotten flowers.

As much as they reinforce the identification between the Verneys and an antiquated, rustic perspective – and between Perdita and a feminine realm outside politics, if not altogether beyond human attention – these secluded spheres and layered landscapes prove more complicated upon closer scrutiny. In the first place, the scenes Lionel observes in the "antique wood" are not straightforwardly relics of the past; they feature "majestic oaks which had grown, flourished, and decayed during the progress of centuries" alongside more recently cleared ground. We may think here of *News from Nowhere*, in which the smoggy, crowded world of Victorian England has been transformed by public gardens and expanded greenery. But the time frames here are even more tangled than in Morris's socialist uprooting of capitalist modernity. Here, those "younger plantations" that now stand in the "pride of maturity" date back to the early *nineteenth* century, two-and-a-half centuries prior to the action of the book but contemporary with its original publication. We might have discerned a Burkean defense of continuity with the past here over the sudden, modernizing breaks associated with radical reform and revolutionary change. Certainly, these scenes resonate with the novel's emphasis on long expanses of time. Yet aside from the ways these multiple temporalities acquire complicated importance in their own right (and even Burke had complicated views on ecological sustainability)[37] the novel's futuristic setting complicates matters. No less than the book's mind-bending preface, which issues in futuristic prophecies from the Sibyl's cave, scenes like that in which Lionel reflects on the forest complicate the relationship between past, present, and imagined future. What counts as traditional and even conservative in the terms of its twenty-first-century appears differently from the moment of Shelley's readers. The book also hearkens to images of monarchy and tradition that transcend time, converging as they do with landscapes associated with chivalric and otherwise antiquated or premodern pasts, which become, in the novel, the locus of idealistic improvement.

Shelley elsewhere described Windsor Forest as "the only spot of English ground" for which she had any affection (quoted in *LM*, 32 n. 35). The site of the accreting histories described in Alexander Pope's poem, the royal hunting ground, as E. P. Thompson demonstrated, also saw clashing visions of the country's moral economies and social structures come together with the legacies of crown rule and a violently repressive legal code.[38] The area also functioned, to some extent, as a microcosm of the nation, offering a cross section of high and low society in tandem with past and present power structures. On July 21, 1818, Hobhouse traversed Windsor Forest on horseback, where he and his companion engaged the locals in conversation, including "a mechanic of the most *liberal* principles" who said meeting the accompanying Whig statesman was the "greatest honour." A week earlier, Hobhouse spelled out his response to a recent discussion of the "corruption of the people," in ways that help to situate this harmonious exchange. Corruption, Hobhouse stated, was an "idle" designation. The *noblesse oblige* that Hobhouse dispensed from horseback (together with his class's embrace of "fine parks" and "sumptuous fare") were entirely compatible, as he saw it, with a progressive political orientation.[39] While he condemned the exchange of hospitality for political favors, continued hierarchy (if not *squire*archy) was naturalized by the kinds of rustic, heroic settings described here. During coming decades, the "mechanic" class would acquire increasing political power, in tandem with changing vistas for progress and reform. Putting Hobhouse's comments together lets us see how he squared a version of patrician rule from horseback with glimpses of a reconfigured society, at once a modern politics and a continuation of the past.

Shelley's novel witnesses a similar conjunction, presenting political modernization in tandem with rustic scenes. Yet that harmony ultimately proves fleeting. As much as Shelley expands the canvas of the novel beyond elite men and palace intrigue, she obscures the contours of popular activity, airbrushing out a larger, untidy population of "mechanic" workers. In the novel, Windsor Forest, like England as a whole, appears largely absent of regular people. These scenes function more obviously to anticipate the uprooting, or growing over, of existing political institutions, without clear indications of how (or whether) they are to be replaced. Although Lionel narrates this transition, his own disjointed story of sudden returns and switched loyalties, serves to complicate and disrupt its significance. While the drama around the novel's men will become fraught and personal, those dynamics are also political. In any case, that drama is ultimately defused of any real potential for upset. Raymond serves to uphold and thereby preserve the constitutional balance. And the salience of his political success, in any case, falls away, as he and, in turn, the country succumb to a plague that makes political institutions beside the point. Lionel's perspective, as the novel's narrator, thus presents us with a sequence of self-erasing prospects. He leaves continental politics behind to return to his "Native England," only to return to political intrigue by way of Adrian and Raymond, only for politics to become largely irrelevant. But those overlapping perspectives also coincide, as in his description of the forest, with more patient attention to the natural environment. Indeed, the role of this natural scenery as "background" or a parallel setting to the courtly scenes of power shifts, as the plague takes hold, to become something more like the novel's foreground and exclusive setting. These rural scenes add to the novel's political indeterminacy while bringing alternative temporalities and even vectors for political change into view.

The Last Man subdues conflict and blunts factious disputes from the outset. The same applies to the prospect for potential upset or conflict between the court and the country at large. The deepening of the novel's plot makes this quietism literal, with a growing emphasis on empty and evacuated scenes and resonant absences. Yet while the prospects for political drama fade, other aspects of the fictional world take on political significance. For Charlotte Sussman, the departure of the characters clustered around Lionel and Adrian from England becomes legible in terms of contemporary debates over emigration policy.[40] For an increasing number of critics, the "human" drama of *The Last Man* recedes altogether to force a reevaluation of interspecies belonging and environmental dwelling. But remaining a little longer with the point of transition from the political to the pandemic – and from the interpersonal to the interspecies – lets us revisit the novel's reformist contexts and politics more narrowly understood. The idealized vistas glimpsed by Lionel and even Raymond, however fleeting, have an important bearing on the novel, even as politics comes to have less to do with hierarchies preserved by elite men than with the management of populations.

After the plague takes hold, Lionel echoes his earlier paean to England. But he does so, crucially, in the context of departure. Earlier, he had bid adieu to Europe and welcomed his native shores ("Farewell to courtly pleasures . . . to the maze of passion and folly! All hail, England!" [*LM*, 32]) but now he inverts the direction of travel: "Farewell to the dead! farewell to the tombs of those we loved! – farewell to giant London and the placid Thames, to river and mountain or fair district, birthplace of the wise and good, to Windsor Forest and its antique castle, farewell! themes for story alone are they, – we must live elsewhere" (*LM*, 258). These superimposed locations – juxtaposing Windsor Forest and the "tombs" of the dead, aligning London with the Thames – instill these abandoned scenes with an uncanny resonance, hollowing out the scenes of the novel's political plot while returning to view the full, massy scope of surrounding natural scenes. Fuson Wang sees this scene of farewells opening onto new kinds of community.[41] But the viability of the communities imagined here is, at best, rather limited. This passage allows us, perhaps more importantly, to perceive the ways these "Farewells" are superimposed, creating a sense of overlapping, discordant loss.

That sense of loss is further deepened and complicated by the novel's female characters. The women in *The Last Man* are, from the outset, associated with absence and decline. Perdita shares her name with the forgotten heroine of Shakespeare's *Winter's Tale* (and recalls Ophelia in her mournful gathering of flowers and death by drowning). Evadne, the recalcitrant Greek exile, succumbs to destitution and decline.[42] Both women may be seen to adopt roles occupied by Shelley herself. In her 1824 journal entry on being the "last man" left behind after the passing of the "beloved race," Shelley alluded to her circle of the "elect." More obliquely, she associated herself – and thereby the novel she went on to write – with a more pervasive sense of lastness, given totemic force by the death of Percy Shelley (and, in turn, that of Byron). Yet her remarks and the title of her novel raise an obvious question: what about women? That identification with the "last man" includes at least one woman, Shelley herself. Yet this need not incorporate women, as full and autonomous partners, into the "race" whose ending she summoned. As the "last man," Shelley may remain subordinated to her male companions, even claiming a secondary male identity as her own, as Eve to Adam, or the wife under her husband's name. *The Last Man*, in which the ending of "a . . . race" extends to the entirety of the species, may seem to transcend this ambiguity: "man" here stands in for "mankind." But *The Last Man*, as we have seen, remains focused (at least at the outset) on a political world still dominated by men – and a select few men at that. The novel hardly countenances the dramatic increase in the franchise demanded by more radically minded reformers, let alone the direct inclusion of women in the political process. Despite the novel's twenty-first-century setting, women are not seen to take any kind of direct political role, whether by voting or taking political office. Her feminist pedigree notwithstanding, Shelley did not build in obvious ways upon Wollstonecraft's feminism. For all her youthful transgressions, she came to occupy a relatively conventional role. Yet as *The Last Man* also demonstrates, women might take up a variety of oblique, implicitly critical relationships to politics, beginning with silent observation.

Gender was front and center when Shelley wrote to Hobhouse, asking to attend debates in the House of Commons. Shelley called attention to her female subordination, while in the process shoring up her correspondent's male superiority. "Since my difficulty arises from restrictions placed by you the virtual majority upon us the weaker portion," she wrote with sly irony, "I feel as if I had some (the shadow of a shade) claim upon your gallantry." By collapsing Hobhouse's role in a political elite that "virtual[ly]" represented the people at large with his gender, she thereby identified herself both with the supposedly weaker sex ("the shadow of a shade") and the wider population denied suffrage, most of whom, across classes, were women. But she also asserted a demand, in the guise of a humble request, conveying her desire to attend the "strangers gallery" where visitors were permitted to observe parliamentary debates. She hastened to underscore her supposed reticence, emphasizing her capacity to remain mute: "I hear that there is a place, over the roof of St. Stephens where you senators permit us to hear, not seen. Could you introduce me to this enviable post? – would you? – I make the request frankly – deny me in the same manner if I be too intrusive."[43]

Shelley planned to draw upon her observation of the parliamentary chamber in the novel she was then completing: "a tale which will certainly be more defective than it would otherwise be," she wrote in the same letter, "if I am not permitted to be present at a debate."[44] That "tale" became *The Last Man*, in whose opening volume, we have seen, political debate plays a central role. But Shelley's letter to Hobhouse also illuminates the novel's gender dynamics and *their* potential political significance. Perdita may appear as a self-consciously weak, subordinated figure. But her character also hints at the buried potential enclosed within feminine roles of quiet observation. Lionel encourages us to see Perdita as a hidden, obscured, absent figure whose bower represents a retreat from the noisy world of public affairs. That world is imagined to have its own plenitude. Crossing its threshold feels like a portal into another realm to Lionel. Raymond, meanwhile, experiences its erotic charge and romantic possibility as another world to conquer. His love for Perdita rivals and for a time outweighs his political and militaristic ambitions. The man who had just persuaded the "legislators of England" that a "scepter was not too weighty" for his hand appears "frolicsome" in its bounds, Lionel observes, even willing to abandon his ambition and cast crowns and scepters in the dust for love. But we do not need to take these accounts of Perdita's rustic retreat as a bower detached from politics (or as a self-enclosed realm of erotic escape) at face value. Locating Perdita in a space of romance completely apart from politics, after all, means following the lead of these male characters and not her female creator.

Perdita's apartness from the world appears in the novel as neither neutral nor inevitable: that characterization comes from the men. Lionel's account of his arrival with Raymond to her cottage, after the victorious debate that sees him resoundingly celebrated, makes the constructed nature of this supposed retreat from politics clear: "We found her in her flower-adorned alcove; she was reading the newspaper report of the debate in parliament, that apparently doomed her to hopelessness" (*LM*, 52). Raymond discourages her from reading on: "Not a word more shall my sweet Perdita read of this contention of madmen and fools," he states (*LM*, 52), not clarifying whether he includes himself among that company. But her continued silence speaks volumes. Shelley may not have been able to attend the Palace of Westminster (Caroline Lamb had only been able to do so by posing as a boy). But Shelley was able to follow parliamentary debates from a distance. She could read about them, as Perdita does, in the newspaper. As the author of a book in which the members of parliament she had pointedly described as "senators" are transfigured into fictional characters, Shelley cultivated her own perspective on the world of political men. Turning now to the novel as a whole will allow us to assess the cumulative impact of these complexly overlapping natural and political scenes, as politics gives way to the plague and the condition of England reverts to a state of nature.

The Last Man and the Spirit of the Age

Muriel Spark posited an urban context for the genesis of Shelley's novel that wedded the darkest fears of Malthus with the onset of industrial capitalism: "As the factory gates nightly emitted their begrimed victims like smoke from their chimney stacks," Spark wrote, "as every whistle-stop on the new railroad engendered its Mechanic's Institute like the germs of an occupational disease; so mankind lost confidence in his natural faculties. Science lined up with Industry to form a force as vast and irrational as Mary's Plague; and all premises seemed to point to a Last Man."[45] *The Last Man* has continued to produce interpretations that oscillate between treating the text as timeless myth and commentary on modernization. Spark vividly ties Shelley's book to the spirit of the age. But the political unconscious of *The Last Man* has less to do with Promethean growth and satanic mills, at least in the book itself, than with the sheer invisibility of the poor. Shelley solves Malthus's predicament by not allowing her futuristic England (or the world at large) to seem plausibly populated in the first place. We can nonetheless use these occluded social contexts – in tandem with the novel's veiled references to contemporary political activity and debate – to develop a fuller account of its engagement with the ends of politics, asking what happens to "England" as the novel's various processes of unwinding take hold.

The onset of the plague in *The Last Man* comes from contact with the East. America shows an early susceptibility to infection. Raymond's voyage to Greece, meanwhile, turns his hubris and vainglory into a vector of disease. In the next chapter, I turn to the expanding global scope of Byron and Shelley's writings, with a view to their bearing on domestic politics. The works of both writers, I propose, sought to marginalize England and its institutions and to imagine the world that would follow from their sidelining and even disappearance. I conclude my account of politics in *The Last Man* here by attending to the implications of the plague for the condition of England. After successive waves of panic, bacchanalia, and unrest, the onset of mass death sees the nation revert to an at once stripped-down and oddly full rustic condition. The significance of this change is far from self-evident. The "tendency of the novel," McWhir writes, "is towards the vindication of subversive, destructive, anti-civilizing power, most vividly symbolized first by plague and finally by the ruins of depopulated Rome" (*LM*, xxv). Other critics have seen the disease as unleashing revolutionary energy against an archaic *ancien régime*. But what these and other accounts miss and obscure, I would suggest, are the ways Shelley's novel operates not by way of totalizing categories – disease equals destruction equals subversion – but overlapping layers of resonance and significance. After all, the scenes in which England gives way under the force of the plague echo scenes from much earlier in the novel. The political condition of the country and the meanings of the English land reverberate in complex ways with each other well before the plague takes hold, in ways that are only deepened and expanded as the novel goes on. In the case of Lionel, for one, the growing desolation recalls his earlier experience in the northern English countryside.

After first arriving back to England early in the novel, Lionel learns about Adrian's decline and seeks him out in his convalescence, taking a flying balloon to his Scottish estate. As they travel back through England together, Adrian makes an encomium to the nation's accomplishments, including the power of men over the elements. But this paean to

"Fertile England" goes beyond technological advancement. Adrian celebrates the "busy towns and cultivated plains" and proceeds to emphasize the challenge that "rustic scenes" pose to "profuse luxuries." Adrian's emphasis on what nature "ministers" includes a subtle glance at the world of male-dominated politicians. Shelley makes that pun more explicitly in the opening lines of the novel, where Lionel writes of man that "Nature herself was only his *first minister.*" Adrian follows his claim about nature's prime ministry with a fulsome declaration: "Oh that death and sickness were banished and that every man might find a brother in his elbow." These scenes, equally indicative of Adrian's philosophical idealism as of his unsuitability to rule, find counterparts in the political ambitions of Raymond. He hails the era of his protectorship as one of prosperity and improvement. "Canals, aqueducts, bridges, stately buildings" – to include a future National Gallery – "and various edifices for public utility, were entered upon," surrounding him with "projectors and projects." More ambitious (and efficacious) than Adrian, he seeks to make England "one scene of fertility and magnificence," with poverty "abolished," labor "lightened of its heaviest burden" and "machines . . . to supply with facility every want of the population." Talking like Adrian about ending disease, he also seeks to inspire the people with his "beneficial will" and by reordering the "mechanism of society" (*LM* 82–3).

But these claims face ironic deflation. When Raymond visits Evadne (after being presented with her plans for the new National Gallery), the novel makes a momentary swerve into altogether different social terrain. As he approaches her derelict quarters, he describes his shock at the surrounding urban scenes: "Poverty, dirt, and squalid misery characterized its appearance." This prompts a wider realization: "Alas! thought Raymond, I have much to do before England becomes a Paradise" (*LM*, 84). While Adrian's idealized schemes for benevolent, perfected governance help to make him a calm and empathetic leader as the plague finally takes hold, prior to this the royal heir spectacularly fails to live up to his political role. The book describes him as a spent wave and dying flame whose belief that man can will evil away appears absurdly utopian. Yet his rural visions are not merely punctured and ironized. The novel also gives us some limited indication, in Raymond's sweeping plans for improvement, that a reforming government *could* implement the more reasonable versions of these agendas (if not his stated goal of banishing disease). The ironic decline of a political world organized around men, coupled with the oblique perspectives of characters marginalized by class and gender, displaces images of politics as usual. At the same time, the book points to other visions of the world, including unspoiled natural scenes and perfected societies, which acquire further sharpened focus, in turn, from the deepening of the plague. These glimpses at "Fertile England," function as idealized futures, which come into focus in the cracks between changing political realities.

The plague, of course, comes to dominate. Cameron offers one way of making sense of the novel's transitions, from flourishing England to uninhabited wasteland, in claiming that *The Last Man* is an "inherently Malthusian work." By this, she suggests that the book sympathizes with conservative cleric Thomas Malthus, whose bleakly pessimistic theories (deplored, among others, by Hazlitt) reduced human life to a grim political economy in which more births meant greater privation, culminating in the mass starvation of the poor. Malthus asserted, further, that mankind was not ultimately capable of improvement, challenging Godwin's vision of perfectible institutions and social regeneration with the blunt assertion that mankind was subject to strict limits. Where Hobbes had asserted that human life was nasty, brutish, and short, Malthus maintained that it was destined to be crowded, malnourished, and miserable. There was not enough food to support an increase in children (the kind of potato-counting political economy Hazlitt despised), and therefore there were inherent limits on population growth. Plagues were a further natural way to keep the human population in check.[46]

As with Spark's nightmarish vision of factories spewing forth uncared-for populations, this vision of scarcity and want offers a suggestive backdrop for *The Last Man*. These accounts principally serve to bring the realities behind Shelley's fiction into view, rather than illuminating the dynamics presented in the novel itself. But we do not, at any rate, need to ask whether the novel "agrees" with Malthus's ideas – merely acknowledging that mankind is susceptible to plague does no such thing – to see the resonance of the novel with broadly Malthusian ways of thinking about politics. That resonance has to do less with those theories per se, I would suggest, than with a consonance between their respective ways of narrating reality. Regardless of its validity as an account of human species growth and decline, that is to say, Malthus advances an approach to political life that entails a strictly limited understanding of human nature, organized around finite resources and the corresponding finitude of "man."[47] Mankind is reduced to a wild or primitive state in *The Last Man*. But that does not, by and large, result in the kind of antagonistic relationship that would follow from a penuriously Malthusian (or combatively Hobbesian) worldview. The dismantling of institutions prompts a reevaluation of human nature as much as a return of the species to a base animal condition. Mankind goes from a population considered in the aggregate to a more dispersed set of relations, unmoored from and no longer bounded by prior institutions and arrangements. To this extent, the version of human nature presented in Malthus's philosophy falls apart.

We come closer to the substance of that worldview by reflecting upon the visions of collective human life from which Malthus's theories arose. He pointed to the squalid conditions in which the poor lived, giving rise to the argument that mankind was destined to live in competitive, meager circumstances. Shelley appears to repudiate this perspective on a crowded human future, as much as she refutes – at once puncturing and sidestepping – Godwin's idealistic schemes for human governance. But her avoidance of this outcome comes, as I have already suggested, from refusing to ever present the country as plausibly populated in the first place. The onset of the plague, for Lionel, does not effect such a massive rupture with what came before, in part because there are so few people around him to begin with. The only way England can appear, in Raymond's words, "a Paradise" is on that basis. *The Last Man* is thus a Malthusian fiction, in the sense that the country only appears to flourish from having a suppressed population. Shelley responds to the plight of the poor by refusing to acknowledge their existence. Rather than foregrounding a Malthusian worldview, however, she cuts out the middleman, removing the need for a response to overcrowding by rarely having crowds on the horizon (except when they are about to be silenced). The novel's earlier equivocation between support for inherited institutions and their revolutionary transformation thus coincides with another pivot point: between Shelley's steadily overcrowding present and an impossibly empty future. These scenes comment upon each other, without settling into an entirely plausible synthesis. Yet in doing so, they create suggestive possibilities that impress upon politics as conceivable visions for the future.

"The picture of England under the plague is curiously modern," Elizabeth Nitchie observed in her mid-twentieth-century reading of *The Last Man*. "When the plague was ravaging the continent of Europe," she continued,

> thousands of refugees fled to England. England helped them as she helped the political refugees of the eighteenth century, and those of the twentieth, of whom Mary never dreamed. "The English spirit awoke to its full entirety, and, as it had ever done, set itself to resist the evil." Taxes were increased. Pleasure grounds and parks were ploughed up and planted, producing employment and food. Great estates became refuges for the poor and

dispossessed. Trees were cut down for lumber to erect temporary dwellings.[48]

Nitchie emphasizes a distinctly post-1945 vision here: an expansive and open welfare state that, while not a communist utopia, presents a modest Keynesian adaptation of Morris's democratic socialism. By contrast, in her early twenty-first-century account, Hilary Strang sees the novel as imagining the leveling out of existence, into a version of "bare life." That apparent flattening results in searching questions about the biopolitical governance that views the ends of politics as the superintendence of populations. "Can there be a democratic equality among persons," Strang asks, "that does not risk the reduction of personhood to the simple equivalence of one biological, animal life with another?"[49] Strang's answer is to view *The Last Man* as "a novel of the politics of common life, a politics to which it is in no way incidental that in the end, that supposedly singular Last Man will have a dog by his side." The question of who counts and on what basis was, she astutely concludes, "a problem central to thinking about what it meant to call for a democratic politics in early nineteenth-century England."[50]

Nitchie's account, tinted by the triumphalism of postwar patriotism, presents an excessively rosy portrait of Romantic-era immigration policies. At any rate, the novel's depiction of England's isolation and decline may equally be imagined as a Brexit-like retreat, pulling up the drawbridge on an island nation. But if the novel's suggestiveness poses challenges, that need not undermine the value of these readings. Strang valuably elaborates a deep historical background, looking back to the 1640s, to illuminate the novel's account of "leveling"; her account expands, in turn, upon long-standing questions about governance, population, and species with a view to ever-more acute questions about human exceptionalism. The capacity of *The Last Man* to speak to such different contexts as postwar jubilation and biopolitical governance (and in its own moment, we might conjecture, the squalid lives of the urban poor, or populations of enslaved and formerly enslaved people) speaks to the rich suggestiveness of a novel that, like other great artworks concerned with unrepeatable human predicaments, invokes timeless themes. Recent accounts of the novel have argued for the relevance of other contexts, including the interest of the novel in population limits, failed revolutions, and wide-ranging questions about epidemics and planetary catastrophe. Shelley's novel provides an abundance of footholds for interpretations of this kind. The appearance of a mysterious black cloud opens the book up to the question of climate change as yet a further context in which the novel's concerns with the ending of species may resonate.

Yet not all contexts are created equal. Politics does not just represent one possible context among many. As the critical readings of Nitchie and Strang demonstrate and intuit, there are more specific political contexts at play in *The Last Man*. The book as a whole, beginning with the procedure-heavy opening, concerns itself with what "politics" means and entails. In the first volume, specific political debates dominate: the epidemic does not make an appearance until much later. These respective facets of the novel are woven together – through Spark illuminatingly terms the novel's "symphonic technique"[51] – to create its structure and, ultimately, its aesthetic. The novel's three volumes thereby ask, as a formal question, what these political contests and debates about the restructuring of human society have to do with the eventual dissolution of mankind. At the same time, the novel draws a more literal connection between the onset of the plague and politics. The unraveling of human society, which takes place in tandem with and even hastens on the dismantling of political structures, thereby points toward the novel's contemporary political referents: a complex moment of political transition and specific changes in the realm of what Strang terms "politics proper."[52]

The current vogue for reading Shelley's novel for its treatment of nonhuman animals and interspecies environments may risk eliding the importance of politics. But those readings, with noted exceptions, also risk not taking their own political insights seriously enough, replacing the ecocritical tendency to privilege modes of engagement outside politics with the Anthropocene-informed impulse to confront man as a species. Late Romantic authors including Shelley, by contrast, inhabited a dynamic field of action and agents, in which politics and political institutions were always already in the mix. Like today, brewing challenges to established political structures (and even the prospect of their ending) not only portended anxious uncertainty, but also the prospect of new political futures. The moment at which things begin to unravel presents an opening, however fleeting or qualified, for alternatives. The image of the isolated Byronic dog has limited utility for thinking about how to transform the basis of human community. The novel's sweeping tableaus pose still greater challenges for making sense of a world filled, unlike that of Shelley's novel, with lots of people, including populations liable to face dismissal and neglect. *The Last Man* locates us in an indeterminate, disaster-free space of questioning. Once the plague has taken over, it is too late for politics. But we find alternative options at the thresholds, where nonpolitical worlds rub up against the sovereign spheres of politics, disrupting, uprooting, and overlaying things as they are.

CHAPTER 5

New Worlds
Frankenstein, The Island, *and the Ends of the Earth*

The Spirit of the Age does not begin with a figure drawn from the front lines of parliamentary politics and popular radicalism, nor with a major presence from the literary world. Instead, William Hazlitt's compendium of Romanticism's last men commences with a portrait of Jeremy Bentham. As "one of those persons who verify the old adage, that 'A prophet has most honour out of his own country,'" Hazlitt writes, Bentham's reputation "lies at the circumference; and the lights of his understanding are reflected, with increasing lustre, on the other side of the globe." His name is "little known in England, better in Europe, best of all in the plains of Chili [*sic*] and the mines of Mexico."[1] The jurist, philosopher, and constitution-writer appears, in this portrait, at a pronounced remove from bookish concerns, with the focus instead on his democratic impulses. These features of his identity collide, spectacularly, in an example of his apparent disregard for literary tradition. Bentham's property adjoined that of John Milton. But he would have been content to knock down the poet's house, a scandalized Hazlitt writes, to create "a thoroughfare ... for the idle rabble of Westminster to pass backwards and forwards ... with their cloven hoofs."[2]

The Spirit of the Age presented Bentham as a man detached from politics, at a distance from the reforms he sought, in theory, to hasten. Bentham appears as an aloof, marginal figure, apart from the rowdiness of the hustings or the noise of the tavern, on the shores of politics. Drawing a contrast with Hobhouse (whom he characterized in the same opening pages as a vigorous political campaigner), Hazlitt locates Bentham's reformist spirit at a double-faceted remove from England's political present. For Hazlitt, Bentham's fame was, above all, in the Americas: he had "offered constitutions for the New World." That geographical detachment was bound up with a temporal remove. The portraits in *The Spirit of the Age* feature a wide variety of orientations toward political and historical time, comprising a "proliferation of simultaneities" in Emily Rohrbach's invaluable phrase. Bentham had, the portrait observes, "legislated for future times."[3] But Hazlitt protested too much when he claimed, dismissively, that Bentham had "once ... stuck up a handbill" in Westminster. Bentham was in fact closely involved in the politics of the borough. His stated aspirations included universal suffrage, annual elections, and the abolition of monarchy and aristocracy. This theoretical commitment to "fundamental constitutional change" as a "necessary condition" for making wider political changes coupled with practical involvement in elections.[4] Bentham was also an influential member of the London Greek Committee that helped send Byron on his final journey, in addition to his other ties to global freedom struggles.[5] Yet even as he overstated the division between theory and practice in Bentham's life, Hazlitt neatly captured the ways that differing temporal scales and geographical sites coincided and overlapped in his thinking, such that epoch-defining, world-altering changes mingled together with day-to-day business. Bentham's distance from "personal intrigues, or party politics," his apparent concern with "humanity at large" (over the contents of "bills of mortality"), and his cultivation of a marginal, eccentric role converge in the portrait's most vividly realized tableau. "When any one calls upon him," Hazlitt's sketch concludes, "he invites them to take a turn around his garden ... and there you may see the lively old man, his mind still buoyant with thought and with the prospect of futurity, in eager conversation with some Opposition Member, some expatriated Patriot, or Transatlantic Adventurer, urging the extinction of Close Boroughs, or planning a code of laws for some 'lone island in the watery waste.'"[6]

This chapter extends the geographical scope of this book to the Americas, the South Seas, and the North Pole. In the early nineteenth century, peoples from Spain and Greece to South America pursued independence, seeking to throw off the yokes of the past to claim self-determination and new freedoms. For centuries, contemplating the "New World" had occasioned visions of communal life not bound by existing political structures or other limits on human society. That included theoretical appeals to prepolitical states of nature and practically minded claims about supposedly endless land and resources (often predicated upon the erasure of native peoples and the perpetuation of "Old World" hierarchies).[7] Turning to the ends of the earth in the late Romantic age, I argue in this chapter, permitted authors to engage interrelated scenes of political beginning and ending. That included paradise-like idylls and unspoiled natural scenes but also barren, ruined landscapes, destitute or abandoned populations, and even empty planets. These visions were bound up with changing conceptions of governance and freedom. But they were not only relevant beyond England's shores or within imagined futures. As the case of Bentham demonstrates, legislating for the "New World" and future times rubbed up against reformist agendas and practical politics in the here and now. The dissolution of political institutions in *The Last Man* returned England to a state of nature, pointing to the alternative communities (and even the alternative ecologies) that might take shape following the suspension of politics as usual. This chapter takes up those reflections across a global canvas.

Hazlitt appropriates a line from Alexander Pope's *Essay on Man* as the focus of Bentham's speculations: a "lone island in the watery waste." At least since John Donne and Daniel Defoe, the island has served as an evocative synecdoche for the relationship between individual and collective, isolated men and mankind as a whole. Islands, archipelagoes, and sheets of ice located amidst the "watery waste" of globe-spanning oceans – at once autonomous and loosely connected, isolated and liminal – also function as complex figures for community, upholding and eliding collective identities. Like the image of atomized man, islands and "watery waste[s]" ultimately give way in the writings I examine here to reflections upon the limits of human community. That includes appeals to fluid multiplicity and submerged layers of connection but also scenes hostile to human flourishing: ruined landscapes, abandoned populations, biblical deluges, and empty planets. In the *Essay on Man*, the island is a Native American's fantasized escape. Pope's "poor Indian" conjures the "island in the watry waste" as an imagined place "where slaves once more their native land behold, / No fiends torment, no Christians thirst for gold."[8] Beginning in the 1820s, the Indigenous peoples of North America became the targets of calculated efforts at "lasting," drawing on supposedly ending lines and lone figures.[9] Britain's West Indian colonies occasioned fantasies about the rural peasantry that might replace the rotten, corrupted plantation system. As with Pope's "poor Indian" (and the "slaves" imagined as his counterparts), those debates invoked islands that straddled the present and imagined futures or fantasized pasts. Building upon the colliding visions of political beginning and ending in this book's previous chapters, this chapter asks how the figure of the island offered a means of reflecting upon possible futures for England, mankind, and the planet at large – including futures in which England and the British Isles more widely had no place.

In *The Last Man*, Shelley located her vision of the evacuated nation in a global framework. The novel showed how unspoiled natural scenes might serve as a proxy for perfected government or as rural (pre- or extrapolitical) idylls where new kinds of community become possible. Those aims also converged in Shelley's first novel. *Frankenstein* was concerned with first men but also prefigured its author's later concerns with isolated men in barren landscapes and included its own oblique reflections on politics and political institutions. The creature proposes an escape, with his newly created bride, to South America, casting those "wilds" as an unspoiled, empty wasteland in which he can forge a new life, in what Diana Reese views as a sardonic appeal to "natural man."[10] The ambition to escape from Europe to South America was shared by Byron, who formulated plans to join its independence struggles (along with hopes of becoming a wealthy "planter"). These fantasized itineraries pursued a familiar trajectory: escaping a worn-out continent for alternative vistas and new freedoms. At the same time, they enclosed sophisticated reflections on political change, including the interrelated ascent of liberal constitutionalism and global empire. The same can be said for Byron's final narrative poem. *The Island* imagined the South Seas as the paradisical site of an unspoiled, "Golden Age" society and thus as the inverse of Europe's entrenched institutions, inhumane laws, and corrupting global trade. At the same time, the poem glimpsed another possibility: a world in which England and its institutions simply no longer existed.

Frankenstein and the Ends of the Earth

In the opening chapter of *The Last Man*, Lionel Verney begins his story from a remote location:

> I am the native of a sea-surrounded nook, a cloud-enshadowed land, which, when the surface of the globe, with its shoreless ocean and trackless continents, presents itself to my mind, appears only as an inconsiderable speck in the immense whole; and yet, when balanced in the scale of mental power, far outweighed countries of larger extent and more numerous population. So true it is, that man's mind alone was the creator of all that was good or great to man, and that Nature herself was only his first minister. England, seated far north in the turbid sea, now visits my dreams in the semblance of a vast and well-manned ship, which mastered the winds and rode proudly over the waves. (*LM*, 7)

We encounter Lionel in a condition akin to that of Robinson Crusoe. But there is a crucial difference: this community of one seems to represent the entirety of the human species. England, the center of the world in happier times, continues to rule the waves of Lionel's subconscious life, visiting his dreams as a "vast and well-manned ship." Yet the resurfacing of anglocentric pride here also marks the end of that nation as such – indeed, the end of all nations whatsoever. Charlotte Sussman, reading the novel with a view to its itinerant populations and their cultural memory, sees Shelley commenting upon the borders of national identity. *The Last Man*, in her account, uses the plague to figure the death of the nation. For Lionel, Sussman writes, "England ... becomes a grave for England's corpse" and by locating "England's mortality in her own territory" he "raises the possibility that human community can survive the death of the nation, that it might be remade on a different principle in a different place."[11] My attention here falls on "England" not as a population but as a political entity. The "nation," in my reading, does not die or disperse like a group of people as much as its institutions disband and expire, vanishing (or sinking) without trace. The plague that befalls the world's human population in *The Last Man* leaves the institutions of Shelley's home nation hollowed out, its lands abandoned. While providing qualified glimpses of political renewal, the onset of plague also calls the assumed eminence of England in the wider world into question.

For Lionel, in his island-like retreat, the anchoring global role assumed by England has been replaced by an "inconsiderable speck" whose lone inhabitant counts (in the "scale of mental power") for the entire world. Victor Frankenstein concludes his story in similarly profound isolation. Walton finds Victor in an icy wasteland on an ill-advised voyage to the North Pole, comparing him to the "Ancient Mariner" of Coleridge's poem. Victor later compares his abject state to a "peasant" when "his family have been massacred before his eyes, his cottage burnt, his lands laid waste, and he is turned adrift, homeless, pennyless, and alone, but free," his circumstances here approximating the deracinated subject of an emergent economic liberalism, in a "freedom" of unconstrained movement.[12] They look ahead, too, to the isolated condition of Verney and other destitute and shipwrecked heroes. The lone men lighting out into the darkness at the conclusion of *Frankenstein* not only recur in the lonely figure of the "last man." They also find their symbolic apogee in the final human being: at once the mythic type of a Romantic individualism and the opening onto a speculative posthuman future. Yet the story of Shelley's "Modern Prometheus" is ultimately one of damning failure. For all their apparent similarities, Shelley inflected the destitute figures and evacuated scenes of these two novels with sharply different political significance.

Frankenstein took up questions of origin: the creation of a new species (or "race") and thereby the creation of a new "man." The novel engaged, in turn, with questions about population and propagation: the new beings that might follow, after the creation of a female companion for the creature, and the putatively uninhabited landscapes that might provide their home. Critical discussions have attributed Frankenstein's creation, both the act and its offspring, with multifaceted political significance. In a narrow sense, the book can be read as an allegory of political innovation in the wake of the French Revolution (looking ahead to the tradition of linking *Frankenstein* to reform and mass politics in nineteenth-century England). Shelley's novel was available in these terms to its original readers, Julia Douthwaite proposes, who understood events in France as heralding the creation of a "new man."[13] Critics have seen the monster as figuring the future existence of the proletariat, whose unleashing cannot be controlled by the novel's bourgeois hero; more recent accounts have tied the novel to depictions of slavery.[14] Shelley's mobilization of the Prometheus myth introduces further complications, creating hierarchies between men and gods that map onto immutable lines of class and race.[15] At the same time as Shelley's novel infamously features new kinds of creation – including the male usurping of female reproductive agency – the book also countenances original kinds of death and destruction. Frankenstein's monster not only fantasizes about the death of his creator, after Victor destroys his female companion, but the destruction of mankind – seemingly the first time that such a prospect, the extinction of the human race, a world without man, had been presented as such.[16]

These dynamics take shape and acquire added resonances through the book's geography. Victor grows up in Switzerland, in some of the same scenes traversed by Rousseau, infusing his idyllic upbringing, Douthwaite notes, with the promise originally associated with the French Revolution (and specifically Godwinian ideals).[17] The events of the novel supplement these scenes with encounters on rain-lashed hillsides, in mountain ravines, and finally in the Arctic, where Walton discovers Victor and hears his tragic story. Critics have proposed that the book's geography can accordingly be read as an allegory of the French Revolution, from its bliss-infused European beginnings to its violent collapse amid "fire and ice."[18] When Victor compares his condition to that of a peasant whose cottage has been burned to the ground, he may recall a scene of post-Napoleonic devastation that Shelley had witnessed firsthand.[19] But the novel also includes some additions to – and surprising deviations within – these broad geopolitical coordinates. Despite being a novel about a Swiss-born, German-educated scientist, Victor makes a voyage to England (the origin point for Walton's voyage). After tracking Victor down on his excursion to the Scottish Hebrides, the creature desires his escape to South America, seeking to propagate his kind in that supposed wilderness.[20] From the idyllic rural scenes of Victor's education to his (and Walton's) doomed travels to the ends of the earth, *Frankenstein* stages the tragic fall of its hero in relation to a complex geography, whose added political significance will come into focus by returning briefly to *The Last Man*.

Lionel Verney grows up in the rugged farmland of northern England, where the dethroned Windsors have an estate. Lionel holds the royal family – who had spurned his father and cast him out from the court – responsible for his own poverty and suffering, "bear[ing] evidence in my very person to the ... ingratitude which had made me the degraded being I appeared" (*LM*, 16). He watches the arrival of Adrian in his home county through jaundiced eyes: "With my mind fully occupied by these ideas, I might be said as if fascinated, to haunt the destined abode of the young Earl. I watched the progress of the improvements, and stood by the unlading wagons, as various articles of luxury, brought from London, were taken forth and conveyed to the mansion." After indulging these vengeful, envious sentiments, Lionel finds himself imprisoned after his plans for revenge issue in daring acts of poaching, culminating in a bloody encounter with a groundskeeper. But the landowner takes mercy. Adrian has great delight watching "the tribes of lovely and almost tame animals" on his lands. With similar benevolence, he grants Lionel clemency for his crime and goes on to provide him with an education, appealing to their "hereditary bond of friendship" (*LM*, 20).

This encounter overpowers Lionel. He was not swayed by Adrian's rank, he reassures us, "nor was it I alone who felt thus intimately his perfections: his sensibility and courtesy fascinated every one. His vivacity, intelligence, and the active spirit of benevolence, completed the conquest." These details are cemented by another: "he was deep read and imbued with the spirit of high philosophy" which gave "a stone of irresistible persuasion to his intercourse with others" (*LM*, 20). The novel comes closest here to lauding Percy Shelley. In much the same way that he elevated Godwinian perfectibility as a sacrosanct worldview and program for living, this portrait interweaves political idealism and fellow feeling. As the novel progresses, the initial failure of Adrian to ascend to a position of leadership redirects the novel's political energies, as we have seen (Chapter 4), to Raymond. Yet this early scene also points us to the ways that Adrian's worldview also presents a locus early on for positive political change in the novel. Were he not rescued by Adrian's clemency, we can assume that Lionel might otherwise have become a murderous criminal. Comparing Adrian's "princely magnificence" ("rich carpets and silken hangings, ornaments of gold") to his own "mean dress" and blaming the prince's father for his deceit and "dereliction . . . of all noble sympathy and generous feeling," he imagines these trappings of wealth being "wrenched" away and entertains more darkly violent thoughts as he views the evidence of inequality "with novel and tormenting bitterness." In contrast with Perdita's admiration of Adrian's generosity (if not her outright royalist sympathies), Lionel earlier asserts that he and Adrian "must be enemies" and that the deposed royal "shall learn to dread my revenge!" (*LM*, 17).

Lionel sounds remarkably similar here to the narrative voice in the central section of *Frankenstein*. The creature deems Victor his "adversary," a word that Lionel also uses of Adrian (whom he terms his "unheeding adversary" [*LM*, 18]). His envy for mankind and despair at his abject, wretched condition boil over into murderous hatred, informed by his social dispossession. There are further parallels between the two books. The episode in which Lionel scornfully watches Adrian from the shadows of the forest replays, in reverse, the – literally – central scene from *Frankenstein* where the creature describes his rejection by a family of cottagers, themselves refugees from the French Revolution. Their repulsed reaction turns him from a basically good creature into a vengeful tyrant who burns their cottage to the ground, thereby underscoring what Percy Shelley, for one, saw as the book's core moral: that society creates its own monsters. *The Last Man* revisits this dynamic, further amplifying its class dimension. Lionel's resentment is ramped up to an almost parodic degree ("I will not suffer like a spaniel!" [*LM*, 18]) and serves, in turn, to accentuate the goodness of Adrian, whose generosity and benevolence not only defuse his anger but convert him, over time, into a strenuous advocate of this worldview. In *Frankenstein*, England and its supposed freedoms serve, by contrast, as an ironic double for the dark failure of Victor's hopes – and his British travels see him destroy the female companion demanded by his creature.[21] *The Last Man* effectively reverses and recuperates the trajectory of Shelley's earlier novel, permitting its burned-out revolutionary ideals and tarnished idealisms to find a home, fleetingly, in the rugged English countryside.

Frankenstein contained its own glimpses of revolutionary idealism. The implication behind its geographic plotting may be that in a perfectly organized world, like that of the childhood idyll enjoyed by Victor, evil would never be created. But *Frankenstein* presents a grim picture of collapsing hopes, bringing the story of the dispossessed monster together with that of Victor and drawing both into a tragic, downward spiral. That plot, which takes shape over a widening global canvas, skewers male romantic ambition and contrasts the neglect of female domesticity and family with destructive Romantic individualism and scientific or political hubris.[22] *Frankenstein* also shows a world spiraling into ruin and destruction. Victor's brother is murdered at the gates of his Swiss town, and his friend Clerval is murdered in Ireland. The destruction of the creature's female companion during Victor's trip to Scotland aborts his hopes to procreate in South America, launching the narrative on its final journey to the North Pole. In Victor's comparison of himself to a ravaged "peasant" and the monster's plans to escape to South America, the legacies of a corrupt "Old World" and the ruinous pursuit of the "New World" emerge as two sides of the same coin.[23]

The 1832 Reform Bill was cast as its own version of Frankenstein's "monster": a dangerous new innovation that promised to end in destruction once the masses were given political sway, with related images and tropes casting the enfranchised body politic as its own monstrous entity, cut loose and set free. We might equally connect the dynamics presented in Shelley's novel, I suggested in Chapter 3, with legislation passed the following year: the Emancipation Bill that promised to end slavery in the British Empire. The British nation, like Victor Frankenstein, sought to run away from and abandon the life its actions had created. Shelley had, with her husband, voiced ardent antislavery sympathies; the monster's self-description as a "slave" may inflect his plight with those associations. The history of American colonization and its afterlives may equally inflect the imagined voyage to the Americas within *Frankenstein* itself. The prospect of an escape to a supposedly empty wasteland offers a last-ditch solution. But the same destructive, scorched-earth logics, Shelley can be seen to imply, will be perpetuated in that imagined wilderness, extended to the attrition of human and nonhuman life. The arrival of Victor at the North Pole confirms this sense of exhaustion and ruin, concluding the book with a vision of the ends of the earth that – read alongside other writings by the Byron circle – presents an oblique glance at the end of the planet.

In *The Last Man*, the North American continent becomes diseased before England, precluding the possibility of a westward escape from the outset. By way of Ireland, inhabitants of Britain's former colonies return to the mother country in search of safety, but become violent marauders. At the same time, as we saw in the previous chapter, Shelley shows how a version of American democracy, combining Godwinian political ideals and Benthamite reform with the return to an expansively imagined rural existence, may provide the prospects for renewal nearer home. But those hopes take shape amidst a growing emphasis on empty landscapes, albeit not entirely unhospitable ones. Early in the book, a resentful Lionel takes some solace from his environment: "each cottage rang with the praises of Adrian ... [but] looking on the sterile rocks about me, [I] exclaimed – '*They* do not cry, long live the Earl!'" (*LM*, 17). These encounters with unspoiled scenes and worlds untouched by man reverberate with a strangely indeterminate political significance. (What might the rocks in fact "cry" back to the world of politics?) The natural scenes in *The Last Man* have all the more resonance when situated in the context of a world where borders have dissolved and nations disbanded. Aside from the fantasized plague, the book thereby provides qualified glimpses of what starting over might look like. While the book does not invest much in Percy Shelley politically (and casts him, at times, as a rather pathetic and cloying figure), Shelley keeps a version of his philosophy alive. But she does so, critically, on the condition that the men embodying his ideals recede from view, disappearing into the foliage or receding to the status of an echoing voice in a barren landscape. *Frankenstein*, by contrast, leaves no such hope. While vindicating, in the abstract, the messages about goodness promoted by her father and husband, Shelley's novel offers no scenes for prospective flourishing. The only escape from the ruined Europe depicted by the book promises its own destruction – by following an itinerary borrowed not from the wan and idealistic Shelley, but from the spirited and impetuous Byron.

New Worlds in *The Island*

"There is no freedom in Europe," Byron wrote in 1819, describing the continent as "a worn out portion of the globe." He voiced plans to seek out a new home in Australia, presumably an ironic suggestion given its emerging reputation as a penal colony. However, his attentions turned more frequently to the Americas. In his remarks on the exhausted, "worn out" status of Europe, Byron celebrated South America as the only remaining site of freedom: he wanted "a country – and a home – and if possible – a free one." Describing the Anglo-Americans as "a little too coarse," he wondered if he could get letters to "Boliver [*sic*] and his government."[24] Byron contemplated political activity nearer home, including England, Spain, and, ultimately, Greece. These imagined itineraries coincided with a temperament that, while volatile as ever, was dulled by a growing sense of malaise and decline. "Exercise & excitement seemed nessessary [*sic*] for both his body – & mind," Trelawny wrote to Hobhouse in 1824, but "both seemed declining in his long inactive and secluded way of living in the south – he became peevish – sickly & indifferent and disenchanted with every thing – he acknowledged this – and I continually urged him with new plans." Trelawny found him a yacht ("for he was always fond of the sea"). But growing weary of this idea, Byron entertained plans of South America "& took some steps for that purpose." He then turned his attentions to North America, "& from repeated & pressing invitation from thence he seemed determined to go their [*sic*]." They had everything prepared, Trelawny claimed, "though this was much against my wishes – as I believed it was the country least suited to him!"[25] But delays materialized. In the meantime, the Greek War of Independence had surfaced as a new locus for his energies. Byron's long-standing partiality to that nation, his ties with Italian revolutionaries, and solicitations from the London Greek Committee led him to his final destination.

The year that Byron embarked for Greece saw the composition and publication of his final narrative poem, *The Island* (1823), which tells the story of the "Mutiny of the Bounty." Following expeditions by Captain Cook earlier in the eighteenth century, Lieutenant William Bligh undertook a series of voyages to the islands of the South Seas, including present-day Tahiti. Aided by botanist Joseph Banks, Bligh sought to collect samples of the native breadfruit (a hearty staple, on whose name Byron punned *ad nauseam*). In 1789, the crew of the Bounty rose up against Bligh, casting him out on the waves – the initiating event of Byron's poem. But *The Island* has other concerns than the mutiny and its aftermath, focusing instead on the perpetrators of the rebellion, the island's people and culture, flora and fauna. Alongside his other planned escapes, Byron had said he meant "to obtain by purchase, or otherwise, some small island in the South Sea, to which . . . he might retire for the remainder of his life." In his poem, the mutineers return to the eponymous island, which the poem casts as a refuge from the outside world. As if in fulfillment of Byron's own desires to escape a corrupted world and its degrading institutions, the island stands as a self-enclosed idyll, outside time.[26]

So it seems, at least. But *The Island* complicates this idealized picture with probing questions about the basis of human society, beginning with its economic foundations. As Tobias Menely has demonstrated, poets from Milton to Charlotte Smith recognized that growing use of carbon-based fuel portended permanent alteration of the Earth's system. The beginnings of capitalism (and thus the origins of the modern-day climate crisis) appear in georgic poetry and its allegorical and lyric counterparts, Menely shows, as reflections on the changing conditions of planetary life. Byron's poem can be seen to engage related questions. But poetic attention falls here on the *absence* of energy transfer and commodity exchange. For the people of Byron's island, "shells, their fruits" are "the only wealth they know." The only resources tapped here are those that grow plentifully on the Earth's surface, locating the island outside cycles of extraction, exhaustion, and exchange. Rather than mining resources to propel endless global trade, Byron's island basks in its own self-sustaining equipoise. Beneath the fires of Milton's hell, Menely contends, was the unleashing of fossil fuels from within the Earth's surface (a darkly damaging counterpart to self-sustaining solar energy).[27] But in *The Island*, buried resources and violent extraction are replaced by endless, inexhaustible wealth, all out in the open: "The Earth, *whose mine was on its face*, unsold / The glowing sun and produce all its gold."[28] Before the corrupting influence of trade and the despoiling of the landscape can take hold, *The Island* cuts them off, at the root.

The simple world of *The Island* recalls Byron's recent treatment of the American wilderness in *Don Juan*. In Canto VIII of that poem, composed the previous year, Byron describes Daniel Boon (the "back-woodsman of Kentucky") as the head of a "sylvan tribe" (VIII.65). In addition to erasing Indigenous peoples, Byron's idealized account of Boon seems almost self-consciously to engage the stereotypical accounts of the "New World" superimposed over the realities of American settlement. But his treatment of Boon's "tribe" also captures an elusive moment of potential, at the cusp between the original encounter and violent settlement. "Simple they were, not savage," Byron writes of Boon's followers, "and their rifles, / Though very true, were not yet used for trifles" (VIII.66). Byron pointedly under-scores the reality of violence here. The "true" rifles are, we can infer, tried and tested. But he also suspends the prospect of endless trade and its accompanying violence. Byron's rhyme sets up the prospective exchange of "rifles" for "trifles" and thus the perpetuation of that cycle. But the poem suspends its movement: exchange has "not yet" supplanted a world in which "the free-born forest found and kept them free, / And fresh as is a torrent or a tree" (VIII.65). The gun-like mechanism that slots "rifles" into "trifles" gives way here to a pleasing bristle: "free-born," "forest," "free," "fresh," "tree." Byron echoed these lines in *The Island*, whose so-called savage inhabitants, he reminds us, live a life characterized by a similarly desirable simplicity and freedom. In *The Island*, natural abun-dance effects an even more absolute suspension of trade, arresting the very prospect of exchange in the enjoyable torpor expressed by Byron's languid poetic language.

In tandem with its abandonment of global commerce, *The Island* revisits fundamental questions about sovereignty and law. Returning to the island helps the mutineers to reshape their ingrained assumptions about hierarchy and governance. Byron expressly disapproves of the mutineers and their "Saturnalia of unhoped-for power" (1.84).[29] But as the poem follows the mutiny's perpetrators back to the island, they achieve a qualified redemption. Tarquil, one of the men, engages in an erotic tryst with a local woman, Neuha. While ultimately doomed, that encounter stands in for a larger process of adaptation and acclimatization. The native breadfruit has a key role in this eroticized ecosystem. Allowing for life without work, the crop ("procurd with no more trouble than that of climbing a tree and pulling it down," in Banks's words) creates abundant time for other pursuits and thus allows for bliss without end.[30] The poem brings these aspects of island life together in an "amalgam of Hesiod's idyllic age of gold with the primitive condition of mankind as envisaged by Rousseau half a century before."[31] Earlier depictions of Tahiti had engaged dubious notions of noble savagery and female availability.[32] Byron engaged related ideas (albeit with a greater sense of self-awareness) and risked casting Tahitian society as a blank slate, without agential subjects or existing power structures.[33] Yet, while saturated by well-worn myths and clichéd tropes, Byron's island differs in important ways from its precursors. His island is not a fantastical escape but an emphatically real place, in which the men make a new life, on the edge of the "known" world. Whatever its accuracy, Byron set out not to imagine a utopia outside but a space within time, another world within this one.

Rather than an unfallen Eden or a fantasized utopia, then, Byron's island describes a real place whose ecology sees the plentiful breadfruit simply grow in the beams of the sun, whose solar energy "bakes its unadulterated loaves / Without a furnace in unpurchased groves" (1.161–2). The trade routes of global commerce nonetheless supply added levels of significance to the poem's location. In the real-life events behind *The Island*, the overthrow of Bligh interrupts a planned voyage to the West Indies. The breadfruit was not merely a self-replenishing curiosity. For Cook and Banks, the discovery of this abundantly growing crop offered a prospective solution to hunger. Bligh sought to transport the breadfruit from the South Seas to the West Indies. His voyage was thereby in the service of slavery, as this transplant to the Caribbean ecosystem became, in practice, a means of perpetuating the use of enslaved labor: botanical fuel for slavery's ruthless biopolitics. Coleridge, Southey, and other Romantics heatedly took issue with Banks's proposal, casting "a network that tied free Tahiti to the enslaved West Indies" as one that "united science with tyranny." Byron can be seen to follow these precursors.[34] But his poem gives these concerns with corrupt modern institutions and complicity with slavery a different inflection. *The Island* focuses upon a *break* in the cycle, addressing not the prospective fulfillment of Banks's scheme but the world that takes shape after its failure.

The poem's emphasis on a self-replenishing, labor-free ecosystem has a counterpart in its aesthetic. *The Island* is a self-consciously minor work. The poem afforded Byron an opportunity to poeticize the lush scenes described in a travel narrative that he admired. Modulating between the scathing tone of his recent satire *The Age of Bronze* (a panoramic attack on Europe, in the wake of the Congress of Verona) and his qualified indulgence of current tastes for "poesy," he adopted an aesthetic register that he characterized as "tameness" in a letter to Leigh Hunt. The poem can thus be seen to mark a waning, or plateauing, of Byron's poetic powers. The poem's fantasies of female availability and languid bliss may, relatedly, be seen as rather lazily indulging (if not promoting) stereotypical images of native women. But the poem also witnesses Byron's cultivation of a newly low-key poetic register, one that echoes and builds upon features of his early poetry. The new poetical itineraries explored in *The Island* thus only emerge fully, I propose, when we conceive of the paradise imagined in the poem as opening out into a complex vision of the political future. That means locating the world imagined by the poem in relation to the world left behind, while also recognizing that its multifaceted significance proves inextricable from its serene but subtly layered aesthetic.

As with the earliest voyages to the New World, travels in the South Seas were shaped by exploratory hubris. From the outset of the poem, Byron casts an eye askance on the ambition of its male political figures (which include, both de facto and de jure, the last Byronic hero). Byron may not expressly disapprove of Bligh. But this "gallant Chief" first appears as a kind of mirror image of Walton, the opening narrator of *Frankenstein*. Where Walton seeks out the North Pole, Bligh seeks out the "arctic sun" of the Southern hemisphere (1.169) and, adopting the "glorious role" of those "who search the storm-surrounded pole," looks back to Europe, dreaming of "Old England's welcome shore" (1.18, 20). Defined by his ties to the British Isles, Bligh echoes Byron, who understood his travels abroad through the lens of his Scottish childhood and the novels of Walter Scott.[35] Later the same decade, *The Last of the Lairds* by John Galt (1826)

and *The Last of the Mohicans* (1826) used lone men to meditate on the end
of dying lineages, as did Scott's genealogical romances. Those books were
concerned with supposedly expiring ways of life. But their reflections on
lastness converged with a growing emphasis on intrepid exploration –
together with a ballooning cast, in fiction and reality, of colonizers and
missionaries. Those "first" and "last" men, braving the seas for faraway
lands or new frontiers, find parallels in the captain and crew of the
"Bounty." As the nineteenth century went on, those identities took
shape in the context of imperialist conquest and an ever-expanding global
empire.

Edward Bulwer-Lytton, the former dandy elected in 1831 as a radical
MP, was the author of *Pelham* (1828) and other political satires. Between
The Last Days of Pompeii (1834) and *The Coming Race* (1871), Bulwer-
Lytton became the bestselling novelist of the period and – in line with
the Victorian age's growing imperial ambitions – was invested in imagining muscular, British-born conquerors. His historical sagas and adventure
stories included attention to antecedent conquests *within* the British Isles.
In *Harold, the Last of the Saxon Kings* (1848), Bulwer-Lytton rehearsed
claims that many English people had both Saxon and Scandinavian ancestors. In an unfinished novel, he described the English "race" as those who
"hope, combat, strive, succeed, everywhere – in the city, in the wild, under
the tropics, at the pole." As "colonizers," these men were, he wrote,
"arrogant in the power of self-government, restless from the longing of
unbounded range" and ready to discover and settle in "new worlds."[36] *The
Island* mobilized related mythologies, activating an awareness of earlier
histories of voyaging and conquest within Britain, describing Torquil as
a "blue-eyed northern child" and "the fair-haired offspring of the
Hebrides" and characterizing him as an inhabitant of "isles more known
to man, but scarce less wild" (11.163–5).[37] Bligh, meanwhile, appears as
a feared, respected "Chief" in terms that glance toward Native Americans.

In the Victorian age, ancestral British identities – including, as Kerstin
Petersen has shown, the qualified rehabilitation of Viking "blood" –
bolstered imperial claims to colonial stewardship and violent conquest.[38]
The Romantic age was already seeing British and especially Scottish administrators assert control in the imperial arena, tightening the Empire's hold
over the Indian subcontinent. Read with hindsight, *The Island* cannot fully
escape these emerging logics. But Byron ultimately subverts and dislocates
them. Rather than affirming racialized hierarchies, moreover, he sets out to
challenge their grasp. Byron had already begun to look askance on the
racialized identities that underpinned supposed British superiority. In *Don*

Juan, Joselyn M. Almeida proposes, he destabilized the epic genre's "formal logic" and the "concept of blood purity that legitimizes both patriarchal and racialist systems" as well as "transmission processes that reproduce and legitimize the legal, political, and exclusionary systems of the state."[39] In *The Island,* Byron was similarly concerned to challenge incipient racial myths and emergent imperial practices. Far from reinforcing or promoting claims of innate superiority, the poem goes out of its way to *de*naturalize conquest. Men may still be on top here, but Byron rejects ideas of blood purity promoted by Lytton and his Victorian successors to emphasize other kinds of lineage and affinity. Torquil's origin in the rugged isles of Scotland (and behind that, Scandinavia or Iceland) does not reinforce his claims to superiority. Rather, Byron uses his background to assert, through emphatic use of anaphora, an *equivalence* with his native love interest, Neuha:

> Both children of the isles, though distant far;
> Both born beneath a sea-presiding star;
> Both nourished amidst Nature's native scenes,
> Lov'd to the last, whatever intervenes.

> (11.274–7)

To be sure, this is not an equal partnership, whether in terms of brute strength or imperial power, and these "wild" origins may equally operate in the service of a civilizing mission. Appreciation for the "noble savage" need not stand in the way of conquest; that designation may in fact accelerate dispossession.[40] But the binaries that sustain these dynamics become pliant in Byron's poem, these distinctions smudged and submerged as the isolated condition of the titular island loosens up, relativizing ties to and between islands back "home."

That smoothing away of division continues as the poem takes up the hoary notion that "rude" societies are more "civilized." *The Island* presents a familiar amalgam of unspoiled scenes, noble savagery, and primitive sophistication. But while perfectly amenable to the naturalizing of conquest, those tropes give rise, in Byron's hands, to clever and playful reversals. The beneficial influence of the island upon Torquil ultimately does "more than Europe's discipline had done, / And civilized Civilization's son!" (11.270–1), and the abundant virtues of this secluded paradise occasion, in turn, critical reflections back on Europe. That contrast gives way to a further deconstruction of old and new worlds:

> The Old World more degraded than the New, –
> Now *new* no more, save where Columbia rears
> Twin giants, born by Freedom to her spheres,

Where Chimborazo, over air, earth, wave,
Glares with his Titan eye, and sees no slave.

(II.74–8)

These lines recall the treatment of history's relentless cycles in *Childe Harold's Pilgrimage* and, more recently, *The Age of Bronze*. In that latter satire, Byron used the Congress of Verona to issue a damning conclusion about recent turns in global politics, which had created an age of perpetual bloody war anchored by the emboldening of reactionary and imperialistic European states. *The Island* would seem to issue in a similar picture of a "degraded" world. But the poem does not set out to belabor the degeneracy and barbarism of Europe at large (or the corruptions of England in particular). These lines also describe a process of gradual, sequential uprooting and change. The "Old World" had been supplanted by "the New." But now *that* world ("*new* no more") confronts assertions of South American freedom. The account of Tarquil's being "civilized," similarly, need not be understood as an inversion – and thus recapitulation – of the binary logic of civilization and barbarism, but as a reinvention. Read in light of the earlier lines identifying him and Neuha as "both children of the isles," the ironized "discipline" of the island restores him to an earlier version of himself, hearkening back to his *own* island roots while also making him anew.

Britain's slave colonies challenged simplistic distinctions between old and new worlds, coupling archaic kinds of hereditary bondage with new guises of violence and terror. Challenges to Britain's role in perpetuating the use of enslaved labor led to contested visions of the worlds that might follow from abolition and emancipation. The year that Byron wrote *The Island* saw the founding of the new antislavery organization committed to the "extinction" of slavery. The premise behind the Society for the Mitigation and Gradual Abolition of Slavery Throughout the British Dominions was that slavery would, with the proper sequence of measures, be softened and displaced. That gave rise, as we saw in Chapter 3, to competing and contradictory visions of slavery's ending. The transition beyond slavery was imagined as a gradual, peaceful withering away. But a newly constituted polity, with enslaved people at the center, could only look like a utopian fantasy (and one widely feared as a dystopian threat). The enslaved populations of the Caribbean risked, in turn, being forgotten or rendered invisible. But in a more open-ended imagining of the future, the entire globe could be envisaged as a clean slate, in which all governmental institutions and existing versions of politics were pulled up root and branch. In Byron's poem and its intersecting geographies, these equivocal endings and newly dawning horizons take on freshly charged significance.

In *The Island*, Byron "embraces the breadfruit," one study has proposed, "to display his conscious opposition not only to slave colonies" – where Bligh sought to transport the fruit as food for enslaved persons – "but to the reactionary turn taken by former liberals in Britain." The poem's reclaiming of the breadfruit thus condemns slavery while mounting a critique of the colonizing turn taken by Byron's Romantic predecessors (whose opposition to the "vices of cultivated society" bled into their embrace of missionary efforts that sought to bring the wider world into line with Western norms).[41] Byron had his own axes to grind with Southey, whose "Church and King" nationalism fed into the "muscular Christianity" shaping British imperialism and its missionary efforts.[42] But beyond these localized antipathies, these wider geographies allow us to see the added resonance of the poem's newly imagined world. While the poem does not allude to Britain's slave colonies directly, the breadfruit scheme means they are silently present as a site in which (as contemporary debates in parliament make clear) the prospect of new worlds had urgent stakes. Byron's poem activates these and other resonances in locating the three sets of islands, Pacific, Caribbean, and British, in relation to each other.[43] The new horizons that become discernible at the ends of the earth are thus intimately related to the changing ends of politics. In practice, that would issue in new phases of imperialism and national supremacy. But in Byron's poem, their entanglement becomes the occasion for an equivocal hope, predicated not upon England bolstering its power but on the nation receding from view.

In a more emphatic version of the dynamics staged in *The Last Man*, Byron's poem suspends and silences the influence of England and its institutions. In *The Island*, the home country and "Old World" are not critiqued or dismantled as much as they are deprived of their presumed centrality and importance. These entities and the global systems that extend their reach are simply forgotten, fading without trace. Byron does not follow the unceremoniously removed captain and his crew on their subsequent voyages but releases them instead into vacant emptiness and scenes that recall "Darkness." But the momentary grimness notwithstanding ("The ills that lessened still their little store, / And starved even Hunger till he wrung no more"), the poem once again proves the polar opposite of that paired text. Where "Darkness" hollows out all visions of communal life, from society and its institutions to the very material infrastructure of the shared world, *The Island* instead asks the reader to reflect on what kinds of new world(s) might emerge through vacancy and emptiness, by the stripping away and even swallowing up of what came before.

That includes the disappearance of politics – and property. The mutineers are criminals, at least under English law. But returning to the island, they reclaim an earlier innocence:

> Once more the happy shores without a law
> Receive the outlaws whom they lately saw;
> Nature, and Nature's goddess – Woman – woos
> To lands where, save their conscience, none accuse.
>
> (1.209–12)

By contrast with the kind of eternal marking staged in the biblical story of Cain, the mutineers' earlier crimes become moot as they are accepted anew by the inhabitants of the island. The lines quoted here imagine a Miltonic paradise, prior to the formation of biblically informed law; they also draw on ideas of primitive goodness, inverting violent accounts of the "state of nature" (and introducing something closer to the simple Indians of Pope's *Essay on Man*). These lines are ground zero for arguments about the poem's indulgence of stereotypes about the wantonness of native women. But pausing to listen more closely also reveals Byron's poetics seeking to undo binary divisions between the respective worlds of the island peoples and the prospective colonists. Beyond the jurisdiction of English courts, the mutineers are literally outside the law. Byron does not let us forget that they are piratical lawbreakers and general lowlifes. But the efforts to spatialize these divisions (as the "outlaws" arrive in a land "without a law" where "none accuse") give way under the sonic rendering of the pleasing scenes ("happy shores" where "Woman woos") to become a kind of pleasing, babbling, seminonsense, as *laws* give way to *shores* in which *outlaws* cannot be *accused* even as they are *wooed*. This is not a fantastical world in which crime or sin have never existed. Instead, the forgetting of England effects an undoing of prior identities, even as they confront a people, Byron makes sure to tell us, with an indwelling "conscience" to guide them.

The women may be said to dissolve the men in *The Island*. That dynamic reaches its apotheosis in the poem's famed concluding watery sex scene. From an outside perspective, the island represents a putatively "feminine" othered and othering space. But whatever essentialism may be at play in these wider discourses – in ways that would have a persistent influence in colonialism as in Byron's personal life – the poem, on its own terms, renders lushly welcoming erotic terrain.[44] If the women serve to unman the men, that unmanning presents less of a threat when British-formed male identities not only have less pull but no meaning. *The Island* imagines the kind of alternative community that might flourish in the space of suspension and forgetting – from letting go. In the process, the poem represents an important node in the fusion between Byron's poetry and his political thought. *The Island* has seemed like an outlier next to the final cantos of *Don Juan* and his various works on biblical themes, including *Cain* and *Heaven and Hell*. But the poem belongs squarely alongside those late writings, I propose, not least given the references to Noah's ark and the poem's debt to Milton. *The Island* acquires further resonances next to Byron's imagined itineraries for his future political life, helping to situate his draw toward the Americas and the ambiguous disappearances associated with his subsequent turn to Greece. At the same time, the poem points to a further set of images and themes that reverberate throughout Byron's final writings. The prospect of giving way to the "watery waste" courses through these late works, in which releasing a hold on human identity, individual life, and even the species as such acquires acute political significance, as images of nations and islands give way to other collectivities and the world gives way to the waves.

The Island joins with *The Last Man* in its concern with the dismantling of institutions and dissolution of identities. Beyond similarities of theme, Shelley's novel also owes a pronounced (if ambient) debt to the aesthetics of Byron's poem, which she had copied out in manuscript two years before writing her own novel.[45] *Paradise Lost* hangs over the exilic narrative of *The Last Man*, providing its epigraph. But the novel also, in some sense, plays out a *return* to Eden. Byron's poem has its own densely intertextual relationship with Milton. Given Shelley's recent engagement with *The Island*, we might view both poems, Milton's and Byron's, as crucial works within the novel's compositional matrix, themselves inextricable from each other. Byron's island, that is to say, mediated Milton's paradise and thereby helped to shape the aesthetics of *The Last Man*. Shelley's novel helps us, in turn, to reread *The Island*. The landscapes described in the poem may resemble Byron's Greece in Polynesian dress, as at least one critic has noted. But in these early lines, Byron wonderfully melds Miltonic Edens and pastoral idylls with the unspoiled scenes that come from abandoning – or simply forgetting – Europe's failed paradises for the "world" of these open waters:

> The waters with *their world* were all before;
> Behind, the South Sea's many an islet shore.

> The quiet night, now dappling, 'gan to wane,
> Dividing darkness from the dawning main;
> The dolphins, not unconscious of the day,
> Swam high, as eager of the coming ray;
> The stars from broader beams began to creep,
> And lift their shining eyelids from the deep.
>
> (1.5–12, emphasis added)[46]

These lines allude to the conclusion of *Paradise Lost*, in which the "world was all before" our ancestral parents in their banishment from paradise. They also invoke Homeric images of long-thirsted-for islands. Yet Byron, reversing the course of biblical exile and heroic quests, presents a scene of intuitive contact between humans, nonhuman creatures, and their environment. Byron sounds like Pope, in related lines, as he conjures a scene untrod by prior human influence: "The courteous manners but from nature caught, / The wealth unhoarded and the love unbought." To recover these tendencies, one needs to shed the influence of "Our means, our birth, our nation, and our name, / Our fortune, temper, even our outward frame" and succumb to "our yielding clay." A voice can still be heard within, whatever land we tread or creed we are taught, which Byron identifies as "conscience" (the "oracle of God!")[47] These redeemed colonizers are tied to the unspoiled natives through a kind of natural law. But Byron's poetic sensorium-cum-aquarium also points to something else: the return of mankind to a shared creaturely condition, sustained by its own justice.

A Sinking Island: Poetry and the Ends of Literature

Despite efforts to hold his earliest poetic persona at a remove, Childe Harold's travels became inextricable from his author's wayward movements and turbulent emotions. That included Byron's early attraction – voiced in poems about the craggy mountains of Scotland – to exile and escape. As the sight of shore gives way, Harold strums a harp and bids farewell to England:

> "Welcome, welcome, ye dark-blue waves!
> And when you fail my sight,
> Welcome, ye deserts, and ye caves!
> My native Land – Good Night!"[48]

Childe Harold's Pilgrimage established geographic and aesthetic itineraries that would continue to shape Byron's life and writings. The welcoming of "waves," "deserts," and "caves," eddying currents of loss, and poignant attachments to ruined pasts all continued to be felt, this book has argued, both in Byron's writings and those of Mary Shelley (an ardent reader and transcriber of *Childe Harold's Pilgrimage*). At the same time, the two writers' shared aesthetic concerns came to include the changing ends of politics, extending to visions of the end of politics and the end of the world as such. In Byron's late writings these concerns with loss and lastness converged to shape his parting reflections on the ends of literature. Byron's final writings supply a further twist to Harold's vision of his "native Land" giving way to a darkening sky and expanding sea: the prospect of the English nation and its people sinking without trace.

In the second canto of *The Island*, Byron delightfully intermixes a translated Polynesian song with Popean rhymed couplets. In the process, he collapses an argument against militarism with an argument for poetry. "A boy Achilles, with the Centaur's lyre" singing a ballad "rung from the rock, or mingled with the wave, / Or from the bubbling streamlet's grassy side" has greater power, these lines assert, than "all the columns Conquest's minions rear" (11.85, 88, 92).[49] Poetry, removed from political barbarism, is identified with natural features: rocks, waves, and streams. Byron's use of an actual song here built upon a precedent established in *Childe Harold's Pilgrimage*, which adapted Albanian and Greek folk music. *Childe Harold* casts a jaundiced eye upon destructive cycles of conquest, which elicit its hero's plaintive woes and the poem's wider reckoning with diminished hopes for the future. *The Island* localizes the primitive power of verse to its Pacific setting, as the "freshest bud of Feeling's soil." Byron thereby underscores the unspoiled, innocent qualities of this hidden paradise by contrast with Europe. But he goes on to claim that *all* poetry harbored, at one point, this potential for fresh beginnings: "Such was this rude rhyme," Byron writes (adding that "rhyme is of the rude"): "But such inspired the Norseman's solitude, / Who came and conquer'd." The will to violent conquest had its origin, these lines claim, in the poetic pursuit of new horizons. Byron's winking reference to the "rude" nature of "rhyme" locates his couplets in the same category. But decoupled from the history of conquest and repressive cycles of violence, poetry maintains the potential to alter the world for the better, aspiring to the condition of inspirational change: "And sweetly now that untaught melodies / Broke the luxurious silence of the skies" (11.103–4). These lines from *The Island* imagine a kind of primitive poetry that dissolves all prior language: babbling and bubbling, mingling back with the elements. But in contrast with the "unheard melodies" sealed within the past by Keats's urn, these "*untaught* melodies" infuse poetic utterance with rapturous, if not also rupturing potential – breaking open the "luxurious silence of the skies" to create richly tinted new horizons.

Byron wrote *Hints from Horace* during the same travels that inspired *Childe Harold's Pilgrimage* and conceived of the poem as an imagined sequel to *English Bards, Scotch Reviewers*, his scathing attack on the entire literary establishment. As its title suggests, *Hints from Horace* eschews Juvenalian harshness for an urbane posture and mellow tone. The poem contains piercing insights into the literary establishment but also adopts a supple, malleable, adaptable view of language:

> New words find credit in these latter days,
> If neatly grafted on a Gallic phrase;
> What Chaucer, Spenser did, we scarce refuse
> To Dryden's, or to Pope's maturer muse.
> If you can add a little, say, why not?
> As well as William Pitt and Walter Scott;
> Since they by force of rhyme and force of lungs
> Enrich'd our islands' ill-united tongues;
> 'Tis then, and shall be, lawful to present
> Reforms in writing, as in Parliament.[50]

Byron locates the capacity to coin new words (or at least "graft" onto foreign ones) in the literary past. In his own belated time, "these latter days," such inventions seem more dubious. But the English language, no less than English politics, remains cheerfully amenable ("why not?") to reinvention. Taking cues from Pitt's forceful vocal performances in parliament and Scott's archaic romances and plaintive lays, Byron identifies "Reforms" with a continuous, enriching process, driven by an ongoing motor of vocally expressed change, twice referred to as a "force."

In referring to that "force," Byron may have an eye on its legal basis: the force of law that, when claimed by foundational political documents and rulers, wrested politics out from a state of nature. That word may equally, with its forward propulsion, register the dynamic and unstoppable nature of change. But whether inevitable as sovereign decree or the product of nature's random swerves, Byron goes on to conjoin this newness with a sense of fadedness. As with the new republic in Shelley's *The Last Man*, these "Reforms" bud only to immediately pale, petrify, and turn to dust:

> As forests shed their foliage by degrees,
> So fade expressions, which in season please;
> And we and ours, alas! are due to fate,
> And works and words but dwindle to a date;

Though as a monarch nods, and commerce calls,
Impetuous rivers stagnate in canals;
Though swamps subdued, and marshes drain'd, sustain
The heavy ploughshare and the yellow grain,
And rising ports along the busy shore
Protect the vessel from old Ocean's roar; –
All, all, must perish; *but, surviving last,*
The love of letters half preserves the past;
True – some decay, *yet not a few revive,*
Though those shall sink, which now appear to thrive,
As custom arbitrates, whose shifting sway
Our life and language must alike obey.

(89–104, emphasis added)

This meditation on the passage of time has a mixed valence. The ability of "letters" to withstand the passage of time (only a "half"-preservation in the first place) remains equivocal. While "some decay," Byron writes, "not a few revive, / Though those shall sink, which now appear to thrive." Yet he leaves us uncertain whether revival supplants the sinking, or vice versa. The line might appear to suggest that some works will "revive" *even though* presently thriving works will, in many cases, sink. But the lines also permit a less optimistic reading, affirming that "not a few" will revive *while also* observing that those books that now "appear to thrive" (the ones that were "revive[d]") shall, still, "sink." Accepting the former reading does not preclude sinking from ultimately winning out: "not a few" (but maybe not all that many) will "revive," only for more (and ultimately all of them) to "sink." Byron's lines grant special power to natural elements subdued by man's influence, here canals and drained farmlands. But while the "monarch" and "commerce" may do their best to stem the tide, the "force of rhyme and force of lungs" has been replaced, here, by "impetuous rivers" and "Ocean's roar." Byron sounds an ambivalent but decisively pessimistic downward slide in Horace's lines. That sense of decline only intensified as his life and writings went on. When Byron voiced these sentiments, in the years of *Childe Harold*, the prospect of repressive cycles being broken was at least on the horizon, while some investments, like Byron's attachments to the Whig elite and aristocratic nostalgia, still maintained a hold. But then came his interrelated personal disappointments and political disillusionment, against the backdrop of continent-wide reaction and dwindling outlets for freedom. As Byron reached his later years, these already chastened hopes gave way to the prospect of everything, "life and language," new and old, politics and literature, being swept away or sinking without trace. The claim that "love of letters half preserves the past" looked more and more like wishful thinking.

Byron returned to *Hints from Horace* in the 1820s. As he continued work on *Don Juan*, he sought to publish the earlier poem, reanimating its subtly damning verdicts in what he viewed as an age of deepened gloom. The poem's reference to "these latter days" acquired an added charge in this context. In the original poem, that phrase claimed a place for Byron in relation to earlier (literary) generations. But a decade later, "these latter days" captured a creeping experience of belatedness: if not the end of days as such, then an encroaching sense of lateness, including a pervasive sense of lastness. Byron had the growing sense, both personal and political, of having reached the end, making the return to the poem both, Jerome J. McGann proposes, a "sort of blessed remembrance of things past" and a pointed reflection on the present.[51] The return to *Hints from Horace* was thus bound up with his developing plans for *Don Juan*, and both works were of a piece with his deepening despair at the state of the literary establishment.

Those reflections on a "sinking" age became inflected, in turn, by politics, beginning with cultural politics.[52] In August 1818, Hobhouse informed Byron that the *Edinburgh Review* had invited the poet to do something that "shall raise [our] age to a level with any Augustan period of literature." In the same letter, he noted that the Whig *Morning Chronicle* "humbly request[ed] you would come home and consent to save this sinking country."[53] The notion that England and its national literature were in decline found archetypal expression with the English Augustans. For Pope, Swift, and the Scriblerian circle, "sinking" became a potent term for con-joined political and cultural decline, with that word's economic register (the "sinking" funds serviced the ballooning national debt) providing an added valence to this critique of modernity. Hobhouse used that term to make a more pointed political claim about collapsing reformist hopes and harden-ing Tory hegemony. These concerns became intertwined as Byron returned to a long-standing preoccupation: the neglect of Alexander Pope.

The sidelining of Pope drove a heated Romantic-era debate about aesthetic and cultural value. For Byron, the neglect of his prized satirical and moral precursor also became a complexly personal and political affair. In his published letter responding to Reverend Bowles, Byron assembled visions of political and poetic declining and falling into an elaborate tableau, culminating with the prospect of mass sinking:

> If any great national or natural convulsion could or should overwhelm your country in such sort as to sweep Great Britain from the kingdoms of the

earth, and leave only that, after all, the most living of human things, a *dead language*, to be studied and read, and imitated by the wise of future and far generations, upon foreign shores; if your literature should become the learning of mankind, divested of party cabals, temporary fashions, and national pride and prejudice; an Englishman, anxious that the posterity of strangers should know that there had been such a thing as a British Epic and Tragedy, might wish for the preservation of Shakespeare and Milton; but the surviving world would snatch Pope from the wreck, and let the rest sink with the People. He is the moral poet of all civilization; and as such, let us hope that he will one day be the national poet of mankind.[54]

This is an image of the nation as a shipwreck. But while imagining a "Convulsion" sufficient to "sweep Great Britain from the kingdoms of the Earth," Byron does not settle on whether this is a "national or natural" catastrophe, a seismic political change and social rupture or an unexpected disaster like an exploding volcano or comet from space. (If the nation were to "sink" far enough, of course, these prospects could converge, combining cultural decline with rising sea levels). Byron plays here, as Shelley would in *The Last Man*, with multiple ideas of England: as a metaphorical island, an island nation, and an entire "world" that may come to an end. But these works also bring another prospect into sharp focus. As the reference to the "surviving world" confirms, this is not the end of the world so much as a world without England, which has been swept from "the kingdoms of the earth."

This is not, however, a world in which the home nation is merely forgotten. There are crucial exceptions to this mass sinking-if-not-extinction event. The survivors here are celebrated literary authors – at least one of them – rescued as "the People" sink (or, more darkly, are allowed to sink) beneath the waves. But what futures are imaginable for literature in this scenario? Reflecting upon literary survival in the third canto of *Don Juan*, Byron pictured the doomed efforts of a writing subject who sees "even his nation / Become a thing, or nothing, save to rank / In chronological commemoration" (iii.89), a chain of forgetting that extends to dead poets, Milton and Shakespeare. In his seminal account of Romantic poetry and the culture of posterity, Andrew Bennett shows how Byron, in this passage from *Don Juan* and elsewhere, ironizes the "redemptive force" claimed for the future reception of literary works, while in the process raising the prospect of future recuperation ("albeit ambivalently") for himself. Byron's writing, in Bennett's deconstructive account, "both questions and disturbs the logic of posthumous fame and, at the same time, in various and complex ways, performatively inscribes that logic within this very rejection."[55] But in contrast with the dark passages in which Byron describes earth as a series of tombs connecting in a cycle of universal death, his defense of Pope presents at once a more damning and more hopeful vision. Pope allows Byron to indulge the fantasy of a last poet whose works endure, against a complexly imagined backdrop of endings. By conjoining "national" and "natural" disasters, he envisions those works being rediscovered in some imagined future world even as he also glimpses the prospect of mankind's extinction.

In tandem with their reflections on posterity and future readerships, Byron's final writings thus raise the prospect of reaching the end of the line. The prospect of literary works surviving in the absence of a national or even – pushing the imagery of disaster and catastrophe to a planetary scale – a global readership to appreciate them might seem to amount to the end of literature. In the context of the "last man," that prospect becomes a philosophical-temporal conundrum, about books without any-one living to read them.[56] But imagined by way of scenarios that do not mean the end of humanity, the "end of the world" might mean that, as some lines of transmission end, other ends for literature emerge: new objectives and fresh beginnings, capable of casting a renovating influence back on the present, in which the prospect of that otherwise daunting future takes shape. Byron spells out one such prospect amidst this vision of a shipwrecked and sinking nation: England's "*dead language*" – divested of factional politics and ephemeral fashions, "pride and prejudice" – being taken up by "the wise of future and far generations upon foreign shores." In imagining how this prospect might be realized, we need not turn to literal questions about the transmission of the English canon. With Byron's reflections on "rude" rhyme and "untaught melodies" in *The Island* we find a different kind of answer. There, a Popean poetics revives upon contact with supposedly unspoiled scenes and foreign peoples, at the ends of the earth but not yet at the end of the world.

Coda
Don Juan *and the Ends of Literature*

As with the death of the sun in Byron's "Darkness," the prospect of Earth being rendered uninhabitable collapses the end of the world with the end of the planet. The discovery of other planets might thus, by extension, represent the discovery of new worlds, including new political worlds. Space becomes the site of new societies in various examples of contemporary science fiction, but we find an example close to the world of this book in two films by Ridley Scott. *Prometheus* (2012) and its sequel *Alien: Covenant* (2017) imagine a group of scientists and engineers tasked with seeking out a new planet that could be home to man. As in their precursor *Alien* (1979), they gruesomely fall prey to the creatures that inhabit the planets they discover after those alien beings take over their bodies as their new hosts. The recent films make several additions to the themes of the original *Alien* trilogy. The space voyagers in *Prometheus* have as their companion an android named David, programmed with a cut-glass English accent. *Alien: Covenant* begins with David greeting *another* android: a replica of himself. In a rebellious gesture against man, his creator, David has here become a creator in his own right. This space-aged remix of *Frankenstein* takes on a still-more perverse cast when David takes control of a planet inhabited by alien creatures, whom he then sentences to death like an emperor hastening on the demise of his own empire.

In a scene where he recalls that act of destruction, David and the replica android quote lines from Percy Shelley's sonnet "Ozymandias." David reads the inscription from the pedestal of the abandoned statue: "My name is Ozymandias, King of Kings, / Look on my Works, ye Mighty, and despair!" The second android continues with the poem's final lines:

> Nothing beside remains. Round the decay
> Of that colossal Wreck, boundless and bare
> The lone and level sands stretch far away.[1]

David responds enthusiastically, but in doing so he makes an uncharacter-
istic error: "Byron. 1818. Magnificent." This is both a misattribution and
a misinterpretation. David reads "Ozymandias" as a poem about a ruler
defiantly outliving his own death. But this "colossal Wreck," discovered in
a desert, not only points to the ruin of an empire; the poem also suggests
the likely absence of anybody to read the statue's inscription (and its plea to
"Look on" the vanished emperor's works "and despair"). David may, of
course, have understood all too well the inscription's appeals to an unyield-
ing human will-to-conquest, as evidenced in his hitching the words of the
deceased "King of Kings" to Byron in 1818. Read as channeling a "Byronic"
defiance of worldly limits, the poem may seem less ironic after all. But
the second set of lines and their eerily barren scenes further compound his
mistaken identification. In quoting the inscription, David allows Byron's
concern with a tortured human spirit seeking to outlive (or at least endure)
the violent cycles of history to supplant Shelley's more ethereally idealistic
claims to a universal history of man. But when it comes to haunting
emptiness, Byron's writings point, this book has suggested, to another
story. As "Darkness" and the late writings examined in this book make
clear, Byron was more concerned with plangent reflections on loss and
resonant endings than with claims to mastery. His natural reaction to
seeing planets from space would not have been imperialistic visions of
worlds to conquer, we might speculate, but poetic meditations on worlds
passing away.

   Byron repeatedly affirmed that European society was exhausted and on
the brink of destruction – a prospect that coupled, in his late writings, with
visions of the world ending. But he also presented flickering glimpses of an
alternative, including by way of void-filling absences. Byron and his circle
contemplated visions of unspoiled new worlds that shade – in ways that
Swift, for one, could never have imagined – into their own fantasies of
escaping the planet. Expanding upon fantasies of this world giving way to
another, recent science fiction (with depressing echoes in the wish lists of
certain billionaires) has engaged technoutopian fantasies of colonizing the
moon or building new worlds on other planets. By contrast, late Romantic
fantasies of reaching or going beyond the ends of the earth were, as with
Walton's voyage to the North Pole in *Frankenstein*, at least subtly critical.
Byron spoke repeatedly of the world deserving its own destruction and
fantasized about escapes, as we have seen, to Australia, South America, and
the South Seas, which he foresaw as an alternative to the ruin of Europe
(even as his plans suggest he was equally invested in bringing peripheral
economies into the European-controlled world-system). His late writings

supplemented these appeals with images of numbing continuity and renewed repression, or fantasies about the onset of biblical deluges and natural disasters.

Wordsworth and his circle provided Byron with one reference point for cultural repression and poetic decline.[2] In scenes later echoed in *The Last Man*, Percy Shelley sought to dose Byron with "Wordsworth physic" upon meeting him at Lake Geneva. For the depressed, recently exiled poet, the cure was worse than the disease. The ascent of the Lake poets marked, so far as Byron was concerned, the nadir of modern poetry. In their seclusion at Keswick and their preoccupation with drab, rain-lashed scenery, Wordsworth and his drizzly company allowed Byron to provide "sinking" with a more literal locus. In the unpublished "Dedication" to *Don Juan*, Byron imagined Wordsworth and his coterie as "shabby" residents on the lower hills of Parnassus, whose belief that "poesy has wreaths for you alone" made him "wish you'd change your lakes for ocean." That phrasing imagined the Wordsworth circle leaving England altogether. The later prose preface identified Southey as a "Pantisocratic apostle," alluding to his abandoned scheme to form a utopian colony in Pennsylvania with Coleridge. Yet the metaphor of lakes becoming ocean also becomes available as an image of flooding, if not drowning. Byron gestured elsewhere in the "Dedication" toward biblical prophecy. Wordsworth's rambling excursions would only become poetry "when the Dog Star rages" and biblical prophets speak again (with Milton "the blind old man, aris[ing] / Like Samuel from the grave"). But these lofty registers serve to mark a bathetic fall. Byron goes on to imagine Southey "tumbl[ing] downward like the flying fish / Gasping on deck." In his scrupulous study of Byron and Percy Shelley, Charles Robinson emphasizes the explicit and ambient debts of both writers to Wordsworth. Relatedly, he sees Torquil in *The Island* as a "Shelleyan hero," whose hopes of a new world look back to the earlier poet's idealism (and behind him, Wordsworth). But rather than Byron finally "accept[ing] the 'Utopian' vision in Shelley's poetry," that poem stages not the reclaiming of an earlier paradise, I have proposed, but the discovery of a new world predicated on the existing world having passed away, sinking without trace.[3]

In a further elaboration of "sinking," the image of the Poet Laureate soaring too high – and floundering when he lands back on board a ship – yokes a Popean language of literary decline together with a complex metaphor for a nation that has become, from Byron's perspective, suffocatingly inhospitable. We do not need to attribute Byron with our own sensitivity to floodplains to recognize that, when he contemplated these writers changing "lakes for ocean," he imagined the British nation "sink-ing" without trace, whether through a bout of especially bad weather or a biblical flood that also amounts to the end of the world. But while Southey, the "flying fish," finds himself gasping for breath, out of his element, the ship on which he lands points at other possibilities. As *Don Juan* goes on, death at sea and biblical deluges shape the swaying progress of its protagonist. The second canto sees Byron's hapless hero cast out on the Mediterranean, barely escaping from a lifeboat after his shipmates feast on his dog and then turn on each other (before their cannibalism leads to their own raving madness). Byron drew upon actual reports of shipwrecks, while perhaps also looking back to the woozy experience of Daniel Defoe's young seafarers. But this episode, which culminates with an ambiguously immanent rainbow, also occasions reference to Noah's ark and Promethean endurance, even as the fate of Juan's dog provides a grim point of comparison with "Darkness" (although we may recall that Byron planned to be entombed with his late canine companion, Boatswain).

As would be the case for *Don Juan* as a whole, contexts proliferate, shunting one another aside in quick succession. Beyond offering an alle-gorical frame for Juan's story, these biblical narratives – together with the poem's plot, such as it is – become equal partners with another voice, as narration of the story gives way in favor of first-person commentary.[4] When Juan embarks upon his voyage, Byron compares his story to a biblical parable ("As if a Spanish ship were Noah's ark, / To wean him from the wickedness of earth" [2.8]) and narrates this voyage out by way of a first-person persona already recognizable (the intermittent Spanish-born narrator of the early cantos having already receded) as that of the English poet. There is a "devil of the sea," the Byronic poet notes, looking back to *Childe Harold*, "As I, who've crossed it oft, know well enough" (2.11). Byron continued to stitch his life and persona into the poem. That included, among other things, a return to the Whig past. The London-based cantos of *Don Juan* and their Whiggish urbanity served to restabilize his persona amidst familiar hierarchies.[5] But that coupled, in what became the poem's final stages, with a more precise sense of time, including time's heterogeneity. The poem's growing emphasis on "narrative presentness," Emily Rohrbach proposes, creates a "rich multiplicity of present possibil-ities," such that, far from narrowing the poem's sense of where things are headed, *Don Juan* ultimately "*resists* the tendency to imagine the present as part of a narrative that leads to the future." The various endings that Byron folded into his freewheeling commentaries on the present further com-pound this sense of multiplicity. The closing of avenues, extending to the prospective demise of mankind, might be expected to create a more restricted sense of the future. But an emphasis on endings, this book has argued, at once redoubles and sharpens the sense of the future's unknowability and plurality, as broken lines and echoing absences reflect backward on the political present.

We find a rough-and-ready analogue for this collision of presents and endings in the personal correspondence where Byron narrated the busy world of his life abroad for readers back home. Writing to his sister Augusta on November 7, 1822, from Genoa, Byron described a series of recent disturbances, beginning with natural disasters. There had been "three slight shocks of an Earthquake" that had "frightened the whole town into the Streets" (though Byron noted that "neither they nor the tumult" had awakened *him*). There had, more significantly, been a "deluge" that had "carried away half the country" and seen his hilltop village "nearly knocked down by lightning and battered by columns of rain."[6] Byron went on to describe jumbled, chaotic, at-once comic and tragic scenes: "the comfortable view of the whole landscape under water – and people screaming out of their garret windows – *two bridges* swept down – and our next door neighbours – a Cobbler and a Wigmaker – and a Gingerbread baker delivering up their whole stock to the elements – which marched away with a quantity of shoes – several perukes – and Gingerbread in all it's [*sic*] branches." The road had been "an impassable cascade." A child had drowned a few feet from the foot of the hill. A "preaching Friar," meanwhile, claimed that "the day of Judgement will take place positively on the *4th* – with all kinds of tempest and what not." The preacher had received gifts and warnings, Byron noted with outrage, from "the *public authorities*." But when the date in question turned out "a very fine day," the villagers had been "exceptionally angry" – and had insisted upon "having the day of Judgement – or their cash again." The letter continued by turning outward, to the wider world: "There seem to have been all kinds of tempests all over the Globe – and for my part it would not surprize me – if the earth should get a little tired of the tyrants and slaves who disturb her surface."[7]

Byron's letter to his sister was a descriptive account of what he had seen. But its narrative procedure resembles that of his comic-epic masterpiece. In *Don Juan*, all the stuff of life – gingerbread and peruke wigs, flooded streets and dead children, shifty friars and angry villagers – becomes part of poetry's lot. The same goes for Byron's treatment of the world to come, or the end of life. In much the same way that the present's multiplicity serves, as Rohrbach deftly argues, to make the future at once unknowable and radically contingent, so the poem's playful inclusion of vistas that go beyond the bounds of human experience works at once to screen and scramble visions of the future world. In Canto I of *Don Juan*, Byron folded the radical unknowability of death into the endless churn of his narrative. "We die, you know – and then – " one stanza concludes. "What then? – " the next stanza begins, before filling these unbridgeable gaps in knowledge and time, with turned pages, vocalized pauses, and ended evenings: "We die, you know – and then – // What then? – I do not know, no more do you – / And so good night. – Return we to our story" (1.133.8, 134.1–2). As the poem went on, Byron folded eschatology into his multifaceted commentary on the present. The thrust of his letter to Augusta was to mock religion. The final reckoning becomes something for which the villagers have paid; having been sold a lemon, they now demand their money back ("the day of Judgement – or their cash again"). Byron gives in to a pessimistic vision of the world that tolerates these transactions, including an incipient sense of political – if not also ecological – exhaustion, which sees "the earth" become "a little tired" of those who "disturb her surface."[8] Byron supplied a cynical (and even a nihilistically Swiftian) cast to statements like this one, including in his final satires. But *Don Juan* was ultimately different. The poem played with the equivalences between (cash) registers: the interplay between economic and religious values, moral economies and sexual ones. Especially in its later cantos, moreover, the poem also permitted Byron to multiply, endlessly, his frames of reference and their bearing on real and imagined worlds.

In Canto IX, the nature of the "worlds" imagined by the poem multiplies in tandem with the prospective ends of the world (or end of the worlds) that would follow from their dissolution. This series of world unmaking and remaking follows, tellingly, from Byron's reflections on writing: the "scribes" behind the "voluminous" publications, whose circulation he equates to the national debt. Byron forgets what he means to advise these "great Authors." But then, finding his point again, he imagines his "lost advice" ("beyond all price," because outside any marketplace) being discovered in another age:

> But let it go: – it will one day be found
> With other relics of "a former world,"
> When this world shall be *former*, underground,
> Thrown topsy-turvy, twisted, crisped, and curled,
> Baked, fried, or burnt, turned inside-out, or drowned,
> Like all the worlds before, which have been hurled
> First out of and then back again to Chaos,

The Superstratum which will overlay us.

So Cuvier says; – and then shall come again
Unto the new Creation, rising out
From our old crash, some mystic, ancient strain
Of things destroyed and left in airy doubt:
Like to the notions *we* now entertain
Of Titans, Giants, fellows of about
Some hundred feet in height, *not* to say *miles*,
And Mammoths, and your winged Crocodiles.

(IX.37–8)

As in *Cain*, Byron drew upon catastrophism here to imagine a spectacular series of dissolutions and reformulations, amounting to transformations of the entire planet. He plays, in turn, with images of the world being swept clean, "burnt ... or drowned" (to which we might compare the letter in which he imagined earth itself "get[ting] a little tired" of its tyrants and slaves). At the same time, Byron harnesses Cuvier's account of worlds before Adam – and future explosions of this world – into an image of sequential *political* worlds. Following "our old crash" (the noun suggesting economic and social collapse, as well as a more general sense of decline and demise), a new world emerges, in which "we" will have the status of myth.[9] That prospect couples with the endurance of select remnants of our political world. The next stanza goes on to imagine George the Fourth being "dug up" by the "new worldlings of the then new East" (IX.38.1–2). Byron thus makes the ending of political lines and even the dissolution of entire societies the source of ambiguous "relics": the political dinosaurs that bewilder a newly constituted political society, located at a supposedly earlier phase of political development, as well as the still more perplexing status of his own poetry, whose imagined rediscovery prompts this extended reflection in the first place.

The reappearance of those relics in a reoriented political world carries an elusive potential for the present tense of reading in which they reverberate ("some mystic, ancient strain"; "things ... left in airy doubt"). At the same time, Byron's appeals to catastrophism make those future worlds, or *any* world, subject to change – and disappearance. The prospect of there having been, as Cuvier posited, multiple "worlds" before this one not only gives rise, after all, to the prospect of multiple future worlds but also of *those* worlds ending, in turn, so as to give way to others. Byron adopts Cuvier's account of the "worlds before, which have been hurled / First out of and then back again to Chaos" into an image of *new* political worlds, taking shape after the clearing away of others. The "worlds before" may look backward to prior worlds but also (as with the "world ... before" in the final lines of *Paradise Lost*) *ahead* to those worlds that take shape amidst the ruins and remnants of others. Those visions of political ending ultimately give way, as in the other works examined in this study, to indeterminate visions of the political future. But *Don Juan*, as ever, gives us more than we had bargained for. This vision of exploding and reforming "worlds" serves, in turn, as a valuable account of Byron's method in that poem and its continued composition. We may thus discern a striking parallel between these energetically busy visions of worlds ending and his endlessly generative use of *ottava rima*, both of which forge new possibilities out of (odds and) ends.

Don Juan accumulates and disperses, builds and ebbs. Rather than an endless process of recycling, however, the sequence acquires distinctive shapes and directions. The poem adapts an askew angle of vision on the world, even if that perspective cannot be reduced either to a stable vantage on the present or orientation toward the future. The (dis)order that Byron finds in and through the world's confusion offers endless pleasures and provocations. But its swerves also have a final, added valence for our own time. Reflecting upon the challenges posed to linear temporality by our current planetary condition, Jeffrey Jerome Cohen proposes a "vorticular topology of reading" as more apt to its mind-bending predicaments and impossible futurities. "A vortex often obliterates," Cohen writes. But he goes on: "its spirals and shifts may also render evident long-standing embroilments, the unexpected touchings of forces and entities within expansive spatial and temporal systems." Vortices are "disjunct histories in contiguity, binding lines into curved motion, a model of temporality that does not easily sediment into discrete layers." While most Anthropocene narratives "embrace linearity" ("hard starts and full stops, plots with rising action, accelerated propulsions, catastrophic denouements") their "currents," Cohen concludes, "swirl with affective detritus, recondite matter, queer fragments, anomalous proximities."[10] This model of reading for our time also presents a rough guide to the stanzas and cantos of *Don Juan*, whose queer energies and collisions of time turn on their own axes while seeking to jolt, bend, shock, screw, tease, tickle, or taunt the world into pursuing a better direction, or just a different one.

Notes

Introduction

1. [Henry Brougham], review of Morris Birkbeck, *Notes on a Journey in America*, *Edinburgh Review* 30 (June 1818), 124, 122, 120, 123, 137.
2. Review of Morris Birkbeck, *Notes on a Journey in America*, 138–9.
3. *The Last Man* explicitly concerns the condition of "England." The English questions engaged in this book were often – and increasingly – also British ones, not least given the continued growth of empire. This book attends to political debates that crystallized at the English metropole but remains conscious, for example, of Scotland's deep involvement in the slave trade (and that Byron's calls for the literal "sinking" of England also entailed the disappearance of the British Isles).
4. The attention to temporal multiplicity and divergent chronologies in this book is especially indebted to Jonathan Sachs, *The Poetics of Decline in British Romanticism* (Cambridge: Cambridge University Press, 2018); James Chandler, *England in 1819: The Politics of Literary Culture and the Case of Romantic Historicism* (Chicago: University of Chicago Press, 1998); and Emily Rohrbach, *Modernity's Mist: British Romanticism and the Poetics of Anticipation* (New York: Fordham University Press, 2015). My discussions of apocalyptic time and historical rupture also draw upon Reinhart Koselleck, *Futures Past: On the Semantics of Historical Time*, trans. Keith Tribe (New York: Columbia University Press, 2004 [1979]) and J. G. A. Pocock, *The Machiavellian Moment: Florentine Political Thought and the Atlantic Republican Tradition* (Princeton: Princeton University Press, 2016 [1975]).
5. The identification of "the world" with this planet may appear uncontroversial. But the image of "Spaceship Earth" that grounds post-1968 environmentalism, Jason Moore argues, privileges a detached, fatalistic view of "man" rather than embracing the entangled "web of life" – a flawed logic repeated, Moore contends, in discussions of "the Anthropocene." Tobias Menely pushes beyond environment to geohistory, arguing that a stratigraphic

understanding of Earth's history (and attunement to the shift from solar to carbon-based fuel regimes) allowed poets from John Milton to Charlotte Smith to recognize the role of changing climates in the making of plural worlds. Anahid Nersessian has proposed an approach to ecocriticism grounded in competing planetary imaginaries and finds in the minimal utopias of Romantic poetry alternatives both to the world as it is and to the abandonment of this planet in pursuit of other, perfect worlds. See Jason Moore, "Who Is Responsible for the Climate Crisis?" *Maize* (November 2019); Tobias Menely, *Climate and the Making of Worlds: Toward a Geohistorical Poetics* (Chicago: University of Chicago Press, 2021); Anahid Nersessian, *Utopia, Limited* (Cambridge: Harvard University Press, 2015).

6. David Remnick, "Obama Reckons with a Trump Presidency," *The New Yorker*, November 18, 2016.

7. Koselleck, *Futures Past*.

8. See David Runciman, *How Democracy Ends* (New York: Basic Books, 2018).

9. Naomi Klein, *The Shock Doctrine: The Rise of Disaster Capitalism* (New York: Picador, 2007). See also Sasha Lilley, ed., *Catastrophism: The Apocalyptic Politics of Collapse and Rebirth* (Oakland: PM Press, 2012).

10. Naomi Klein, *The Battle For Paradise: Puerto Rico Takes On the Disaster Capitalists* (Chicago: Haymarket Books, 2018).

11. Alan Weisman plays out this scenario at greater length in *The World Without Us* (New York: St. Martin's Press, 2007). Writing in July 2020, Lawrence Wright combined realism about the return of economic activity ("traffic will necessarily resume, oil will be pumped, airplanes will take off") with the hope that the experience of living with less pollution would come to be seen as an "achievable destiny." "How Pandemics Wreak Havoc – and Open Minds," *The New Yorker*, July 20, 2020.

12. For the "impasse," see Lauren Berlant, *Cruel Optimism* (Durham: Duke University Press, 2011). See also Berlant's discussion of the "glitch" in *On the Inconvenience of Other People* (Durham: Duke University Press, 2022), 24–6.

13. Remnick, "Obama Reckons with a Trump Presidency." Echoing his remarks on the "end of the world," Obama added that he did not believe in adopting "apocalyptic" ways of thinking "until the apocalypse comes."

14. Hannah Arendt, *The Origins of Totalitarianism* (New York: Harcourt, Brace, Jovanovich, 1973 [1951]). For the bearing of Arendt's arguments on the 2010s, see Masha Gessen, *Surviving Autocracy* (New York: Riverhead, 2020) and Anne Applebaum, *Twilight of Democracy: The Seductive Lure of Authoritarianism* (New York: Doubleday, 2020).

15. For Keats, notions of historical progress, informed by the stadial theory of the Scottish Enlightenment and his brother's emigration to America, had a less

direct bearing on politics in England. See Nicholas Roe, *John Keats and the Culture of Dissent* (Oxford: Oxford University Press, 1998); Chandler, *England in 1819*; Denise Gigante, *The Keats Brothers: The Life of John and George* (Cambridge, MA: Harvard University Press, 2013). As Rohrbach emphasizes in *Modernity's Mist*, despite Keats's investment in the "grand march of intellect," his poetry made room for "lyrical dilation of the moment" in such a way as to interrupt the smooth glide of progress (71).

16. "Introduction" to *Frankenstein*, 3rd ed. (1831). Mary Shelley, *Frankenstein*, ed. J. Paul Hunter (New York: Norton, 2012), 168.

17. *LMS*, 1.466.

18. I adopt this phrase from Sir Llewellyn Woodward, *The Age of Reform, 1815–1870* (Oxford: Oxford University Press, 1962).

19. Jean M. O'Brien, *Firsting and Lasting: Writing Indians Out of Existence in New England* (Minneapolis: University of Minnesota Press, 2010), 10.

20. O'Brien, *Firsting and Lasting*, 109. See also Fiona J. Stafford, *The Last of the Race: The Growth of a Modern Myth from Milton to Darwin* (Oxford: Clarendon Press, 1994).

21. See Sachs, *The Poetics of Decline in British Romanticism*.

22. See Chandler, *England in 1819* and Rohrbach, *Modernity's Mist*.

23. Quoted in Sachs, *The Poetics of Decline in British Romanticism*, 12–13.

24. See, inter alia, Doris Langley Moore, *The Late Lord Byron* (London: John Murray, 1961); Francis Wilson, ed., *Byromania: Portraits of the Artist in Nineteenth- and Twentieth-Century Culture* (Basingstoke: Macmillan, 1999); Tom Mole, *Byron's Romantic Celebrity* (Basingstoke: Palgrave, 2007); Susan Wolfson, *Romantic Interactions: Social Being and the Turns of Literary Action* (Baltimore: Johns Hopkins University Press, 2010); Clara Tuite, *Lord Byron and Scandalous Celebrity* (Cambridge: Cambridge University Press, 2014).

25. Thomas Moore, ed., *Letters and Journals of Lord Byron*, 2 vols. (London: John Murray, 1830), 2.718–19.

26. See "Byron's Success," chapter 8 in Andrew Bennett, *Romantic Poets and the Culture of Posterity* (Cambridge: Cambridge University Press, 1999). For Byron's experience of feeling like "the dead" and its implications for the disaffected stance adopted by his poetry, see "Byron's Opposition," chapter 6 in my *Disaffected Parties: Political Estrangement and the Making of English Literature, 1760–1830* (Oxford: Oxford University Press, 2019), 137.

27. Quoted in Phyllis Grosskurth, *Byron: The Flawed Angel* (London: Hodder & Stoughton, 1979), 378.

28. See Roderick Beaton, *Byron's War: Romantic Rebellion, Greek Revolution* (Cambridge: Cambridge University Press, 2013), 219–20. Compare Jerome J. McGann, *Don Juan in Context* (Chicago: University of Chicago

Press, 1968), 152–4 and Louis Crompton, *Byron and Greek Love: Homophobia in 19th-Century England* (Berkeley: University of California Press, 1985), 326–7.

29. Byron wrote "The best of Prophets of the future is the Past" as a parenthetical aside in a tortured 1821 journal passage about fear and doubt. The passage continued: "It is useless to say *where* the Present is, for most of us know; and as for the Past, *what* predominates in memory? – *Hope baffled.*" *BLJ*, 8.37.

30. For Rohrbach in *Modernity's Mist*, a sense of indeterminacy around the future anterior (what "will have been") insinuates itself into Romantic reckonings with things as they are: a conjuncture apparent in the figure of the "mist" that obscures the present but thereby materializes an ambiguous futurity. See also Chandler, *England in 1819*.

31. Jacques Khalip, *Last Things: Disastrous Form from Kant to Hujar* (New York: Fordham University Press, 2018), 6.

32. Sachs, *The Poetics of Decline in British Romanticism*, 7.

33. I draw here from the valuable discussion of Godwin's text in Julie A. Carlson, *England's First Family of Writers: Mary Wollstonecraft, William Godwin, Mary Shelley* (Baltimore: Johns Hopkins University Press, 2007).

34. Hobhouse also introduced the poet to the other face of reform: "The famous Jeremy Bentham whom you may have read of in the Edinbro' Review has engaged me to put some political work of his into English." Hobhouse to Byron, June 5, 1818. *Byron's Bulldog: The Letters of John Cam Hobhouse to Lord Byron*, ed. Peter W. Graham (Columbus: Ohio State University Press, 1984), 231.

35. Quoted in *His Very Self and Voice: Collected Conversations of Lord Byron*, ed. Ernest J. Lovell, Jr. (New York: Macmillan, 1954), 269.

36. See, for example, Nicholas Hudson, *A Political Biography of Samuel Johnson* (London: Pickering & Chatto, 2013).

37. Havard, *Disaffected Parties*, 137.

38. Colin Jager, "Reading by the Light of Common Day: Politics, Society, Romanticism," *European Romantic Review* 32 (2021), 76–83 (p. 80).

39. Indeed, my account of Johnson in *Disaffected Parties* goes on to emphasize the *disjuncture* between Johnson's stated political convictions and his authorial reputation, as evidenced in pamphlets and ephemeral texts that stressed the instability of Johnson's writings and the volatility of his authorial persona. That disjuncture became crucial, I propose, to Johnson's *literary* identity – an identity that comes into focus in the complex intermediary zone between the living author and the "words on the page." Those words can and do take on a life of their own. If Jane Austen's *Mansfield Park* "cannot be considered a conservative novel," I write in another chapter, "then no such thing as a conservative novel exists. But perhaps no such thing does exist" (228).

40. Building upon scholars including Anne-Lise François, Anahid Nersessian, Amanda Jo Goldstein, and Lily Gurton-Wachter, I thus set out to trace buried agencies, erased presences, vibrant energies, and minimized impacts in late Romantic writing and to follow their resonances deep into the thicket of political activity and debate. As these scholars have shown, these modes of engagement did not belong to an extrapolitical realm (nor to a budding domain of "ecological" consciousness) but to that ever-shifting and historically contingent print-political and cultural-affective field we call "Romantic."

41. The nature of her upbringing, Carlson contends in *England's First Family*, was such that Shelley could not, in important respects, know where she as "a distinct individual" began, whether in terms of the ideas behind her writing or the formation of her habits of mind and personality. As a result, she was "conflicted," Carlson concludes, over matters of "originality, imagination, femininity, and adherence to family." In the same way, I suggest, that we can recover slyly critical engagements with Godwinian political thought in Shelley's writings (alongside the noted absence of engagement with the ideas or writings of her mother), we can also discern her distance from the men in her immediate circle.

42. In the essays collected as *A Life With Mary Shelley* (Stanford: Stanford University Press, 2014), Barbara Johnson reads Shelley's biography into writings that seem to foreclose that possibility. For a suggestive account of the "fracture" that allowed feminist writers to inhabit a space outside the historical present (and thereby write, in some sense, from an imagined future), see David Sigler, *Fracture Feminism: The Politics of Impossible Time in British Romanticism* (Albany: SUNY Press, 2021).

43. *JMS*, 2.476–7. I discuss this entry at greater length in Chapter 4.

44. Hobhouse, Journal, May 4, 1822. British Library Add. MS 56544. Hobhouse was not entirely inattentive to the women on the outskirts of his circle "Went upstairs to Mrs Ricardo," he recorded in the same journal, "she told me that Malthus and her husband would sometimes sit up till three in the morning, defining 'rent'!!"

45. For various post-Bloomian approaches to these questions, see, inter alia, Jack Stillinger, *Multiple Authorship and the Myth of Solitary Genius* (Oxford: Oxford University Press, 1991); Wolfson, *Romantic Interactions*; and Lucy Newlyn, *William and Dorothy Wordsworth: "All in Each Other"* (Oxford: Oxford University Press, 2013).

46. Anna Mercer examines Shelley's intellectual and textual relationship with her husband in *The Collaborative Literary Relationship of Percy Bysshe Shelley and Mary Wollstonecraft Shelley* (New York: Routledge, 2020).

47. Will Bowers, *The Italian Idea: Anglo-Italian Radical Literary Culture* (Cambridge: Cambridge University Press, 2020), 1. Bowers shows how, in the immediate post-Waterloo period, literary culture associated with Italian

exiles in London and English authors sympathetic with Italy challenged state hegemony through innovation and dissent.

48. "The poorer class of manufacturers can earn no more than three shillings and sixpence a week," Hobhouse (then an aspiring reformist politician) wrote to Byron on June 16, 1819, noting that thousands of men were "starving in all the manufacturing districts." There had been "an assemblage of some thousand weavers." But Hobhouse suspected the government would "soon send the horse and a hangman amongst them" (the workers had "swor[n] their oath, broke some windows, and sent a petition to the prince regent asking him to give them all passage to America"). Hobhouse to Byron, June 5, 1818. *Byron's Bulldog,* 273 and 274n.6, The image of an emboldened *ancien régime* spreading state-sponsored terror here was prophetic: Two months later came violence in Manchester's St. Peter's Field – the "Peterloo massacre," in which cavalry wielding sabers descended on a crowd of proreform protestors.

49. After Peterloo, the popular movement championed by Cobbett and Hunt entered a precarious new phase. The violence in 1819 and emergence of "middle-class" priorities among reformers comprised major setbacks for the radical cause. But to a degree neglected in existing accounts of the period, the 1820s were characterized by not only stagnation and disappointment but dynamism and hopes for change (including the revival of a long-dormant interest in ending slavery). E. P. Thompson stresses the betrayal of radical hopes in *The Making of the English Working Class* (New York: Vintage, 1966 [1963]). As Robert Poole notes, however, the massacre exerted a "formative influence" on the reform movement. *Peterloo: The English Uprising* (Oxford: Oxford University Press, 2019), 4. For the wider literary-cultural field in the decade, see Angela Esterhammer, *Print and Performance in the 1820s: Improvisation, Speculation, Identity* (Cambridge: Cambridge University Press, 2020). Esterhammer resists the tendency to see the period as transitional, describing a period of "breathtaking changes" in technology, transportation, and accelerating media.

50. For 1832 as a break that severed a long-standing union of church and state, see J. C. D. Clark, *English Society, 1660–1832: Religion, Ideology and Politics during the Ancien Régime,* 2nd ed. (Cambridge: Cambridge University Press, 2000). Far from representing an *ancien régime,* Boyd Hilton sees the heightened emphasis on "Church and King" during the age of revolutions as a "neo-conservative" reaction to progressive ideology. *A Mad, Bad, and Dangerous People? England 1783–1846* (Oxford: Oxford University Press, 2006), 30. Compare my account of "Late Toryism" in *Disaffected Parties.* As Mandler has shown, complex coalitions of Whigs, Tories, liberals, and moderates

steered the country past Reform into the Victorian age. See Peter Mandler, *Aristocratic Government in the Age of Reform: Whigs and Liberals, 1830–1852* (Oxford: Oxford University Press, 1990). I use "Reform" when referring specifically to the Reform Act, "reform" when referring to the wider movement for legislative change.

51. Ryland in *The Last Man* shares features with Hunt and has been identified by critics with Cobbett. "The people at present are very quiet waiting anxiously for the meeting of parliament," Shelley wrote to Byron in January 1817, adding that "Cobbett boldly prophesies a reform will certainly take place" (*LMS*, 1.26).

52. *Hansard*, March 15, 1832.

53. *Hansard*, March 15, 1832.

54. *Recollections of a Long Life, by Lord Broughton (John Cam Hobhouse)* . . ., ed. Lady Dorchester, 6 vols. (London: J. Murray, 1909–11), 4.113.

55. *Hansard*, March 15, 1832.

56. As Chris Baldick notes, while the "most vicious" *Frankenstein* caricatures were reserved for Irish nationalists ("always regarded in Britain as mindless and primitive brutes"), numerous prints imagined the threats posed by the working classes in both England and Ireland with reference to Victor's creation. See *In Frankenstein's Shadow: Myth, Monstrosity, and Nineteenth-Century Writing* (Oxford: Oxford University Press, 1987), 91 and Lee Sterrenburg, "Mary Shelley's Monster: Politics and Psyche in *Frankenstein*," in *The Endurance of Frankenstein: Essays on Mary Shelley's Novel*, ed. George Levine (Oakland: University of California Press, 1982), 143–71. I discuss the relation between images based on *Frankenstein* and the emancipation of formerly enslaved populations in Chapter 3.

57. See especially Foucault, *Security, Territory, Population: Lectures at the Collège de France, 1977–1978*, trans. Graham Burchell (New York: Palgrave, 2007) and *The Birth of Biopolitics: Lectures at the Collège de France, 1978–1979*, trans. Graham Burchell (New York: Palgrave, 2008).

58. See Elaine Hadley, *Living Liberalism: Practical Citizenship in Mid-Victorian Britain* (Chicago: University of Chicago Press, 2010) and Amanda Anderson, *Bleak Liberalism* (Chicago: University of Chicago Press, 2016).

59. See Ina Ferris, *The Achievement of Literary Authority: Gender, History, and the Waverley Novels* (Ithaca: Cornell University Press, 1991) and Ian Duncan, *Scott's Shadow: The Novel in Romantic Edinburgh* (Princeton: Princeton University Press, 2007).

60. *Recollections of a Long Life, by Lord Broughton (John Cam Hobhouse)*, 4.3 (emphasis added).

61. See Catherine Hall, *Macaulay and Son: Architects of Imperial Britain* (New Haven: Yale University Press, 2012).

62. See David Stewart, *The Form of Poetry in the 1820s and 1830s: A Period of Doubt* (Basingstoke: Palgrave, 2018).

63. See Wolfson, *Romantic Interactions*, 262. Aside from her Byronic poetry, Landon wrote *Stanzas* that appeared beneath West's portrait of Byron and an 1836 *Elegy*. Landon's fascinating life saw her die under mysterious circumstances in Africa. Lucasta Miller, *L.E.L.: The Lost Life and Scandalous Death of Letitia Elizabeth Landon, the Celebrated "Female Byron"* (New York: Knopf, 2019).

64. Wolfson, *Romantic Interactions*, 258, 272.

65. See Andrew Elfenbein, "Silver-Fork Byron and the Image of Regency England," in *Byromania*, ed. Wilson, 77–85.

66. See Tom Mole, *What the Victorians Made of Romanticism: Material Artifacts, Cultural Practices, and Reception History* (Princeton: Princeton University Press, 2017).

67. The index to Moore's edition of Byron's writings cites his parenthetical remark as "Past, the best prophet of the future." That condensed version of the line ("The best prophet of the future is the past") begins to be attributed to Byron in works including the novel *Loyella* by Mrs Harry Bennett-Edwards (London, 1879) and to be quoted in the House of Representatives from the 1880s onwards.

68. Malcolm Chase, *Chartism: A New History* (Manchester: Manchester University Press, 2007).

69. The core of the Earth, in *The Coming Race*, has been the home to "various forms of government." The US-born narrator notes that "the most enlightened European politicians" look forward to democracy "as the extreme goal of political advancement" and the system that prevailed "among other subterranean races." But those races are "despised as barbarians" by the loftier "tribe" at the planet's core who look back to democracy as "one of the crude and ignorant experiments which belong to the infancy of political science": "the age of envy and hate, of fierce passions, of constant social changes more or less violent, of strife between classes, of war between state and state." The end of politics, framed here as the end of democracy, results from the discovery of an electricity-like substance that occasions technological mastery over surplus resources and vanquishes subordinate "races."

70. As Fredrik Albritton Jonsson has shown, whether or not coal could sustain current and future generations became an object of heated public concern and political contestation during the 1820s and 1830s (when those debates intersected with calls for Reform). "The Coal Question Before Jevons," *The Historical Journal* 63 (2020), 107–26.

71. Francis Fukuyama, "The End of History?" *The National Interest* 16 (1989), 3–18.
72. Francis Fukuyama, *The End of History and the Last Man* (New York: Free Press, 2006 [1992]), 46 (emphasis original). Fukuyama's contentious assertion was memorably skewered by Jacques Derrida, who denounced Fukuyama for his come-lately Hegelianism while ridiculing the premise that the conflicts organizing the past can so readily be filed away. See *Specters of Marx: The State of the Debt, the Work of Mourning & the New International*, trans. Peggy Kamuf (London: Routledge, 1994).
73. As Stephen D. King has argued in *Grave New World: The End of Globalization, the Return of History* (New Haven: Yale University Press, 2017), the recent backlash against internationalism and global trade has reopened debates about the nation state and free market. In both hopeful and ominous fashion, these developments have also reintroduced a greater sense of contestation around politics more widely. The coda to King's book imagines a 2044 Republican fundraiser, presided over by presidential candidate Ivanka Trump.
74. See Yascha Mounk, *The People vs. Democracy: Why Our Freedom Is in Danger and How to Save It* (Cambridge, MA: Harvard University Press, 2018). Mounk helpfully anatomizes the recent "populist moment" and prescribes a renovated liberalism, including a focus on civics education, as the solution. The book carries Fukuyama's enthusiastic endorsement.
75. Fukuyama, *The End of History and the Last Man*, 46.
76. Emmett Rensin, "The Blathering Superego at the End of History," *Los Angeles Review of Books,* June 18, 2017.
77. In *The Machiavellian Moment*, Pocock describes the pivot from an eternal, divine perspective into a series of contingent happenings: the "time-dimension" that would eventually come to be known as "history." The "Machiavellian moment," in turn, names the capacity for man to act (that is, to act politically) amidst "a stream of irrational events, conceived as essentially destructive of all systems of secular stability." In what I am terming the "Anthropocenean moment," mankind confronts its incapacity to shape events – events that we, as a species, have been responsible for setting in motion (and whose effects will continue long beyond our passing away).

1 The End of Politics and the End of the World

1. *A Leaf from the Future History of England, on the Subject of Reform in Parliament* (1831), 1–2.
2. *A Leaf from the Future History of England,* 3–4.

3. "Yesterday was Sunday but I've been a little unfocused recently and I thought it was Monday. So I came here like it was going to work. And the whole place was empty. And at first I couldn't figure out why, and I had this moment of incredible ... fear and also ... It just flashed through my mind: the whole Hall of Justice, it's empty, it's deserted, it's gone out of business. Forever." Tony Kushner, *Angels in America: A Gay Fantasia On National Themes* (New York: Theatre Communications Group, 2013 [1994]), 75.

4. Cut off from the outside world and forced to confront his immediate surroundings – a small Pennsylvania town – with limited opportunities to exploit his wealth or status, Frank decides, at different stages in *Groundhog Day*, to give his money away, to devote himself to good deeds, and to forge bonds with the local community. In everyday life, we can assume he is a Republican.

5. An exception was Percy Shelley. For an account of Shelley that takes seriously his engagement with contemporary politics, see Timothy Michael, *British Romanticism and the Critique of Political Reason* (Baltimore: Johns Hopkins University Press, 2015).

6. William Morris, *News from Nowhere*, ed. Stephen Arata (Peterborough: Broadview, 2003), 53.

7. See Steve Pincus, *1688: The First Modern Revolution* (New Haven: Yale University Press, 2011) and "*Gulliver's Travels*, Party Politics, and Empire," in *New Perspectives on the History of Political Economy*, eds. Robert Fredon and Sophus A. Reinert (Basingstoke: Palgrave, 2018), 131–70.

8. Swift to Pope, November 26, 1725. *Letters to and From Dr. J. Swift, D.S.P.D.* (Dublin, 1741), 55.

9. Arbuthnot to Swift, August 6, 1715. Quoted in Gregory Lynall, *Swift and Science: The Satire, Politics and Theology of Natural Knowledge, 1690–1730* (Basingstoke: Palgrave, 2012), 91.

10. Hannah Arendt, *On Revolution* (London: Penguin, 2006 [1963]), 37.

11. *Gulliver's Travels. The Cambridge Edition of the Works of Jonathan Swift 16*, ed. David Womersley (Cambridge: Cambridge University Press, 2012), 150–1.

12. I make this case at greater length in "Swift's Political Climates," *Eighteenth-Century Theory and Interpretation* (forthcoming).

13. Carole Fabricant, *Swift's Landscape*, rev. ed. (Notre Dame: University of Notre Dame Press, 1995 [1982]), 72, 75.

14. Jason W. Moore, "Anthropocene or Capitalocene? Nature, History, and the Crisis of Capitalism," in *Anthropocene or Capitalocene?* ed. Jason W. Moore (Oakland: PM Press, 2016).

15. Dipesh Chakrabarty, "Climate and Capital: On Conjoined Histories," *Critical Inquiry* 41 (2014), 1–23.

16. Swift was not hostile to all areas of capitalist growth and imperial expansion. He was in favor of colonies for dedicated resources. Swift and members of his circle were investors in slavery. But his criticism of Anglo-Irish trade and hostility to "modern colonies" also gestured toward alternative trajectories for the British Empire. See my "Swift's Political Climates."

17. We find an illuminating contrast with Swift in the entry on "Optimism" in the *Philosophical Dictionary*, where Voltaire writes that we do not live in the best of all possible worlds and notes that Alexander Pope's vision of a world operating by immutable laws offers "pleasant consolation." Swift differed both from Pope's equipoise and Voltaire's begrudging acceptance, refusing to accept the world as it was.

18. *News from Nowhere*, 53. My discussion of *News from Nowhere*, especially its repudiation of politics and recovery of passion, is indebted to Stephen Arata's introduction.

19. Richard Jeffries, *After London; Or Wild England* (London: Cassell, 1885).

20. John Plotz, "Speculative Naturalism and the Problem of Scale: Richard Jefferies's *After London*, After Darwin," *MLQ* 76 (2015), 31–56.

21. Quoted in Plotz, "Speculative Naturalism and the Problem of Scale."

22. Lawrence Wright, "How Pandemics Wreak Havoc – and Open Minds."

23. Compare Rohrbach, *Modernity's Mist*.

24. See Benjamin Morgan, "Fin du Globe: On Decadent Planets," *Victorian Studies* 58 (2016), 609–35.

25. Jon Mee, *Print, Publicity, and Popular Radicalism in the 1790s: The Laurel of Liberty* (Cambridge: Cambridge University Press, 2016). That conviction was not necessarily driven by a democratic belief in the people achieving a unified public opinion, by way of the rational public sphere. The notion of an end to political contention, Mee writes, building on Kevin Gilmartin, was "often shaped by a Christian sense of millenarian revelation as much as by anything like Rousseau's notion of the ultimately transparent authority of the 'general will'" (12).

26. See Wil Verhoeven, *Americomania and the French Revolution Debate in Britain, 1789–1802* (Cambridge: Cambridge University Press, 2013).

27. Jonathan Roberts, "Wordsworth's Apocalypse," *Literature and Theology* 20 (2006), 361–78 (p. 363).

28. 1805 *Prelude*, x.140–3. William Wordsworth, *The Prelude: 1799, 1805, 1850*, eds. Jonathan Wordsworth, M. H. Abrams, and Stephen Gill (New York: Norton, 1979), 398.

29. See David Bromwich, *Disowned by Memory: Wordsworth's Poetry of the 1790s* (Chicago: University of Chicago Press, 1998); Chandler, *Wordsworth's Second Nature: A Study of the Poetry and Politics* (Chicago: University of Chicago

Press, 1984); Alan Liu, *Wordsworth: The Sense of History* (Stanford: Stanford University Press, 1989).

30. Roberts, "Wordsworth's Apocalypse," quoting Geoffrey H. Hartman, *Wordsworth's Poetry, 1787–1814* (New Haven: Yale University Press, 1964) and M. H. Abrams, *Natural Supernaturalism: Tradition and Revolution in Romantic Literature* (New York: Norton, 1971).

31. "Wordsworth's Apocalypse," quoting *The Prelude*, IV.563–4.

32. Lee Sterrenburg notes that "decline-and-fall themes took on a new resonance and intensity" after 1815. *"The Last Man*: Anatomy of Failed Revolutions," *Nineteenth-Century Fiction* 33 (1978), 324–47.

33. See *The Forms of Informal Empire: Britain, Latin America, and Nineteenth-Century Literature* (Baltimore: Johns Hopkins University Press, 2020).

34. See, for example, *The Age of Bronze*: "The Infant World redeems her name of 'New.' / 'Tis the old Aspiration breathed afresh, / To kindle Souls within degraded flesh" (267–9).

35. Amanda Jo Goldstein, *Sweet Science: Romantic Materialism and the New Logics of Life* (Chicago: University of Chicago Press, 2017), 167.

36. Dates for the onset of the "Anthropocene" vary. As S. L. Lewis and M. A. Maslin note, Crutzen and Stoermer originally proposed "that the start of the Anthropocene should be coincident with the beginning of the Industrial Revolution and James Watt's 1784 refinement of the steam engine. Others followed, including stratigraphers, suggesting that 1800 should be the beginning of the Anthropocene despite a lack of corresponding global geological markers, and the presence of well-known stratigraphic evidence suggestive of different dates." "Defining the Anthropocene," *Nature* 519 (2015), 171–80.

37. Andreas Malm, *Fossil Capital: The Rise of Steam Power and the Roots of Global Warming* (New York: Verso, 2016).

38. See David Higgins, *British Romanticism, Climate Change, and the Anthropocene: Writing Tambora* (Basingstoke: Palgrave, 2017).

39. Melissa Bailes, "The Psychologization of Geological Catastrophe in Mary Shelley's *The Last Man,"ELH* 82 (2015), 671–99. This was dropped from later editions. In the prophetic preface to *The Last Man*, Bailes notes, Shelley alludes to the later versions of Cuvier's theory, in which he localized "revolutions" to volcanos and earthquakes.

40. Martin J. S. Rudwick, *Worlds Before Adam: The Reconstruction of Geohistory in the Age of Reform* (Chicago: University of Chicago Press, 2008), 6. See also *Bursting the Limits of Time: The Reconstruction of Geohistory in the Age of Revolution* (Chicago: University of Chicago Press, 2005).

41. Rudwick, *Worlds Before Adam*, 1–2.

42. *CPW*, 6.229.

43. *CPW*, 6.229–30.

44. *Conversations of Lord Byron with Thomas Medwin, Esq.*, 2 vols. (London, 1832), 2.13–15 (emphasis added).

45. Bailes, "The Psychologization of Geological Catastrophe in Mary Shelley's *The Last Man*," 684–5. In her illuminating discussion, Bailes addresses Shelley's own belief in the viability or otherwise of certain hypotheses about the coming end of the world or the human species. But we do not need to reach any conclusion about their viability to see the implications of these converging endings for the politics and the aesthetics of Shelley's novel.

46. "Darkness," *CPW*, 4.40–3, lines 2–4.

47. The world of "Darkness" can thus be seen to mark the running backward or turning inward of a carbon-driven economy and thus the culmination – or antithesis – of the developments tracked by Menely in *Climate and the Making of Worlds*. This world in collapse is also a collapsed economy. Shelley and Byron would reimagine this situation in *The Last Man* and *The Island respectively*, interrelated works that see the demise of existing economic arrangements on the way to a new world.

48. Examining a passage from Cormac McCarthy's dystopian novel *The Road*, James concludes that its "alliterative cascade . . . propels us at the same time toward the picture of *another* world, a world whose 'alien' appearance isn't straightforwardly comforting, to say the least, but whose sonorous depiction counterpoints the very 'desolation' that inspires it." "Critical Solace," *New Literary History* 47 (2016), 481–504 (pp. 481–2).

2 The Last Whigs

1. John Cam Hobhouse to Francis Place, December 11, 1827. British Library Add. MS 35148; Francis Place to John Cam Hobhouse, December 19, 1827. British Library Add. MS 35148.

2. Place to Hobhouse, December 19, 1827.

3. Place to Hobhouse, December 19, 1827.

4. For the shifting political landscape in the first half of the nineteenth century, see Thompson, *The Making of the English Working Class*; Hilton, *A Mad, Bad, and Dangerous People?*; William Anthony Hay, *The Whig Revival 1808–1830* (New York: Palgrave, 2005); James Vernon, *Politics and the People: A Study in English Political Culture, 1815–1867* (Cambridge: Cambridge University Press, 1993); Mandler, *Aristocratic Government in the Age of Reform*. For "liberal" subjectivity and its antecedents in the Romantic age, see Hadley, *Living Liberalism*; Anderson, *Bleak Liberalism*; Jonathan David Gross, *Byron: The Erotic Liberal* (Lanham: Rowman & Littlefield, 2001); Saree Makdisi, *William Blake and the Impossible History of the 1790s* (Chicago: University of Chicago

Press, 2003); Daniel M. Stout, *Corporate Romanticism: Liberalism, Justice, and the Novel* (New York: Fordham University Press, 2017).

5. The new Whig generation that spearheaded passage of the Reform Act did not overlap meaningfully with the "Abolition" party in parliament. Although these groups inevitably came together in the passage of legislation, they are best conceived as distinct. See Izhak Gross, "The Abolition of Negro Slavery and British Parliamentary Politics, 1832–3," *Historical Journal* 23 (1980), 63–85. Brougham was a critical exception, as I discuss in Chapter 3.

6. See "Aristocratic Styles in the Age of Reform: 11. Liberals and Moderates," chapter 3 in Mandler, *Aristocratic Government in the Age of Reform.*

7. Koselleck, *Futures Past*, 1–2 (emphasis added).

8. See J. G. A. Pocock, "The Varieties of Whiggism from Exclusion to Reform: A History of Ideology and Discourse," in *Virtue, Commerce, and History: Essays on Political Thought and History, Chiefly in the Eighteenth Century* (Cambridge: Cambridge University Press, 1985), 221.

9. See Bernard Bailyn, *The Ideological Origins of the American Revolution* (Cambridge: Harvard University Press, 1967) and Steve Pincus, *The Heart of the Declaration: The Founders' Case for an Activist Government* (New Haven: Yale University Press, 2016).

10. Mandler, *Aristocratic Government in the Age of Reform*, 13.

11. Byron to Hobhouse, October 1819, *BLJ*, 6.228.

12. See, inter alia, Malcolm Kelsall, *Byron's Politics* (Sussex: Harvester Press, 1987); Gross, *Byron: The Erotic Liberal*; Jerome Christensen, *Lord Byron's Strength: Romantic Writing and Commercial Society* (Baltimore: Johns Hopkins University Press, 1993). As Mandler has emphasized in *Aristocratic Government in the Age of Reform*, Fox's legacy was one complex crosscurrent within Whig culture. The connection sustained by Lord Holland, Fox's nephew, was, similarly, only one node within a wider network. While Mandler claims that Hobhouse was effectively a Foxite Whig, he straddled the divide between Holland House and radical Westminster while also displaying early "liberal" tendencies. Mandler's observation nonetheless remains accurate in the sense that Hobhouse *did* seek to mobilize a version of Foxite opposition; what that meant in the 1820s was another question.

13. See "Byron's Opposition," chapter 6, in Havard, *Disaffected Parties.*

14. Francis Place to John Cam Hobhouse, January 29, 1829. British Library Add. MS 35148.33.

15. Hobhouse to Byron, June 5, 1818. *Byron's Bulldog*, 231.

16. *Byron's Bulldog*, 231.

17. *Byron's Bulldog*, 232.

18. *Byron's Bulldog*, 232.

19. See Robert E. Zegger, *John Cam Hobhouse: A Political Life* (Columbia: University of Missouri Press, 1973).
20. British Library Add. MS 47235. I quote from Peter Cochran's transcription.
21. British Library Add. MS 47235. May 23, 1818.
22. British Library Add. MS 47235. May 23, 1818.
23. British Library Add. MS 47235. May 23, 1818 (emphasis added).
24. Hobhouse to Byron, September 28, 1818. *Byron's Bulldog*, 247.
25. Cochran's note to transcription of British Library Add. MS 47235.
26. See Jon Mee, "'Bread & Cheese & Porter Only Being Allowed': Radical Spaces in London, 1792–1795," in *Sociable Places: Locating Culture in Romantic-Period Britain*, ed. Kevin Gilmartin (Cambridge: Cambridge University Press, 2017), 51–69, and *Print, Publicity, and Popular Radicalism in the 1790s*. See also Ian Newman, "Edmund Burke in the Tavern," *European Romantic Review* 24 (2013), 125–48, and *The Romantic Tavern: Literature and Conviviality in the Age of Revolution* (Cambridge: Cambridge University Press, 2021).
27. Hobhouse to Byron, July 16, 1818. *Byron's Bulldog*, 240.
28. British Library Add. MS 47235. July 13, 1818 (emphases added).
29. Hobhouse to Byron, June 16, 1819. *Byron's Bulldog*, 273.
30. Quoted in *Byron's Bulldog*, 273.
31. *Byron's Bulldog*, 273.
32. [John Cam Hobhouse], *Letter to Canning* (London, 1818).
33. "The Englishman is nowhere so degraded an animal as at a borough election," Hobhouse noted, observing that the franchise was "the greatest curse that can befall a town." British Library Add. MS 47235. July 17, 1818. George Eliot mounted related critiques of electoral practice in her mid-Victorian novel *Felix Holt*. See Chapter 4.
34. British Library Add. MS 47235. July 13, 1818.
35. *Byron's Bulldog*, 286.
36. Aside from Lord Holland's west London home, Byron was a frequent attendee at Melbourne House, where he began his ill-fated romance with Caroline Lamb.
37. "Detached Thoughts," in *Byron: A Self-Portrait, Letters and Diaries 1798 to 1824*, ed. Peter Quennell (Oxford: Oxford University Press, 1990), 29 [618–19]. Subsequent references are abbreviated *DT* and given by entry and [page] number in the main text.
38. Quoted in *His Very Self and Voice*, 269 (emphasis added).
39. For the changing resonances of extinct "tribes" and myths around the "last of the race" between the seventeenth and nineteenth centuries, see Stafford, *The Last of the Race*.
40. For differing accounts of Byron's level of political commitment during the later years of his life, see David V. Erdman, "Lord Byron and the Genteel

Reformers," *PMLA* 56 (1941), 1065–94; Kelsall, *Byron's Politics*; Beaton, *Byron's War*; Christensen, *Lord Byron's Strength*.

41. See the discussion of *The Vision of Judgment* in my "Byron's Opposition," chapter 6 of Havard, *Disaffected Parties*.

42. See David Francis Taylor, "Byron, Sheridan, and the Afterlife of Eloquence," *Review of English Studies* 65 (2014), 474–94 (p. 457). With a focus on Byron's attachment to Sheridan as a political figure, Taylor discusses Byron's elegy for Sheridan, "Detached Thoughts," and his return to Sheridan in *Don Juan*, XI.77.

43. *Monody on the Death of the Right Honourable R. B. Sheridan*, CPW, 4.18–22, lines 23–32. Further citations given by line number in the main text. "My feelings were never more excited than while writing the Monody on Sheridan," Byron said, "every word that I wrote came direct from the heart" (*CPW*, 4.454). The poem was completed in 1816 at Lake Geneva in the same months as "Darkness," "Prometheus," "Churchill's Grave," and "The Dream."

44. The poem nonetheless presents a highly qualified account of literary posterity, in which authors remain subject to distortion and vilification, even in the grave.

45. With an eye on questions about actual political efficacy, by contrast, Taylor sees the poem instantiating a "discernable friction between the competing imperatives of two modes of address, the parliamentary oration and the monody." The influence of the *Monody* was thereby circumscribed: whether we locate the theater in the poem or the poem in the theater, its influence remains confined to a delineated literary sphere and a "theatrical rather than parliamentary economy of rhetorical performance." "Byron, Sheridan, and the Afterlife of Eloquence," 486–7.

3 Byron, Brougham, and the End of Slavery

1. The novel, presented as "a volume published in 'Yankeedoodoolia' in the year 2227," contains satire of political "bigwigs" including the Duke of Wellington, "parody on the contemporary second-rate historical novel," and "burlesques on many other literary forms." See Ralph M. Wardle, "The Authorship of *Whitehall* (1827)," *Modern Language Notes* 56 (1941), 207–9.

2. *Whitehall, or the Days of George IV* (London: W. Marsh, 1827), 29–30, 54, and 22.

3. *Don Juan*, IV.115. Mark Canuel identifies Byron's "jokey urbanity" here with a "self-consciously constructed racial hierarchy" apparent in both the politics and the aesthetics of *Don Juan*. In his probing discussion of Byron's engagement with

slavery and race, Canuel points to Byron's support for abolition, including his praise for Wilberforce in *Don Juan*. Noting that Byron voiced outrage at the barbaric treatment of Black flesh, Canuel also emphasizes his attachment to a "subtle yet profound logic that insistently privileges the purity and beauty of white bodies," apparent in the refusal in this stanza to grant the dark-skinned Nubian women any "inherent aesthetic value" or interest beyond the exchange rate of the market. See "Race, Writing, and *Don Juan*," *Studies in Romanticism* 54 (2015), 303–28.

4. See Christopher Leslie Brown, *Moral Capital: Foundations of British Abolitionism* (Durham: University of North Carolina Press, 2006).

5. *Don Juan*, IV.115.

6. Brown, *Moral Capital*, 37–40.

7. In *Capitalism and Slavery*, Eric Williams presented an institution in irrecoverable decline. But revisiting the "last stages of amelioration" through the case of John Gladstone – a wealthy plantation owner in Demerara – Trevor Burnard and Kit Candlin maintain that "notions of a reformed slavery were not illusory fantasies but a realistic possibility in the protean politics of slavery and antislavery in the British Empire of the 1820s." See *Capitalism and Slavery*, rev. ed. (Durham: University of North Carolina Press, 2021 [1944]) and "Sir John Gladstone and the Debate over the Amelioration of Slavery in the British West Indies in the 1820s," *Journal of British Studies* 57 (2018), 760–82 (p. 762). Burnard and Candlin point to the successful introduction of reformist measures in the Dutch colonies to argue that slavery could have continued for decades beyond 1833 in Britain's sugar colonies.

8. See J. R. Ward, "The Amelioration of British West Indian Slavery: Anthropometric Evidence," *The Economic History Review* 71 (2018), 1199–226; Christa Dierksheide, *Amelioration and Empire: Progress and Slavery in the Plantation Americas* (Charlottesville: University of Virginia Press, 2014); Christopher Taylor, *Empire of Neglect: The West Indies in the Wake of British Liberalism* (Durham: Duke University Press, 2018). With an eye on visual culture, Sarah Thomas has shown how images of robust health and fertility (coupled with appeals to the supposedly benevolent treatment of the enslaved) demonstrated that slavery could be sustained through reproduction. "Envisaging a Future for Slavery: Agostino Brunias and the Imperial Politics of Labor and Reproduction," *Eighteenth-Century Studies* 52 (2018), 115–33. See also George Boulukos, *The Grateful Slave: The Emergence of Race in Eighteenth-Century British and American Culture* (Cambridge: Cambridge University Press, 2012). Burnard and Candlin tie Gladstone's efforts to reform and modernize his plantation workforce to an "expansive imperial vision" echoed by his son, the future Victorian prime minister. "Sir John Gladstone and the Debate over the Amelioration of Slavery," 761.

9. Even the most vehement antislavery campaigners, in Taylor's stringent accounting, failed to imagine a present tense for enslaved people, who fell between their current immiserated condition and a future political economy that understood their worth only as labor value. See "'Them Worthless Ones': Emancipatory Liberalism in Jamaica," chapter 2 of *Empire of Neglect*.

10. While initially "cautious," Robin Blackburn notes, the "rebirth of organized abolitionism soon aroused a significant popular response, accompanied by the emergence of fresh forces and far more radical perspectives." See *The Overthrow of Colonial Slavery: 1776–1848* (New York: Verso, 1988) 439, 436. Female-led organizing played a crucial role in this vocal popular movement. See Clare Midgley, *Women against Slavery: The British Campaigns, 1780–1870* (London: Routledge, 1992). Popular organizing worked in concert with print culture. *The History of Mary Prince* (1831) was published with the assistance of Thomas Pringle – editor of the *Anti-Slavery Register* – and female campaigners. See Juliet Shields, *Mary Prince, Slavery, and Print Culture in the Anglophone Atlantic World* (Cambridge: Cambridge University Press, 2021).

11. Blackburn, *The Overthrow of Colonial Slavery*, 439, 436.

12. [Henry Brougham], review of Morris Birkbeck, *Notes on a Journey in America*.

13. "Brougham, Henry Peter," *The History of Parliament: The House of Commons 1820–1832*, 7 vols., ed. D. R. Fisher (Cambridge: Cambridge University Press, 2009).

14. Tanya Agathocleous, *Disaffected: Emotion, Sedition, and Colonial Law in the Anglosphere* (Ithaca: Cornell University Press, 2021). My account of the wider affective public sphere in this chapter builds upon Agathocleous, Lauren Berlant, Julie Ellison, Joseph Rezek, and Ann Laura Stoler among others, in viewing the public sphere of British politics as structured by feeling and inclusive of a wider imperial polity: the political was always affective and politicized affect always racialized.

15. Quoted in Emilia Viotti Da Costa, *Crowns of Glory, Tears of Blood: The Demerara Slave Rebellion of 1823* (Oxford: Oxford University Press, 1994), 299 n. 10.

16. See Burnard and Candlin, "Sir John Gladstone and the Debate over the Amelioration of Slavery"; Da Costa, *Crowns of Glory, Tears of Blood;* Tom Zoellner, *Island on Fire: The Revolt That Ended Slavery in the British Empire* (Cambridge, MA: Harvard University Press, 2020).

17. *The Spirit of the Age: or Contemporary Portraits*, 2nd ed. (London: Henry Colburn, 1825), 324–5.

18. Debates persist about the continued economic viability of slavery and Williams's use of data. But "economic" explanations are inextricable from the competing time frames that I discuss here: Assessments about economic

viability were necessarily bound up with thinking about the future. Debates about the "profitability" of slavery were not only a matter of simple calculation but inseparable from speculations about future value and thus informed by the evolving horizons of imperial activity and changing conceptions of governance.

19. Williams, *Capitalism and Slavery*, 143.
20. Byron to Hobhouse, January 25, 1819, *BLJ*, 6.96–7.
21. "Brougham, Henry Peter."
22. See William Christie, "Going Public: Print Lords Byron and Brougham," *Studies in Romanticism* 38 (1999), 443–75. As Christie notes, Brougham had also given a "savage" review to Byron's first public collection, *Hours of Idleness*. The poet seems not to have been aware of Brougham's authorship until after the period discussed here.
23. Chimney sweepers became the site of anxieties about contaminating "Blackness" associated with enslaved persons overseas. See Jeremy Goheen, "'Soot in One's Soup': Transitory Blackness in British Romantic Chimney-Sweep Literature," *Studies in Romanticism* 61 (2022), 57–65.
24. *CPW*, 5.13, *Don Juan*, 1.15.7–8. Romilly was a noted legal reformer and abolitionist.
25. See my "'Blustering, Bungling, Trimming': Byron, Hobhouse, and the Politics of *Don Juan* Canto 1," *The Byron Journal* 49 (2021), 29–41. See also McGann, *Don Juan in Context* and Truman Guy Steffan, *Byron's Don Juan, Volume 1: The Making of a Masterpiece* (Austin: University of Texas Press, 1957). "Hatred for Brougham, Romilly, Southey, and even Castlereagh" had "moved Byron to the politics of his manifesto," McGann proposes. But rather than simply moving beyond these localized animosities – and in part *by* having but then releasing them – the poem "would only become more serious and thoughtful in its political purposes as it developed." *CPW*, 5.669.
26. See "Byron's Opposition," chapter 6 in my *Disaffected Parties*.
27. "Henry Brougham," *ODNB*. The "shortage of effective Whig speakers in the Commons" turned the party back to Brougham.
28. "Henry Brougham."
29. Quoted in *CPW*, 5.668.
30. "Henry Brougham."
31. *CPW*, 5.85–8 and n. Subsequent references to the "Brougham stanzas" by line number in the main text.
32. Quoted in my "'Blustering, Bungling, Trimming.'"
33. Byron scathingly dismisses Brougham, for example, as "a Lawyer by trade – and Orator by chance" (a variant for line 21). This succinct characterization is highly effective in isolation. But Byron undermines this and other lines, across these stanzas as a whole, piling insult upon insult.

34. Hobhouse to Byron, January 5, 1819.

35. Blackburn, *The Overthrow of Colonial Slavery*, 438–9.

36. Measures to reform slavery were seen, both by supporters of abolition and its opponents, as paving the way for emancipation. But the kind of amelioration promoted by John Gladstone, Burnard and Candlin argue, represented a "rearguard" attempt to preserve slavery and ensure its continuation, perhaps indefinitely. Following Dierksheide, they note that "rational arguments in favor of planter-led abolitionism appealed to Tory and antislavery M.P.s alike, suggesting to conservatives that the more wide-eyed abolitionist plans for emancipation were untried 'experiments.'" "Sir John Gladstone and the Debate over the Amelioration of Slavery," 763 and Dierksheide, *Amelioration and Empire*. For my purposes here, these rhetorics were, to some extent, inseparable, in holding off the end.

37. For the packaging of the contemporary Caribbean in print and visual culture by way of a "planter picturesque" that assimilated the West Indies to the English countryside, see Elizabeth A. Bohls, *Slavery and the Politics of Place: Representing the Colonial Caribbean, 1770–1833* (Cambridge: Cambridge University Press, 2014).

38. Blackburn, *The Overthrow of Colonial Slavery*, 438, 439.

39. Gross, "The Abolition of Negro Slavery and British Parliamentary Politics, 1832–3." Lord Bathurst, Secretary of State for War and the Colonies, for example, was "willing to adapt to new circumstances rather than offering rigid resistance to reform." But he remained "strongly protectionist, was opposed to Catholic emancipation, and was temperamentally skeptical of change." Like Gladstone and Canning, he remained a Tory at last. Burnard and Candlin, "Sir John Gladstone and the Debate over the Amelioration of Slavery," 774.

40. Quoted in Blackburn, *The Overthrow of Colonial Slavery*, 451.

41. Reproduced as the "Preface" to *Substance of the Debate in the House of Commons, on the 15th May, 1823, on a Motion for the Mitigation and Gradual Abolition of Slavery Throughout the British Dominions* (London, 1823), vii–viii, x–xi.

42. *Substance of the Debate . . . on the 15th May, 1823*, 11.

43. *Substance of the Debate . . . on the 15th May, 1823*, 16.

44. Cast out from existing structures of belonging and recognition and no longer made to live in the service of slavery's ruthless political economy, the enslaved may not have been worked to death any longer, but they were, Taylor demonstrates, effectively left to die. See *Empire of Neglect*.

45. *Substance of the Debate . . . on the 15th May, 1823*, 23, 30 (emphasis added).

46. *Substance of the Debate . . . on the 15th May, 1823*, 4.

47. *Substance of the Debate . . . on the 15th May, 1823*, 83 (emphasis added).

48. Blackburn, *The Overthrow of Colonial Slavery*, 423. The pamphlet *Immediate Not Gradual Emancipation* was by Elizabeth Heyricke.

49. *Hansard*, April 15, 1831.

50. *Hansard*, April 15, 1831.

51. Quoted in Da Costa, *Crowns of Glory, Tears of Blood*. Freed persons in Jamaica demanded rights that same year. Blackburn, *The Overthrow of Colonial Slavery*, 428, 425.

52. "The present deranged state of our Colony renders it difficult for the writer to arrange his ideas," the same soldier wrote back to England, "so as to communicate fully and explicitly in a manner that too seriously concerns us all, having in common with every individual white and free person in the Colony, experienced nothing but exposure, fatigue, and want of rest for the last five days, and he is even now, in this exercise, subject to the unpleasant anxiety of instant alarm." The writer of this missive could achieve no salve for his agitated spirits, no restoration of tranquility. In the process, he points to a wider breakdown in available structures of feeling, together with an escalation of habitual vigilance to "anxiety."

53. Blackburn, *The Overthrow of Colonial Slavery*, 436. See also Andrew Porter, "Trusteeship, Anti-Slavery, and Humanitarianism," in *The Oxford History of the British Empire: Volume III: The Nineteenth Century*, ed. Andrew Porter (Oxford: Oxford University Press, 1999), 198–221, and Taylor, *Empire of Neglect*.

54. In fact, Brougham had been surprised by the growing support for immediate emancipation when the Anti-Slavery Society was relaunched in May 1830. Blackburn, *The Overthrow of Colonial Slavery*, 436.

55. Catherine Hall, Nicholas Draper, Keith McClelland, Katie Donington, and Rachel Lang, *Legacies of British Slave-Ownership: Colonial Slavery and the Formation of Victorian Britain* (Cambridge: Cambridge University Press, 2014). See also the "Legacies of British Slavery" database: www.ucl.ac.uk/lbs/.

56. For the 1831 "Christmas Day" or "Baptist" rebellion in Jamaica and its role in hobbling the proslavery cause in parliament, see Zoellner, *Island on Fire* and my "Burn It Down," *The New Rambler* (2021). That same year saw "Swing" riots in English counties, including similar kinds of labor disturbance and property destruction.

57. Lee Sterrenburg, reproducing a version of this image, claims that Parry depicts the "Satanic giant 'Bill' (no little William!) . . . eclipsing worthier causes such as the abolition of slavery and free trade." See "Mary Shelley's Monster: Politics and Psyche in *Frankenstein*," 167. In the version of the image that I examine here, however, abolition is clearly identified (together with the rotten boroughs that the Reform Act set out to eradicate) as a *cause* of reform. The energies of

abolitionists, that is to say, were part of the dangerously experimental energies that helped to give rise, in this retroactive account, to the Reform Act in the first place.

58. *Recollections of a Long Life, by Lord Broughton*, 5.125, 128, 135.

59. While the depiction of Brougham as Othello makes the question of race explicit, that image has the least direct tie with Blackness, depicting Brougham with the kind of "tawny tinge" of brown that Edmund Kean introduced to the character (thereby distancing Shakespeare's Moor from Black Africans). By contrast, the images of Brougham as a specimen of the "Black Style" and as the freestanding "Black Sheep" – when read in dialogue with the image of Othello – invoke the use of "burnt-cork blackface" to portray characters of African descent, including enslaved West Indians. See Kim Hall, "*Othello* and the Problem of Blackness," in *A Companion to Shakespeare's Works: The Tragedies*, eds. Richard Dutton and Jean E. Howard (Malden, MA: Blackwell, 2005), 357–74, and Ashley Cohen, *The Global Indies: British Imperial Culture and the Reshaping of the World, 1756–1815* (New Haven: Yale University Press, 2021), 86. As Michèle Mendelssohn has shown, images of Oscar Wilde in proximity to Black Americans offered a means of mocking his out-of-place status as an Irish author. The scandalous Victorian playwright and dandy wore those associations as a badge of pride, Mendelssohn maintains, as a stigmatized outsider who leveraged his marginality for other ends. *Making Oscar Wilde* (Oxford: Oxford University Press, 2018).

60. Vincent Brown, *The Reaper's Garden: Death and Power in the World of Atlantic Slavery* (Cambridge: Harvard University Press, 2010), 199.

61. These images might thereby approximate Alexander G. Weheliye's account of "racializing assemblages" that traverse the space between legally instituted (white) personhood and abjected, disposable (Black) nonlife with multiple, interlocking kinds of enfleshment, affect, and speciation. *Habeas Viscus: Racializing Assemblages, Biopolitics, and Black Feminist Theories of the Human* (Durham: Duke University Press, 2014).

62. See Chapter 5.

63. In her ingenious reading of *Frankenstein*, Maureen N. McLane emphasizes Victor's failure to recognize the monster as a "fellow creature." Victor's "Malthusian panic" about his creature propagating ensures, in turn, that "the conflict of monster and man will be imagined as a species or race conflict" – an outcome McLane ultimately reads as a failure of humanism and the humanities. *Romanticism and the Human Sciences* (Cambridge: Cambridge University Press, 2000), 107–8. This discussion of inclusion and exclusion, extinction and propagation, individual and population subtends my discussion here.

64. Baldick, *In Frankenstein's Shadow*, 89.
65. *Hansard*, April 15, 1831.
66. See C. L. R. James, *The Black Jacobins: Toussaint L'Ouverture and the San Domingo Revolution* (London: Secker & Warburg, 1938); Susan Buck-Morss, *Hegel, Haiti, and Universal History* (Pittsburgh: University of Pittsburgh Press, 2009); and David Kazanjian, *The Brink of Freedom: Improvising Life in the Nineteenth-Century Atlantic World* (Durham: Duke University Press, 2016).
67. Latin American independence movements also factored into abolition debates. As Blackburn notes, "reports of the emancipation proclamations made by Bolívar and other leaders of the Spanish American liberation movements helped to put British abolitionists on their mettle." *The Overthrow of Colonial Slavery*, 421. South American markets saw Britain seek to reconcile calls for independence with new guises of imperial rule. See Jessie Reeder, *The Forms of Informal Empire*.

4 "Crowns in the Dust"

1. *JMS*, 2.476–7.
2. *JMS*, 2.477 n.
3. Barbara Johnson, *A Life with Mary Shelley*, 9.
4. McWhir, "Introduction," *LM*, xv.
5. McWhir, for example, takes the centrality of Percy Shelley to *The Last Man* as read, tracing the novel's concern with Greece to his Hellenism. But the novel also looks to modern Greece and the freedom struggles that shaped the end of Byron's life.
6. Fuson Wang intriguingly reads the assembling of the prophetic sibylline leaves in the preface to *The Last Man* as a displaced autobiographical effort, on Shelley's part, to claim the agency of editing her late husband's poems. "We Must Live Elsewhere: The Social Construction of Natural Immunity in Mary Shelley's *The Last Man*," *European Romantic Review* 22 (2011), 235–55 (pp. 238–9).
7. McWhir deftly concludes that the book is "neither merely conventional nor merely personal" and that it ultimately eludes definition, "weav[ing] the particular and the general together, making personal meaning out of the breadth of Shelley's reading and out of the resonance of a range of literary conventions" ("Introduction," xv).
8. For the constitutive role of engagement with Byron for the poetic identities of "L.E.L.," Felicia Hemans, and other female authors, see Wolfson, "Byron and the Muse of Female Poetry," chapter 8 of *Romantic Interactions*, 253–90. Wolfson identifies traces of Byron in *Frankenstein*, where his presence channels an interest in "scientific conquest" (257).

9. Johnson, "My Monster/My Self," 18. In *A Life with Mary Shelley*, 15–26.

10. Butler, "Afterword, Animating Autobiography: Barbara Johnson and Mary Shelley's Monster," 37–8. In Johnson, *A Life with Mary Shelley*, 37–50.

11. Johnson, *A Life with Mary Shelley*, 18.

12. Adrian shares Percy Shelley's lithe figure and his love for animals (together with his intermittent frailty and frequent neediness). Critics have identified Adrian as an idealized version of Percy Shelley and also as an "Alastor" figure, referring to the self-critical Wordsworthian avatar in his poem of that title. In his ardent admiration for Adrian, Lionel has been identified with Mary Shelley. Following the death of Raymond and progress of the plague, Adrian succeeds in becoming a kind of wartime hero, notable for his compassionate leadership (succeeding Ryland, who hoards wealth and stokes prejudice). But this eventual ascent is ironized: Percy Shelley's ideals become prominent at precisely the moment that the inevitability of mass death renders them largely beside the point.

13. There are important similarities and differences between Ryland and Cobbett. As McWhir points out, Cobbett was neither, like Ryland, a man of "immense wealth inherited from his father, who had been a manufacturer," nor was he a republican (*LM*, 42 n. 47). Like Ryland, Cobbett took his rural oratory to the United States and was known for his pugnacious support of the white working class.

14. Leslie Marchand, *Byron: A Biography*, 3 vols. (Alfred A. Knopf: New York, 1957), 2.841–2.

15. John Wilson Croker, quoted in *The Letters of John Murray to Lord Byron*, ed. Andrew Nicholson (Liverpool: Liverpool University Press, 2007), 317 n. Croker heard the letter discussed at a dinner with Walter Scott, among other "people of note."

16. See Andrew Elfenbein, "Silver-Fork Byron and the Image of Regency England," in *Byromania*, ed. Wilson, 77–92. "The formulaic plot of the fashionable novel," Elfenbein notes, "is one of supersession: the glittering show of aristocratic Regency society gives way to the sturdy happiness of the bourgeois, companionate marriage" (79). *Venetia* (1837) by Benjamin Disraeli, for example, sees the "heady world of Regency romanticism" give way to a "conservative, aristocratic, and heterosexual couple who represent the hopes for an England purged of the radicalism of poets like Byron and Shelley" (85). Disraeli, the future Conservative prime minister, was a great admirer of Byron in his youth but later sought to distance himself from the radical implications of his dandyish poses (80–2).

17. See "Spurgeon, Byron, and the Contingencies of Mediation," chapter 9 in Tom Mole, *What the Victorians Made of Romanticism*, 117–30. Spurgeon's sermons, Mole concludes, presented a mixed view of Byron's poetry.

18. Quoted in *Felix Holt, The Radical*, eds. William Baker and Kenneth Womack (Peterborough: Broadview, 2000), 96 n.

19. Cohen-Vrignaud sees Eliot's novel foregrounding "sober" liberal principles of individual and social responsibility over aristocratic license and aesthetic pleasure. See "Byron and Oriental Love," *Nineteenth-Century Literature* 68 (2013), 1–32 (pp. 1–2). Cohen-Vrignaud's account of *The Last Man* relatedly sees Shelley framing the novel in political-economic terms as countering Eastern sensuality and excess with an ironic liberal productivity – ironic because the plague sees efforts at rationing and regulation give way to superfluity and excess. *Radical Orientalism: Rights, Reform, and Romanticism* (Cambridge: Cambridge University Press, 2015), 163–77.

20. Raymond was, as the narration elaborates, "perfectly self-possessed; he accosted us both with courtesy, seemed immediately to enter into our feelings, and to make one with us. I scanned his physiognomy, which varied as he spoke, yet was beautiful in every change. The usual expression of his eyes was soft, though at times he could make them glare with ferocity; his complexion was colourless; and every trait spoke predominant self-will; his smile was pleasing, though disdain too often curled his lips – lips which to female eyes were the very throne of beauty and love. His voice, usually gentle, often startled you by a sharp discordant note, which shewed that his usual low tone was rather the work of study than nature" (*LM*, 37). In *The Last Man*, Raymond's contradictions have a clear toll when it comes to women: "gentle, yet fierce, tender and again neglectful ... now caressing and now tyrannizing over them according to his mood, but in every change a despot" (*LM*, 37).

21. *Shelley and Byron: The Snake and Eagle Wreathed in Flight* (Baltimore: Johns Hopkins University Press, 1976), 12.

22. *Shelley and Byron*, 16.

23. *His Very Self and Voice: Collected Conversations of Lord Byron*, ed. Ernest J. Lovell, Jr. (New York: Macmillan, 1954), 269. Byron himself portrayed Shelley as a down-to-earth visionary, braving the waves, as it were, but not seeking to ascend above them: "He, alone, in this age of humbug, dares stem the current, as he did to-day the flooded Arno in his skiff, although I could not observe that he made any progress. The attempt is better than being swept along as all the rest are, with the filthy garbage scoured from its banks" (269).

24. *JMS*, 2.478.

25. "I am melancholy," Shelley wrote in her journal, upon reading canto III of *Childe Harold's Pilgrimage*, before winding her thoughts toward its author: "How a powerful mind can sanctify past scenes and recollections – His is a powerful mind. one that fills me with melancholy yet mixed with pleasure

as is always the case when intellectual energy is displayed. I think of our excursions on the lake." *JMS*, 171–2.

26. Quoted in *JMS*, 2.476 n.

27. *JMS*, 1.172.

28. For the novel's Godwinian contexts, see Sterrenburg, "*The Last Man*: Anatomy of Failed Revolutions," 333–5.

29. See, inter alia, Muriel Spark, *Child of Light: A Reassessment of Mary Wollstonecraft Shelley* (Hadleigh, Essex: Tower Bridge Publications, 1951); Elizabeth Nitchie, *Mary Shelley: The Author of "Frankenstein"* (New Brunswick: Rutgers University Press, 1953); Sterrenburg, "*The Last Man*: Anatomy of Failed Revolutions"; Steven Goldsmith, "Of Gender, Plague and Apocalypse: Mary Shelley's Last Man," *Yale Journal of Criticism* 4 (1990), 129–73; Hilary Strang, "Common Life, Animal Life, Equality: *The Last Man*," *ELH* 78 (2011), 409–31; Wang, "We Must Live Elsewhere"; Lauren Cameron, "Mary Shelley's Malthusian Objections in *The Last Man*," *Nineteenth-Century Literature* 67 (2012), 177–203; Bailes, "The Psychologization of Geological Catastrophe in Mary Shelley's *The Last Man*"; Charlotte Sussman, "'Islanded in the World': Cultural Memory and Human Mobility in *The Last Man*," in *Peopling the World: Representing Human Mobility from Milton to Malthus* (Philadelphia: University of Pennsylvania Press, 2020), 157–77.

30. Sussman examines the book's ties to the "vogue for last-man narratives" in *Peopling the World*, 157–8, 170–1.

31. "Review of The Last Man," *The Panoramic Miscellany* (March 1826), 380–1.

32. F. Rosen, *Bentham, Byron, and Greece: Constitutionalism, Nationalism, and Early Liberal Political Thought* (Oxford: Clarendon Press, 1992), 76. Bentham "saw the only solution to a corrupt and oppressive constitution in the people rising up to change the form of government" (76).

33. My approach to *The Last Man* thus differs from the otherwise-valuable account of Lee Sterrenburg in "*The Last Man*: Anatomy of Failed Revolutions." Sterrenburg sees the book advancing equivalences between the "social organism" and nature and concludes that the advance of the plague – the inverse of a successful revolution – confirms the "antipolitical" bent of Shelley's novel. Although *The Last Man* was in dialogue with the various contexts that Sterrenburg outlines, the novel works not through metaphor, I suggest here, but through attention to the changing layers of politics, past, present, and to come – even though that does entail evident challenges to certain utopian ideals.

34. Review of Morris Birkbeck, *Notes on a Journey in America*, 121.

35. Raymond talks of the "triennial" contests (*LM*, 47).

36. *The Last Man* was apparently begun on the model of *Valperga*, in which Shelley had depicted courtly intrigue in European settings.

37. See Astra Taylor, "A Ruin and a Habitation," in *Democracy May Not Exist But We'll Miss It When It's Gone* (New York: Verso, 2019), 276–306.

38. See E. P. Thompson, *Whigs and Hunters: The Origin of the Black Act* (New York: Pantheon, 1975).

39. British Library Add. MS 47235.

40. Sussman, *Peopling the World*.

41. The novel "strives with great difficulty," Wang claims, "to reconstruct both subject ('we') and place ('elsewhere') in a new framework of cosmopolitan community and political radicalism." The novel's efforts to rewrite redemptive narratives and to imagine a place for an as-yet-unformed "us" recover the novel, in this account, from the charge of nihilism or anti-Romantic conservatism. Wang looks to a buried genealogy of characters that do not meet the qualities of humanness (or man-kind) as affirming the transformative agency of "Romantic imagination" and providing a "surprisingly material and social basis for a reclaimed politics of possibility" ("We Must Live Elsewhere," 236–7).

42. Wang characterizes Evadne as a rational, Wollstonecraftian figure, in whom Shelley mobilized skepticism toward her husband's ideas. Where the Greek exile Evadne represents an exoticized figure – who encodes stereotypes about the corrupting influence of the Eastern other, further tainted by her own transgressive conduct – Perdita also represents a kind of racialized femininity with political implications. Inasmuch as the men set her up as a kind of ideal, she also conceives of herself as representing a kind of unspoiled world. She finds an analogue – and may even have had one point of origin – in Byron's late poem, *The Island*, which features a romance between a Byronic outlaw and a native Tahitian woman. See Chapter 5.

43. *LMS*, 1.466. For the "strangers gallery" in parliament, see Christopher Reid, *Imprison'd Wranglers: The Rhetorical Culture of the House of Commons 1760–1800* (Oxford: Oxford University Press, 2012).

44. *LMS*, 1.466.

45. *Child of Light*, 165.

46. Cameron, "Mary Shelley's Malthusian Objections in *The Last Man*."

47. Compare Michel Foucault on the dawn of this worldview: "At every moment of its history, humanity is ... labouring under the threat of death: any population that cannot find new resources is doomed to extinction ... *Homo oeconomicus* is not the human being who represents his own needs to himself, and the objects capable of satisfying them; he is the human being who spends, wears out, and wastes his life in evading the imminence of death. He is

a finite being." *The Order of Things: An Archaeology of the Human Sciences* (New York: Vintage Books, 1994 [1970]), 279–80, and McLane, *Romanticism and the Human Sciences.*

48. Nitchie, *Mary Shelley: The Author of "Frankenstein,"* 37–8.
49. "Common Life, Animal Life, Equality: *The Last Man,*" 409.
50. "Common Life, Animal Life, Equality: *The Last Man,*" 409.
51. Spark, *Child of Light,* 158.
52. "Common Life, Animal Life, Equality: *The Last Man,*" 411.

5 New Worlds

1. "Jeremy Bentham," in *The Spirit of the Age,* 3.
2. "Jeremy Bentham," 3.
3. "Jeremy Bentham," 6, 4. In *Modernity's Mist*, Rohrbach concludes that Hazlitt's portraits in *The Spirit of the Age* amount to "a collection of balkanized contemporary histories rather than a unified, grand historical narrative." Hazlitt went on to fault Bentham, as Rohrbach notes, for his rigid systematicity. But the multiple temporalities that she elucidates – such that the age's "Spirit" only comes into focus as a cluster of heterogeneous and incommensurate relationships to the present – helps make sense of Bentham's placement as the opening portrait: Hazlitt's emphasis on the nonsynchrony between speculative (international) futures and available formulations of the political present made him not the exception but the exemplar of a general rule.
4. *Selected Writings: Jeremy Bentham*, ed. Stephen Engelmann (New Haven: Yale University Press, 2010), 4–5.
5. In 1823, Bentham's protégés presented his draft recommendations for a new constitution to the faltering Greek government. As Hazlitt's reference to the "New World" acknowledges, he was active in writing South American constitutions too. He also wrote circular letters that appeared in a number of newspapers in the United States. See Rosen, *Bentham, Byron, and Greece* and "Jeremy Bentham," *ODNB*. Bentham challenged the expansionist, civilizing thrust of the British Empire, calling for the nation to cut its colonies loose. *Emancipate Your Colonies!* was written in the 1790s, Christopher Taylor notes, within "a doubled revolutionary conjuncture in which a postimperial utopia seemed realizable." But by the time of its publication in 1830, Bentham's pamphlet "mapped so neatly onto the British discursive environment in which it was published that it was all but redundant." Bentham's call to sever ties with colonies had become compatible with the liberalizing logic that, in Taylor's account, allowed Britain to forget its ongoing responsibility to Black West Indians living in the wake of slavery. See *Empire of Neglect*, 78–9. See also

Jennifer Pitts, "Legislator of the World? A Reading of Bentham on Colonies," *Political Theory* 31 (2003), 200–34.

6. "Jeremy Bentham," 5.

7. The "Pantisocracy" scheme of Coleridge and Southey imagined a settlement in North America, for example, while Mary Wollstonecraft's lover Gilbert Imlay advanced related projects for Kentucky. See Verhoeven, *Americomania and the French Revolution Debate in Britain.*

8. Pope, *An Essay on Man* (London, 1743), 11 (1.106–8).

9. O'Brien, *Firsting and Lasting.*

10. Diana Reese, "A Troubled Legacy: Mary Shelley's *Frankenstein* and the Inheritance of Human Rights," *Representations* 96 (2006), 48–72. As Jessie Reeder has shown, South America was beginning to appear in British political-economic thought in its own right – but as a vast, readily colonizable wasteland. Even the Arctic is more populous than South America in *Frankenstein*, Reeder notes, looking ahead to depictions of Latin America in nineteenth-century British fiction "as either empty or unrepresentable." Reeder, *The Forms of Informal Empire.*

11. Charlotte Sussman, "'Islanded in the World': Cultural Memory and Human Mobility in *The Last Man*," in *Peopling the World*, 162.

12. *The Novels and Selected Works of Mary Shelley: Volume 1: Frankenstein, or the Modern Prometheus*, ed. Nora Crook (London: Pickering, 1996), 145. Further citations of this edition appear in the main text. Compare Celeste Langan, *Romantic Vagrancy: Wordsworth and the Simulation of Freedom* (Cambridge: Cambridge University Press, 1995).

13. Julia V. Douthwaite, "The Frankenstein of the French Revolution: Nogaret's Automaton Tale of 1790," *European Romantic Review* 20 (2009), 381–411. See also Ronald Paulson, *Representations of Revolution, 1789–1820* (New Haven: Yale University Press, 1983).

14. See Franco Moretti, *Signs Taken for Wonders: Essays in the Sociology of Literary Forms*, trans. Susan Fischer, David Forgacs, and David Miller (London: Verso, 1988 [1983]) and Patrick Brantlinger, "Race and *Frankenstein*," in *The Cambridge Companion to Frankenstein*, ed. Andrew Smith (Cambridge: Cambridge University Press, 2016), 228–42. Moretti sees Shelley's novel as anticipating capitalist exploitation, with the race of demons (promised by allowing the monster's "race" to propagate) figuring the proletariat.

15. See Jared Hickman, *Black Prometheus: Race and Radicalism in the Age of Atlantic Slavery* (Oxford: Oxford University Press, 2017).

16. I thank Tobias Menely for alerting me to this point.

17. Julia Douthwaite notes a parallel between "the chronological movement" of the French Revolution and the "narrative movement in *Frankenstein* – from an initial moment of optimism lived in a rural idyll, into an epic of suffering in

which the oppressed turns into the oppressor" – and points to the ways the monster's blissful coexistence with the De Laceys "bespeaks nostalgia for the lost possibility of creating a new polis." Douthwaite, "The Frankenstein of the French Revolution," 384–5.

18. Fred V. Randel, "The Political Geography of Horror in Mary Shelley's *Frankenstein,*" *ELH* 70 (2003), 465–91. Randel proposes that Shelley accepts the "metaphoric equivalence between the French Revolution and [the] monster."

19. *Novels and Selected Works of Mary Shelley: Volume 1: Frankenstein,* 145 n.

20. Victor also lands accidentally in Ireland after leaving Scotland, where he encounters traces of colonial tyranny that Shelley casts as complex mirror images of English freedom. See my "'What Freedom?' *Frankenstein,* Anti-Occidentalism, and English Liberty," *Nineteenth-Century Literature* (2019), 305–31.

21. See my "What Freedom?"

22. See, for example, Anne K. Mellor, *Mary Shelley: Her Life, Her Fiction, Her Monsters* (New York: Methuen, 1988).

23. See my "What Freedom?"

24. Byron to Hobhouse, October 3, 1819, *BLJ,* 6.225–7.

25. Trelawny to Hobhouse, April 30, 1824. National Library of Scotland, Murray Archive.

26. Byron quoted in *CPW,* 7.134.

27. See Menely, *Climate and the Making of Worlds.*

28. *CPW,* 7.27, 1.39–40 (emphasis added). Subsequent references to the poem are given by canto and line number in the main text.

29. The mutineers are described as "men without country, who, too long estranged, / Had found no native home, or found it changed" (1.29–30). At the same time, Byron condemns the "new-born heroes" and their "self-elected Chief" (1.97, 103) for their tyrannical Satanic, if not Promethean, power.

30. Joseph Banks, quoted in Tim Fulton, Debbie Lee, and Peter J. Kitson, *Science and Exploration in the Romantic Era: Bodies of Knowledge* (Cambridge: Cambridge University Press, 2004), 112. The verbal play afforded by the name breadfruit ("scarcely can it be said that they earn their bread with the sweat of their brow") allowed Banks to locate this paradisical scene within interrelated political-economic and religious schemas. Byron eschewed those registers, which were later conscripted to colonizing rhetorics, instead employing his yeasty poetic imagination to describe a crop growing beyond the bounds of biblical geographies or capitalistic logics and the legal regimes they sponsored.

31. Beaton, *Byron's War,* 121.

32. See Matt K. Matsuda, *Pacific Worlds: A History of Seas, Peoples, and Cultures* (Cambridge: Cambridge University Press, 2012), 134–6; Vladimir Kapor, "Shifting Edenic Codes: On Two Exotic Visions of the Golden Age in the Late Eighteenth Century," *Eighteenth-Century Studies* (2008), 217–30.

33. For the power structures of Tahitian society – including the positions held by women – and the engagement of Pacific peoples in global circuits of exchange, see "Navigators of Polynesia and Paradise," chapter 10 in Matsuda, *Pacific Worlds*, 127–43.

34. Fulton, Lee, and Kitson, *Science and Exploration in the Romantic Era*, 108.

35. In 11.284–97, Byron talks about his "Celtic memories" mixing with his encounters abroad, especially Greece. In a related note reminiscing about his childhood, Byron dates his "love of mountainous countries" to his convalescence in the Highlands during a childhood illness (*CPW*, 7.145 n.).

36. Quoted in Kerstin Petersen, "Blood Will Show Out: Vikings and the Construction of White National Identity and Masculinity in Scholarly and Literary Works of the Victorian Age," doctoral dissertation, Binghamton University (2020), 101–2.

37. Byron gestures toward the scenes, including Greece and the East, which might have realized his ambition. But he suffers from the absence of another outlet than the sea: "But grant his vices, grant them all his own, / How small their theatre without a throne?"

38. Petersen, "Blood Will Show Out." In a version of this dynamic, the hybrid scout character in *The Last of the Mohicans* appears as "a man of native goodness, removed from the temptations of civilised life, though not entirely forgetful of its prejudices and lessons, exposed to the customs of barbarity and yet perhaps more improved than injured by this association, and betraying the weaknesses as well as the virtues both of his situation and of his birth." This "lone trapper" proves uniquely equipped to engage the enterprise of the "half wild beings who hang between society and the wilderness" and testifies "to the truth of those wonderful alterations which distinguish the progress of the American nation." James Fenimore Cooper, "Introduction" to *The Last of the Mohicans* (London: Henry Colburn & Richard Bentley, 1831 [1826]), viii–ix.

39. Joselyn M. Almeida, "More Heirs in Love Than Law': Epic, Race, and Alternative Filiations in Byron's *Don Juan*," *ELH* 86 (2019), 997–1025.

40. Compare James Fenimore Cooper: "The Mohicans were the possessors of the country first occupied by the Europeans in this portion of the continent. They were, consequently, the first dispossessed; and the seemingly inevitable fate of all these people, who disappear before the advances, or it might be termed the inroad, of civilisation, as the verdure of their native forests fall before the nipping frosts, is depicted as having already befallen them." "Introduction" to

The Last of the Mohicans, viii. While they are identified as the original possessors of a verdant landscape, Cooper casts the Mohicans' fate here as a "seemingly inevitable" natural process, rendered in a present-perfect tense that has always "already befallen them."

41. Fulton, Lee, and Kitson, *Science and Exploration in the Romantic Era*, 123, 118.

42. Fulton, Lee, and Kitson, *Science and Exploration in the Romantic Era*, 126. In a further example of this biblically informed colonization, the "increasingly received Evangelical wisdom" expressed by Southey and Coleridge took cues from the fact that the breadfruit plant grew in "a society ignorant of the biblical injunction to work" (123). The supposedly unspoiled, biblical paradise represented by Tahiti thus underscored its need of civilization by Christian imperialism.

43. Fulton, Lee, and Kitson see the three locations "in dynamic redefinition": "Britain-the-coloniser becomes oppressive and guilty; the West Indies become sadistic labour camps; Tahiti an idyll of pre-colonised indigenous life; revolutionary France a place of illicit freedoms that can be symbolized by Tahiti" (and, we might add, Haiti). That redefinition, they continue, "takes effect first at the imperial centre: the tropical islands were shaped by the demands of debate back in Britain" (124). Yet while that may have been the case in actuality, it was not true for Byron's poem, which takes nothing for granted about the perpetuation of European power or the durability of English institutions.

44. As Fulton, Lee, and Kitson write, with an eye to the role even of anti-imperialist discourses in fostering cultural imperialism, "there were no innocent fantasies in a world in which Britons could increasingly impose their wills" (124–5). Byron sought to imagine a world in which such fantasies were indeed innocent, I propose here, even as it became ever-more apparent that he could not, in fact, write from one.

45. *CPW*, 7.131.

46. For Milton, see *CPW*, 7.26.

47. These lines, McGann notes, also echo Pope: Compare *An Essay on Man*, III.305–6.

48. *CPW*, 2.16, 1.194–7.

49. *CPW*, 7.138.

50. *CPW*, 1.292, lines 79–88. Subsequent references to the poem are given by line number in the main text. As McGann notes, the publication "occurred in the context of his prose defences of Pope and his own *Don Juan*" and at a time when Byron was also "seriously renewing his attack upon contemporary English social and literary culture."

51. *Don Juan in Context*, 69.

52. See James Chandler, "The Pope Controversy: Romantic Poetics and the English Canon," *Critical Inquiry* 10 (1984), 481–509.
53. Hobhouse to Byron, August 1818, *Byron's Bulldog*, 242–3.
54. *Letter [. . .] on the Rev. W.L. Bowles' Strictures on the Life and Writings of Pope*, 3rd ed. (London: John Murray, 1821), 54.
55. Bennett, *Romantic Poets and the Culture of Posterity*, 198.
56. In *The Last Man*, Lionel mulls the fate of his own story as he contemplates the Western classics and the ruins of Rome. Sussman, "'Islanded in the World,'" 174–7. "Although we run up against the end of his documentation of the literary future," Sussman reminds us, "he continues to preserve the literary past, reading Homer and Shakespeare on his perpetual voyage" (177).

Coda

1. *Shelley's Poetry and Prose*, eds. Donald H. Reiman and Neil Fraistat (New York: Norton, 2002), 109–10.
2. That critique also had a bearing on imagined futures. As Bennett details in *Romantic Poets and the Culture of Posterity*, Byron took issue with what he saw as Wordsworth's cultivated obscurity and the hubris of his and Southey's belief that they would find a future readership. As McGann has shown in *Don Juan in Context*, the resulting account of the Lake poets' works as "trash" ironically validated Byron's own embrace of showy ephemerality and contingent fame.
3. Robinson, *Shelley and Byron*, 234–5.
4. The poem's multiple frames serve to compound the unpredictability of its narrative, Emily Rohrbach emphasizes, and thus the unknowability of the future: "The fact that Byron's narrator professes never to grasp a coherent poetic (let alone historical) picture leaves doubt not only about Juan's possibilities of self-knowledge (Juan is deeply dopey in this respect) but also about the narrator-poet's – indeed, perhaps even Byron's – knowledge of his own project." The poem's added emphasis on digression and counterfactual speculation ultimately gives way to "a multidimensional simultaneity that resists linearity." *Modernity's Mist*, 150, 152. Sachs similarly emphasizes the capacity of poetry to "integrate linear time with other nonlinear, irregular, and contradictory temporal experiences." Poetry, he writes, "struggles with futurity and gives shape and form to the heterochrony so central to the experience of modernity." That "shaping quality" allows poetry "to sustain multiple possibilities and contradictions without resolution, both in its content, but also in its formal qualities." *The Poetics of Decline in British Romanticism*, 21.
5. See Peter W. Graham, *Don Juan and Regency England* (Charlottesville: University of Virginia Press, 1990).

6. *BLJ*, 10.28.
7. *BLJ*, 10.29.
8. For the "overtaxing of the earth's resources" in one of the precursor texts to *The Last Man*, see Sussman, "'Islanded in the World': Cultural Memory and Human Mobility in *The Last Man*," in *Peopling the World*, 170.
9. Graham, *Don Juan and Regency England* and Rohrbach, *Modernity's Mist*, respectively, read these stanzas and the London cantos of *Don Juan* as capturing the generative potential of a once-buried past and highlight the failure of retroactive histories to capture the heterogeneous potential of the present (even as that present becomes a determinate future). By contrast, I see these diminished futures as, however paradoxically, instilling an overburdened political present with a sense of alternative possibilities.
10. Jeffrey Jerome Cohen, "Anarky," in *Anthropocene Reading: Literary History in Geologic Times*, eds. Tobias Menely and Jesse Oak Taylor (University Park: Penn State University Press, 2017), 25–42.

Bibliography

Abrams, M. H. *Natural Supernaturalism: Tradition and Revolution in Romantic Literature.* New York: Norton, 1971.

Agathocleous, Tanya. *Disaffected: Emotion, Sedition, and Colonial Law in the Anglosphere.* Ithaca: Cornell University Press, 2021.

Almeida, Joselyn M. "'More Heirs in Love Than Law': Epic, Race, and Alternative Filiations in Byron's *Don Juan.*" *ELH* 86 (2019), 997–1025.

Anderson, Amanda. *Bleak Liberalism.* Chicago: University of Chicago Press, 2016.

Applebaum, Anne. *Twilight of Democracy: The Seductive Lure of Authoritarianism.* New York: Doubleday, 2020.

Arendt, Hannah. *On Revolution.* London: Penguin, 2006 [1963].

  The Origins of Totalitarianism. New York: Harcourt, Brace, Jovanovich, 1973 [1951].

Bailes, Melissa. "The Psychologization of Geological Catastrophe in Mary Shelley's *The Last Man.*" *ELH* 82 (2015), 671–99.

Bailyn, Bernard. *The Ideological Origins of the American Revolution.* Cambridge: Harvard University Press, 1967.

Baldick, Chris. *In Frankenstein's Shadow: Myth, Monstrosity, and Nineteenth-Century Writing.* Oxford: Oxford University Press, 1987.

Beaton, Roderick. *Byron's War: Romantic Rebellion, Greek Revolution.* Cambridge: Cambridge University Press, 2013.

Bennett, Andrew. *Romantic Poets and the Culture of Posterity.* Cambridge: Cambridge University Press, 1999.

Bentham, Jeremy. *Selected Writings: Jeremy Bentham.* Ed. Stephen Engelmann. New Haven: Yale University Press, 2010.

Berlant, Lauren. *Cruel Optimism.* Durham: Duke University Press, 2011.

  On the Inconvenience of Other People. Durham: Duke University Press, 2022.

Blackburn, Robin. *The Overthrow of Colonial Slavery: 1776–1848.* New York: Verso, 1988.

Bohls, Elizabeth A. *Slavery and the Politics of Place: Representing the Colonial Caribbean, 1770–1833.* Cambridge: Cambridge University Press, 2014.

Boulukos, George. *The Grateful Slave: The Emergence of Race in Eighteenth-Century British and American Culture.* Cambridge: Cambridge University Press, 2012.

Bowers, Will. *The Italian Idea: Anglo-Italian Radical Literary Culture.* Cambridge: Cambridge University Press, 2020.

Brantlinger, Patrick. "Race and *Frankenstein.*" In *The Cambridge Companion to Frankenstein.* Ed. Andrew Smith. Cambridge: Cambridge University Press, 2016, 228–42.

Bromwich, David. *Disowned by Memory: Wordsworth's Poetry of the 1790s.* Chicago: University of Chicago Press, 1998.

[Brougham, Henry]. Review of Morris Birkbeck, *Notes on a Journey in America. Edinburgh Review* 30 (June 1818).

"Brougham, Henry Peter." *The History of Parliament: The House of Commons 1820–1832.* 7 vols. Ed. D. R. Fisher. Cambridge: Cambridge University Press, 2009. Accessed online at www.historyofparliamentonline.org/volume/1820-1832/member/brougham-henry-1778-1868.

Brown, Christopher Leslie. *Moral Capital: Foundations of British Abolitionism.* Durham: University of North Carolina Press, 2006.

Brown, Vincent. *The Reaper's Garden: Death and Power in the World of Atlantic Slavery.* Cambridge: Harvard University Press, 2010.

Buck-Morss, Susan. *Hegel, Haiti, and Universal History.* Pittsburgh: University of Pittsburgh Press, 2009.

Burnard, Trevor and Kit Candlin. "Sir John Gladstone and the Debate over the Amelioration of Slavery in the British West Indies in the 1820s." *Journal of British Studies* 57 (2018), 760–82.

Byron, George Gordon, Lord. *Byron: A Self-Portrait, Letters and Diaries 1798 to 1824.* Ed. Peter Quennell. Oxford: Oxford University Press, 1990.

Byron's Letters and Journals. Ed. Leslie Marchand. 12 vols. London: J. Murray, 1973–82.

Complete Poetical Works. Ed. Jerome J. McGann. 7 vols. Oxford: Oxford University Press, 1980–93.

Conversations of Lord Byron with Thomas Medwin, Esq. 2 vols. London, 1832.

His Very Self and Voice: Collected Conversations of Lord Byron. Ed. Ernest J. Lovell, Jr. New York: Macmillan, 1954.

Letter [. . .] on the Rev. W.L. Bowles' Strictures on the Life and Writings of Pope, 3rd ed. London: John Murray, 1821.

Cameron, Lauren. "Mary Shelley's Malthusian Objections in *The Last Man.*" *Nineteenth-Century Literature* 67 (2012), 177–203.

Canuel, Mark. "Race, Writing, and *Don Juan.*" *Studies in Romanticism* 54 (2015), 303–28.

Carlson, Julie A. *England's First Family of Writers: Mary Wollstonecraft, William Godwin, Mary Shelley.* Baltimore: Johns Hopkins University Press, 2007.

Chakrabarty, Dipesh. "Climate and Capital: On Conjoined Histories." *Critical Inquiry* 41 (2014), 1–23.

Chandler, James. *England in 1819: The Politics of Literary Culture and the Case of Romantic Historicism.* Chicago: University of Chicago Press, 1998.

"The Pope Controversy: Romantic Poetics and the English Canon." *Critical Inquiry* 10 (1984), 481–509.

Wordsworth's Second Nature: A Study of the Poetry and Politics. Chicago: University of Chicago Press, 1984.

Chase, Malcolm. *Chartism: A New History*. Manchester: Manchester University Press, 2007.

Christensen, Jerome. *Lord Byron's Strength: Romantic Writing and Commercial Society*. Baltimore: Johns Hopkins University Press, 1993.

Christie, William. "Going Public: Print Lords Byron and Brougham." *Studies in Romanticism* 38 (1999), 443–75.

Clark, J. C. D. *English Society, 1660–1832: Religion, Ideology and Politics during the Ancien Régime*. 2nd ed. Cambridge: Cambridge University Press, 2000.

Cohen, Ashley. *The Global Indies: British Imperial Culture and the Reshaping of the World, 1756–1815*. New Haven: Yale University Press, 2021.

Cohen, Jeffrey Jerome. "Anarky." In *Anthropocene Reading: Literary History in Geologic Times*. Eds. Tobias Menely and Jesse Oak Taylor. University Park: Penn State University Press, 2017, 25–42.

Cohen-Vrignaud, Gerard. "Byron and Oriental Love." *Nineteenth-Century Literature* 68 (2013), 1–32.

  Radical Orientalism: Radical Orientalism: Rights, Reform, and Romanticism. Cambridge: Cambridge University Press, 2015.

Cooper, James Fenimore. *The Last of the Mohicans*. London: Henry Colburn & Richard Bentley, 1831 [1826].

Crompton, Louis. *Byron and Greek Love: Homophobia in 19th-Century England*. Berkeley: University of California Press, 1985.

Da Costa, Emilia Viotti. *Crowns of Glory, Tears of Blood: The Demerara Slave Rebellion of 1823*. Oxford: Oxford University Press, 1994.

Derrida, Jacques. *Specters of Marx: The State of the Debt, the Work of Mourning & the New International*. Trans. Peggy Kamuf. London: Routledge, 1994.

Dierksheide, Christa. *Amelioration and Empire: Progress and Slavery in the Plantation Americas*. Charlottesville: University of Virginia Press, 2014.

Douthwaite, Julia V. "The Frankenstein of the French Revolution: Nogaret's Automaton Tale of 1790." *European Romantic Review* 20 (2009), 381–411.

Duncan, Ian. *Scott's Shadow: The Novel in Romantic Edinburgh*. Princeton: Princeton University Press, 2007.

Elfenbein, Andrew. "Silver-Fork Byron and the Image of Regency England." In *Byromania: Portraits of the Artist in Nineteenth- and Twentieth-Century Culture*. Ed. Francis Wilson. Basingstoke: Macmillan, 1999, 77–85.

Eliot, George. *Felix Holt, The Radical*. Ed. William Baker and Kenneth Womack. Peterborough: Broadview, 2000.

Erdman, David V. "Lord Byron and the Genteel Reformers." *PMLA* 56 (1941), 1065–94.

Esterhammer, Angela. *Print and Performance in the 1820s: Improvisation, Speculation, Identity*. Cambridge: Cambridge University Press, 2020.

Fabricant, Carole. *Swift's Landscape*. Rev. ed. Notre Dame: University of Notre Dame Press, 1995 [1982].

Ferris, Ina. *The Achievement of Literary Authority: Gender, History, and the Waverley Novels*. Ithaca: Cornell University Press, 1991.

Foucault, Michel. *The Birth of Biopolitics: Lectures at the Collège de France, 1978–1979*. Trans. by Graham Burchell. New York: Palgrave, 2007.

The Order of Things: An Archaeology of the Human Sciences. New York: Vintage Books, 1994 [1970].

Security, Territory, Population: Lectures at the Collège de France, 1977–1978. Trans. by Graham Burchell. New York: Palgrave, 2007.

Fukuyama, Francis. "The End of History?" *The National Interest* 16 (1989), 3–18.

The End of History and the Last Man. New York: Free Press, 2006 [1992].

Fulton, Tim, Debbie Lee, and Peter J. Kitson. *Science and Exploration in the Romantic Era: Bodies of Knowledge*. Cambridge: Cambridge University Press, 2004.

Gessen, Masha. *Surviving Autocracy*. New York: Riverhead, 2020.

Gigante, Denise. *The Keats Brothers: The Life of John and George*. Cambridge, MA: Harvard University Press, 2013.

Goheen, Jeremy. "'Soot in One's Soup': Transitory Blackness in British Romantic Chimney-Sweep Literature." *Studies in Romanticism* 61 (2022), 57–65.

Goldsmith, Steven. "Of Gender, Plague and Apocalypse: Mary Shelley's *Last Man*." *Yale Journal of Criticism* 4 (1990), 129–73.

Goldstein, Amanda Jo. *Sweet Science: Romantic Materialism and the New Logics of Life*. Chicago: University of Chicago Press, 2017.

Graham, Peter W. *Don Juan and Regency England*. Charlottesville: University of Virginia Press, 1990.

Gross, Izhak. "The Abolition of Negro Slavery and British Parliamentary Politics, 1832–3." *Historical Journal* 23 (1980), 63–85.

Gross, Jonathan David. *Byron: The Erotic Liberal*. Lanham: Rowman & Littlefield, 2001.

Grosskurth, Phyllis. *Byron: The Flawed Angel*. London: Hodder & Stoughton, 1979.

Hadley, Elaine. *Living Liberalism: Practical Citizenship in Mid-Victorian Britain*. Chicago: University of Chicago Press, 2010.

Hall, Catherine. *Macaulay and Son: Architects of Imperial Britain*. New Haven: Yale University Presss, 2012.

Hall, Catherine, Nicholas Draper, Keith McClelland, Katie Donington, and Rachel Lang. *Legacies of British Slave-Ownership: Colonial Slavery and the Formation of Victorian Britain*. Cambridge: Cambridge University Press, 2014.

Hall, Kim. "*Othello* and the Problem of Blackness." In *A Companion to Shakespeare's Works: The Tragedies*. Eds. Richard Dutton and Jean E. Howard. Malden, MA: Blackwell, 2005, 357–74.

Hartman, Geoffrey H. *Wordsworth's Poetry, 1787–1814*. New Haven: Yale University Press, 1964.

Havard, John Owen. "'Blustering, Bungling, Trimming': Byron, Hobhouse, and the Politics of *Don Juan* Canto 1." *The Byron Journal* 49 (2021), 29–41.

"Burn It Down." *The New Rambler.* August 2021. Accessed online at https://newramblerreview.com/book-reviews/history/burn-it-down.

Disaffected Parties: Political Estrangement and the Making of English Literature, 1760–1830. Oxford: Oxford University Press, 2019.

"Swift's Political Climates." *Eighteenth-Century Theory and Interpretation.* Forthcoming.

"What Freedom? *Frankenstein*, Anti-Occidentalism, and English Liberty." *Nineteenth-Century Literature* 74 (2019), 305–31.

Hay, William Anthony. *The Whig Revival 1808–1830.* New York: Palgrave, 2005.

[Hazlitt, William]. *The Spirit of the Age: or Contemporary Portraits.* 2nd ed. London: Henry Colburn, 1825.

Hickman, Jared. *Black Prometheus: Race and Radicalism in the Age of Atlantic Slavery.* Oxford: Oxford University Press, 2017.

Higgins, David. *British Romanticism, Climate Change, and the Anthropocene: Writing Tambora.* Basingstoke: Palgrave, 2017.

Hilton, Boyd. *A Mad, Bad, and Dangerous People? England 1783–1846.* Oxford: Oxford University Press, 2006.

Hobhouse, John Cam. *Byron's Bulldog: The Letters of John Cam Hobhouse to Lord Byron.* Ed. Peter W. Graham. Columbus: Ohio State University Press, 1984.

[Hobhouse, John Cam]. *Letter to Canning.* London, 1818.

Hobhouse, John Cam. *Recollections of a Long Life, by Lord Broughton (John Cam Hobhouse) . . ..* Ed. Lady Dorchester. 6 vols. London: J. Murray, 1909–11.

Hudson, Nicholas. *A Political Biography of Samuel Johnson.* London: Pickering & Chatto, 2013.

Jager, Colin. "Reading by the Light of Common Day: Politics, Society, Romanticism." *European Romantic Review* 32 (2021), 76–83.

James, C. L. R. *The Black Jacobins: Toussaint L'Ouverture and the San Domingo Revolution.* London: Secker & Warburg, 1938.

James, David. "Critical Solace." *New Literary History* 47 (2016), 481–504.

Jeffries, Richard. *After London; Or Wild England.* London: Cassell, 1885.

Johnson, Barbara. *A Life With Mary Shelley.* Stanford: Stanford University Press, 2014.

Kapor, Vladimir. "Shifting Edenic Codes: On Two Exotic Visions of the Golden Age in the Late Eighteenth Century." *Eighteenth-Century Studies* 41 (2008), 217–30.

Kazanjian, David. *The Brink of Freedom: Improvising Life in the Nineteenth-Century Atlantic World.* Durham: Duke University Press, 2016.

Kelsall, Malcolm. *Byron's Politics.* Sussex: The Harvester Press, 1987.

Khalip, Jacques. *Last Things: Disastrous Form from Kant to Hujar.* New York: Fordham University Press, 2018.

King, Stephen D. *Grave New World: The End of Globalization, the Return of History.* New Haven: Yale University Press, 2017.

Klein, Naomi. *The Battle For Paradise: Puerto Rico Takes On the Disaster Capitalists.* Chicago: Haymarket Books, 2018.

The Shock Doctrine: The Rise of Disaster Capitalism. New York: Picador, 2007.

Koselleck, Reinhart. *Futures Past: On the Semantics of Historical Time.* Trans. Keith Tribe. New York: Columbia University Press, 2004 [1979].

Kushner, Tony. *Angels in America: A Gay Fantasia On National Themes.* New York: Theatre Communications Group, 2013 [1994].

Langan, Celeste. *Romantic Vagrancy: Wordsworth and the Simulation of Freedom.* Cambridge: Cambridge University Press, 1995.

A Leaf From the Future History of England, on the Subject of Reform in Parliament (1831).

Lewis, S. L. and Maslin, M. A. "Defining the Anthropocene." *Nature* 519 (2015), 171–80.

Lilley, Sasha, ed. *Catastrophism: The Apocalyptic Politics of Collapse and Rebirth.* Oakland: PM Press, 2012.

Liu, Alan. *Wordsworth: The Sense of History.* Stanford: Stanford University Press, 1989.

Lynall, Gregory. *Swift and Science: The Satire, Politics and Theology of Natural Knowledge, 1690–1730.* Basingstoke: Palgrave, 2012.

[Maginn, William]. *Whitehall, or the Days of George IV.* London: W. Marsh, 1827.

Makdisi, Saree. *William Blake and the Impossible History of the 1790s.* Chicago: University of Chicago Press, 2003.

Malm, Andreas. *Fossil Capital: The Rise of Steam Power and the Roots of Global Warming.* New York: Verso, 2016.

Mandler, Peter. *Aristocratic Government in the Age of Reform: Whigs and Liberals, 1830–1852.* Oxford: Oxford University Press, 1990.

Marchand, Leslie. *Byron: A Biography.* 3 vols. New York: Alfred A. Knopf, 1957.

Matsuda, Matt K. *Pacific Worlds: A History of Seas, Peoples, and Cultures.* Cambridge: Cambridge University Press, 2012.

McGann, Jerome J. *Don Juan in Context.* Chicago: University of Chicago Press, 1968.

McLane, Maureen N. *Romanticism and the Human Sciences.* Cambridge: Cambridge University Press, 2000.

Mee, Jon. "'Bread & Cheese & Porter Only Being Allowed': Radical Spaces in London, 1792–1795" In *Sociable Places: Locating Culture in Romantic-Period Britain.* Ed. Kevin Gilmartin. Cambridge: Cambridge University Press, 2017, 51–69.

Print, Publicity, and Popular Radicalism in the 1790s: The Laurel of Liberty. Cambridge: Cambridge University Press, 2016.

Mellor, Anne K. *Mary Shelley: Her Life, Her Fiction, Her Monsters.* New York: Methuen 1988.

Mendelssohn, Michèle. *Making Oscar Wilde.* Oxford: Oxford University Press, 2018.

Menely, Tobias. *Climate and the Making of Worlds: Toward a Geohistorical Poetics.* Chicago: University of Chicago Press, 2021.

Mercer, Anna. *The Collaborative Literary Relationship of Percy Bysshe Shelley and Mary Wollstonecraft Shelley.* New York: Routledge, 2020.

Michael, Timothy. *British Romanticism and the Critique of Political Reason.* Baltimore: Johns Hopkins University Press, 2015.

Midgley, Clare. *Women Against Slavery: The British Campaigns, 1780–1870.* London: Routledge, 1992.

Miller, Lucasta. *L.E.L.: The Lost Life and Scandalous Death of Letitia Elizabeth Landon, the Celebrated "Female Byron."* New York: Knopf, 2019.

Mole, Tom. *Byron's Romantic Celebrity.* Basingstoke: Palgrave, 2007.

What the Victorians Made of Romanticism: Material Artifacts, Cultural Practices, and Reception History. Princeton: Princeton University Press, 2017.

Moore, Doris Langley. *The Late Lord Byron.* London: John Murray, 1961.

Moore, Jason W. "Anthropocene or Capitalocene? Nature, History, and the Crisis of Capitalism." In *Anthropocene or Capitalocene?* Ed. Jason W. Moore. Oakland: PM Press, 2016.

"Who Is Responsible for the Climate Crisis?" *Maize* (November 2019). Accessed online at www.maize.io/magazine/what-is-capitalocene/.

Moore, Thomas, ed. *Letters and Journals of Lord Byron.* 2 vols. London: John Murray, 1830.

Moretti, Franco. *Signs Taken for Wonders: Essays in the Sociology of Literary Forms.* Trans. Susan Fischer, David Forgacs, and David Miller. London: Verso, 1988 [1983].

Morgan, Benjamin. "Fin du Globe: On Decadent Planets." *Victorian Studies* 58 (2016), 609–35.

Morris, William. *News from Nowhere.* Ed. Stephen Arata. Peterborough: Broadview, 2003.

Mounk, Yascha. *The People vs. Democracy: Why Our Freedom Is in Danger and How to Save It.* Cambridge, MA: Harvard University Press, 2018.

Murray, John. *The Letters of John Murray to Lord Byron.* Ed. Andrew Nicholson. Liverpool: Liverpool University Press, 2007.

Nersessian, Anahid. *Utopia, Limited.* Cambridge, MA: Harvard University Press, 2015.

Newlyn, Lucy. *William and Dorothy Wordsworth: "All in Each Other."* Oxford: Oxford University Press, 2013.

Newman, Ian. "Edmund Burke in the Tavern." *European Romantic Review* 24 (2013), 125–48.

The Romantic Tavern: Literature and Conviviality in the Age of Revolution. Cambridge: Cambridge University Press, 2021.

Nitchie, Elizabeth. *Mary Shelley: The Author of "Frankenstein."* New Brunswick: Rutgers University Press, 1953.

O'Brien, Jean M. *Firsting and Lasting: Writing Indians Out of Existence in New England.* Minneapolis: University of Minnesota Press, 2010.

Paulson, Ronald. *Representations of Revolution, 1789–1820.* New Haven: Yale University Press, 1983.

Petersen, Kerstin. "Blood Will Show Out: Vikings and the Construction of White National Identity and Masculinity in Scholarly and Literary Works of the Victorian Age." Doctoral Dissertation, Binghamton University (2020).

Pincus, Steve. *1688: The First Modern Revolution*. New Haven: Yale University Press, 2011.

"*Gulliver's Travels*, Party Politics, and Empire." In *New Perspectives on the History of Political Economy*. Eds. Robert Fredona and Sophus A. Reinert. Basingstoke: Palgrave, 2018, 131–70.

The Heart of the Declaration: The Founders' Case for an Activist Government. New Haven: Yale University Press, 2016.

Pitts, Jennifer. "Legislator of the World? A Reading of Bentham on Colonies." *Political Theory* 31 (2003), 200–34.

Plotz, John. "Speculative Naturalism and the Problem of Scale: Richard Jefferies's *After London*, After Darwin." *MLQ* 76 (2015), 31–56.

Pocock, J. G. A. *The Machiavellian Moment: Florentine Political Thought and the Atlantic Republican Tradition*. Princeton: Princeton University Press, 2016 [1975].

Virtue, Commerce, and History: Essays on Political Thought and History, Chiefly in the Eighteenth Century. Cambridge: Cambridge University Press, 1985.

Poole, Robert. *Peterloo: The English Uprising*. Oxford: Oxford University Press, 2019.

Porter, Andrew. "Trusteeship, Anti-Slavery, and Humanitarianism." In *The Oxford History of the British Empire: Volume III: The Nineteenth Century*. Ed. Andrew Porter. Oxford: Oxford University Press, 1999, 198–221.

Randel, Fred V. "The Political Geography of Horror in Mary Shelley's *Frankenstein*." *ELH* 70 (2003), 465–91.

Reeder, Jessie. *The Forms of Informal Empire: Britain, Latin America, and Nineteenth-Century Literature*. Baltimore: Johns Hopkins University Press, 2020.

Reese, Diana. "A Troubled Legacy: Mary Shelley's Frankenstein and the Inheritance of Human Rights," *Representations* 96 (2006), 48–72.

Reid, Christopher. *Imprison'd Wranglers: The Rhetorical Culture of the House of Commons 1760–1800*. Oxford: Oxford University Press, 2012.

Remnick, David. "Obama Reckons with a Trump Presidency." *The New Yorker*, November 18, 2016. Accessed online at www.newyorker.com/magazine/201 6/11/28/obama-reckons-with-a-trump-presidency.

Rensin, Emmett. "The Blathering Superego at the End of History." *Los Angeles Review of Books*, June 18, 2017. Accessed online at https://lareviewofbooks.org /article/the-blathering-superego-at-the-end-of-history/.

Roberts, Jonathan. "Wordsworth's Apocalypse." *Literature and Theology* 20 (2006), 361–78.

Robinson, Charles E. *Shelley and Byron: The Snake and Eagle Wreathed in Flight*. Baltimore: Johns Hopkins University Press, 1976.

Roe, Nicholas. *John Keats and the Culture of Dissent*. Oxford: Oxford University Press, 1998.

Rohrbach, Emily. *Modernity's Mist: British Romanticism and the Poetics of Anticipation*. New York: Fordham University Press, 2015.

Rosen, F. *Bentham, Byron, and Greece: Constitutionalism, Nationalism, and Early Liberal Political Thought*. Oxford: Clarendon Press, 1992.

Rudwick, Martin J. S. *Bursting the Limits of Time: The Reconstruction of Geohistory in the Age of Revolution*. Chicago: University of Chicago Press, 2005.

Worlds Before Adam: The Reconstruction of Geohistory in the Age of Reform. Chicago: University of Chicago Press, 2008.

Runciman, David. *How Democracy Ends*. New York: Basic Books, 2018.

Sachs, Jonathan. *The Poetics of Decline in British Romanticism*. Cambridge: Cambridge University Press, 2018.

Shelley, Mary. *Frankenstein*. Ed. J. Paul Hunter. New York: Norton, 2012, 168.

The Journals of Mary Shelley, 1814–1844. 2 vols. Eds. Paula R. Feldman and Diana Scott-Kilvert. Oxford: Oxford University Press, 1987.

The Last Man. Ed. Anne McWhir. Peterborough: Broadview: 1996.

The Letters of Mary Wollstonecraft Shelley. 3 vols. (Baltimore: Johns Hopkins University Press, 1980).

The Novels and Selected Works of Mary Shelley: Volume 1: Frankenstein, or the Modern Prometheus. Ed. Nora Crook. London: Pickering, 1996.

Shelley, Percy Bysshe. *Shelley's Poetry and Prose*. Eds. Donald H. Reiman and Neil Fraistat. New York: Norton, 2002.

Shields, Juliet. *Mary Prince, Slavery, and Print Culture in the Anglophone Atlantic World*. Cambridge: Cambridge University Press, 2021.

Sigler, David. *Fracture Feminism: The Politics of Impossible Time in British Romanticism*. Albany: SUNY Press, 2021.

Spark, Muriel. *Child of Light: A Reassessment of Mary Wollstonecraft Shelley*. Hadleigh, Essex: Tower Bridge Publications, 1951.

Stafford, Fiona J. *The Last of the Race: The Growth of a Modern Myth from Milton to Darwin*. Oxford: Clarendon Press, 1994.

Steffan, Truman Guy. *Byron's Don Juan, Volume 1: The Making of a Masterpiece*. Austin: University of Texas Press, 1957.

Sterrenburg, Lee. "*The Last Man*: Anatomy of Failed Revolutions." *Nineteenth-Century Fiction* 33 (1978), 324–47.

"Mary Shelley's Monster: Politics and Psyche in *Frankenstein*." In *The Endurance of Frankenstein: Essays on Mary Shelley's Novel*. Ed. George Levine. Oakland: University of California Press, 1982, 143–71.

Stewart, David. *The Form of Poetry in the 1820s and 1830s: A Period of Doubt*. Basingstoke: Palgrave, 2018.

Stillinger, Jack. *Multiple Authorship and the Myth of Solitary Genius*. Oxford: Oxford University Press, 1991.

Stout, Daniel M. *Corporate Romanticism: Liberalism, Justice, and the Novel*. New York: Fordham University Press, 2017.

Strang, Hilary. "Common Life, Animal Life, Equality: The Last Man." *ELH* 78 (2011), 409–31.

Substance of the Debate in the House of Commons, on the 15th May, 1823, on a Motion for the Mitigation and Gradual Abolition of Slavery Throughout the British Dominions. London, 1823.

Sussman, Charlotte. *Peopling the World: Representing Human Mobility from Milton to Malthus*. Philadelphia: University of Pennsylvania Press, 2020.

Swift, Jonathan. *Gulliver's Travels*. Ed. David Womersley. Cambridge: Cambridge University Press, 2012.

Letters to and From Dr. J. Swift, D.S.P.D. Dublin, 1741.

Taylor, Astra. "A Ruin and a Habitation." In *Democracy May Not Exist But We'll Miss It When It's Gone*. New York: Verso, 2019, 276–306.

Taylor, Christopher. *Empire of Neglect: The West Indies in the Wake of British Liberalism*. Durham: Duke University Press, 2018.

Taylor, David Francis. "Byron, Sheridan, and the Afterlife of Eloquence." *Review of English Studies* 65 (2014), 474–94.

Thomas, Sarah. "Envisaging a Future for Slavery: Agostino Brunias and the Imperial Politics of Labor and Reproduction." *Eighteenth-Century Studies* 52 (2018), 115–33.

Thompson, E. P. *The Making of the English Working Class*. New York: Vintage, 1966 [1963].

Whigs and Hunters: The Origin of the Black Act. New York: Pantheon, 1975.

Tuite, Clara. *Lord Byron and Scandalous Celebrity*. Cambridge: Cambridge University Press, 2014.

Verhoeven, Wil. *Americomania and the French Revolution Debate in Britain, 1789–1802*. Cambridge: Cambridge University Press, 2013.

Vernon, James. *Politics and the People: A Study in English Political Culture, 1815–1867*. Cambridge: Cambridge University Press, 1993.

Wang, Fuson. "We Must Live Elsewhere: The Social Construction of Natural Immunity in Mary Shelley's *The Last Man*." *European Romantic Review* 22 (2011), 235–55.

Ward, J. R. "The Amelioration of British West Indian Slavery: Anthropometric Evidence." *The Economic History Review* 71 (2018), 1199–226.

Wardle, Ralph M. "The Authorship of *Whitehall* (1827)." *Modern Language Notes* 56 (1941), 207–9.

Weheliye, Alexander G. *Habeas Viscus: Racializing Assemblages, Biopolitics, and Black Feminist Theories of the Human*. Durham: Duke University Press, 2014.

Weisman, Alan. *The World Without Us*. New York: St. Martin's Press, 2007.

Williams, Eric. *Capitalism and Slavery*. Rev. ed. Durham: University of North Carolina Press, 2021 [1944].

Wilson, Francis, ed. *Byromania: Portraits of the Artist in Nineteenth- and Twentieth-Century Culture*. Basingstoke: Macmillan, 1999.

Wolfson, Susan. *Romantic Interactions: Social Being and the Turns of Literary Action*. Baltimore: Johns Hopkins University Press, 2010.

Woodward, Sir Llewellyn. *The Age of Reform, 1815–1870*. Oxford: Oxford University Press, 1962.

Wordsworth, William. *The Prelude: 1799, 1805, 1850*. Ed. Jonathan Wordsworth, M. H. Abrams, and Stephen Gill. New York: Norton, 1979.

Wright, Lawrence. "How Pandemics Wreak Havoc – and Open Minds." *The New Yorker*, July 20, 2020. Accessed online at www.newyorker.com/magazine/2020/07/20/how-pandemics-wreak-havoc-and-open-minds.

Zegger, Robert E. *John Cam Hobhouse: A Political Life*. Columbia: University of Missouri Press, 1973.

Zoellner, Tom. *Island on Fire: The Revolt That Ended Slavery in the British Empire*. Cambridge, MA: Harvard University Press, 2020.

Index

CAMBRIDGE STUDIES IN ROMANTICISM

General Editor

JAMES CHANDLER, *University of Chicago*

Printed by Printforce, the Netherlands